The
Spanish-American War:
A Compact History

Books by Allan Keller

MADAMI (with Anne Putnam)
GRANDMA'S COOKING
THUNDER AT HARPER'S FERRY
MORGAN'S RAID
THE SPANISH-AMERICAN WAR: A COMPACT HISTORY

The
Spanish-American War:
A Compact History

by Allan Keller

Hawthorn Books, Inc.   Publishers   New York

1 2 3 4 5 6 7 8 9 10

To
I. E. K.
an Everest among sand dunes

Foreword

Seventy years after the event, our war with Spain in 1898 is as difficult to justify on moral grounds as it was in the days of President William McKinley and the first President Roosevelt. The sad plight of the Cuban insurgents was no worse than the oppression imposed upon other peoples in other lands which we ignored then and have continued to ignore.

The United States was younger just before the turn of the century, and there seemed to be an eagerness to prove our strength. It was not actually truculence—rather the prideful assurance a boy knows when he first realizes that he is a man. We had grown big and we wanted the nations of the world to know it. There were also simple greed, political opportunism, and personal advantage behind the pressures that led to war.

Many will say that we would not react the same way today, that we are wiser and have eschewed expansion as a national policy. That may be true. There are less drastic ways of achieving the same goals.

But we did go to war in 1898.

This is a story of that war, with its hidden causes, its unexpectedly swift victories and its blunders, its incredible humor and its bizarre personalities. If we must continue to have wars— a pathetic thought—then conflicts like this one would be preferable to the bloody holocausts of the twentieth century.

An author owes many things to many persons—too many to acknowledge fully. But special thanks must go to a few. No writer on the Spanish-American War can overemphasize the aid implicit in the monumental history written by the late Admiral French Ensor Chadwick. Few men have equaled his masterful coverage of every aspect of a major war. All other historical works on that conflict are pigmies standing in the shadow of a giant.

Three old friends, who gave unstintingly of their time, knowledge and kindness, are the late Miss Beatrice Kelly, librarian emeritus of the Ferguson Library, Stamford, Connecticut; Wade Doares, librarian at the Arthur Hays Sulzberger Library at the Graduate School of Journalism, Columbia University; and Monroe Stearns, Executive Editor of Hawthorn Books. Kershaw Burbank was most kind to lend me documents and newspaper clippings belonging to, or written about his father, Robert Burbank. I am heavily indebted to four ladies who smoothed the path that leads from rough copy to final typescript: Patricia Schifini, Angela Brennan, Carol Erickson and, most loyal of all, Nevia Sorz.

Whatever faults there are, are mine alone, but without the understanding and wisdom of my wife there would have been many more, and I gladly acknowledge the incalculable support only an author truly understands.

ALLAN KELLER

Darien, Connecticut

Contents

Foreword   vii
1. Freedom Is a Holy Cause   1
2. "I Will Furnish the War"   9
3. Shadow over Havana   27
4. The Bugle Sounded Taps   34
5. Machining an Army   45
6. "You May Fire When Ready, Gridley"   54
7. The Bottle Is Corked   72
8. *Gussie* Goes to War   86
9. Hobson Scuttles the *Merrimac*   97
10. Landing at Daiquirí   112
11. First Blood at Las Guásimas   128
12. "Don't Bother with the Little Blockhouses"   145
13. San Juan Hill   157
14. Colonel Roosevelt, the Critic   168
15. Courage Is Not Enough   182
16. The Flags Change over Santiago   199
17. Picnic on Puerto Rico   213
18. Manila Falls into the American Basket   220
19. Silent Now, the Guns   238
Select Bibliography   247
Index   251

War . . . is such a terrible, such an atrocious, thing, that no man, especially no Christian man, has the right to assume the responsibility of beginning it.

—TOLSTOI,
Anna Karenina

1 ★ ★ ★ ★ ★ ★

Freedom Is
a Holy Cause

On the morning of March 8, 1895, the American steamer *Aliança*, of 3,000 tons register, Captain Crossman commanding, steamed into the Windward Passage between Cuba and Haiti on her way north to New York from Colón. A Spanish gunboat fired a shot across her bow, followed this with other shots, and chased the passenger ship for twenty-five miles.

Four days later the *Aliança* arrived in New York, her passengers irate at Spanish effrontery, her captain sure the attack had been aggressive and intentional because the American flag was clearly visible, and the ship news reporters delighted to have another story dealing with Spanish arrogance.

Dark ribbons across the front pages of American newspapers announced the story, but the articles beneath them were forced to admit that no harm had been done to anything but American national pride. In more normal times polite diplomatic exchanges might have sufficed to end the matter, but the years just before the turn of the century were hardly normal.

An insurrection in Cuba against the oppressive rule of Spanish colonial governors had been under way for three years.

1

A goodly number of Americans were not only sympathetic to the downtrodden natives but seemed eager to use the revolt as a justification for annexation of the island.

On the same newsstands that carried the extras about the latest insult to the Stars and Stripes were copies of *Forum* magazine in which Henry Cabot Lodge, the Republican Senator from Massachusetts and a leading hawk of the era, plumped for outright annexation of Cuba:

From the Rio Grande to the Arctic Ocean there should be but one flag and one country. . . . For the sake of our commercial supremacy in the Pacific we should control the Hawaiian Islands and maintain our influence in Samoa. England has studded the West Indies with strong places which are a standing menace to our Atlantic seaboard. We should have among those islands at least one strong naval station, and when the Nicaragua Canal is built, the island of Cuba, still sparsely settled and of almost unbounded fertility, will become to us a necessity.

With these sugarplums dangled before the American people, any pretext for driving the Spaniards off the island just below Florida seemed fortuitous. The western frontier had just about disappeared, and many citizens of a nation that had been moving outward from early lodgments on the Atlantic coast for more than two and a half centuries saw Cuba as a small, but eminently desirable, promised land.

The *Alliança* affair did not immediately lead to war with Spain. Many other incidents had to occur before the fire became so hot that the pot boiled over, but it was the sort of incident people could understand much more clearly than they could the nuances of diplomatic debate.

Interventionists in Congress leaped happily to their feet to worry the *Alliança* bone. Senator John T. Morgan of Alabama said that if he had the right to do so he would immediately "despatch a fleet of warships to Havana," and Senator Shelby M. Cullom was even more warlike: "It is time that some one woke up and realized the necessity of annexing some property. We want all this northern hemisphere."

Fortunately for all at that particular moment in history, it was not up to politicians like Lodge, Cullom, and Morgan to order the American fleet into enemy ports or to annex territory belonging to others just because it would enhance American maps. Grover Cleveland, a Democrat, was in his second term as President, had both feet planted solidly on the ground, and saw no benefits accruing from a war with Spain. During the three years the insurrection had been going on, the President had done a commendable job of blanketing the little fires his opponents had touched off in their interventionist fervor.

It was more than passing strange that so many decent, God-fearing men assumed it was this country's divine right to pick up various pieces of international real estate. Those most often mentioned for this illicit honor were Hawaii, Samoa, Cuba, and even bits of mainland China. The dying out of the frontier had much to do with creating this expansionist fever. Moreover, the long period of peace following the Civil War had seen a new generation come along, a generation not personally familiar with the bloody tragedy of war, and thus not as averse to courting its dangers.

Nations fighting for their own survival in the early years of their existence seldom have time to think of annexation or, for that matter, any involvement in affairs outside their own borders. The American Civil War had prevented any fragmenting of the United States, and the thirty years that followed had seen the rise of industrialization as the nation became strong and re-united. With this maturity came a feeling of strength and power and, in the minds of many, a willingness to play a larger role on the world stage.

This was the atmosphere that existed in the closing decade of the nineteenth century. It paralleled in many ways the consciousness of strength that sustains a man in his early twenties. The world is his oyster and the fears that come with age have not yet taught him caution. The United States too had come of age, had survived a hideous fratricidal conflict, and could feel the sap running strong in its limbs.

So when news came from the cane fields of Cuba that under-privileged peasants had revolted against their Spanish overlords, many Americans saw no reason for sitting back and avoiding involvement. This era was also the period when hundreds of thousands of refugees from various European brands of tyranny migrated to America in search of golden opportunity. These people—Irish, German, Italian, Polish, Jewish, and others—felt a kinship with the oppressed Cubans. "Freedom" was a word of holy significance to them, and any people raising that cry were sure of at least moral support.

At first the news was spotty and motives anything but clear. It seemed to be just another flare-up like the many that had tortured Cuba since the days when the Spanish Empire in the New World began to disintegrate under the hammer blows of Simón Bolívar and José de San Martín.

There had been an abortive rebellion led by General Narciso Lopez in 1850 which had failed, followed by another a year later with Lopez leading an "army" of four hundred American, German, and Irish adventurers. This was an even greater disaster, because of bad planning and lack of popular support among the natives that would be duplicated more than a hundred years later at a cove called the Bay of Pigs.

There had been another insurrection which boasted the sonorous title of the Ten Years' War, but the excitement and tension in the cigar factories of Tampa and New York outpaced that of the revolt in Cuba. The ten-year conflict, which was little more than a series of hit-and-run skirmishes between guerrillas and Spanish soldiery, produced one incident which might have led to war but did not, for a number of reasons.

An itinerant steamship named *Virginius* had been engaged for several years in the dirty business of gun-running, providing rifles and ammunition to any and all groups in the Caribbean who could get money on the barrel head to pay for them. The skipper was an American who would sell to both sides in a political imbroglio, caring nothing at all for ethics or noble causes.

A Spanish gunboat caught the *Virginius* on the high seas off Jamaica and, with a total lack of concern for international law, seized the cargo of guns and all the crew. Before a British man-of-war could prevent the slaughter, firing squads mowed down the sailors in the plaza at Santiago, Cuba.

Cuban sympathizers in the United States, some of the newspapers, and quite a few men in Congress called for war, or at least a show of force by the U.S. Navy. There was a touch of irony here, for the Navy was in such a state of disrepair that it would have been unsafe to order most of its units to sea.

Common sense triumphed over the bellicose protests when even the noisiest of jingoists realized that they had no holy cause. The *Virginius* affair was a tawdry one and hardly respectable enough to stand the light of inquiry. When the excitement simmered down, diplomats went to work behind the scenes, where they function best, and finally closed out the Ten Years' War with an agreement between Spain and the insurgents signed in early 1878.

Treaties and solemn pacts drawn up by learned statesmen do not always remedy conditions that are deeply rooted within the lives and consciences of a nation. The Pact of Zanjon was no better than those signed in Vienna, Versailles, Rheims, and elsewhere before and after 1878. It left the sores of oppression open in Cuba even if it did put a stop to a formal state of war.

But guerrilla skirmishing, burning of rich planters' cane fields, and retaliatory measures introduced at the point of Spanish bayonets went on as before all over the Gem of the Antilles. Conditions grew steadily worse, international trade nearly disappeared, and hunger stalked many of the poorer provinces. Gun-runners did a brisk business, although how the patriots scratched together enough money to buy arms is still an unsolved mystery. Many a Cuban child must have gone hungry so its father could possess a rifle and a pocketful of cartridges.

Spain herself was wracked by so many internal dissensions that she could pay little attention to righting wrongs in her last Caribbean possession, even if the officials had had a mind to do so. From the earliest voyages of Columbus to the end of the nineteenth century, Spain had always looked upon overseas colonies as a source of revenue, not as areas for social change or constitutional betterment for mankind.

With the ink barely dry on the Pact of Zanjon, Cuban stalwarts in the United States went back to their plotting. José Martí, the leader of the patriots who lived in New York, organized still another expeditionary force which American

authorities scotched as it was readying for a descent on the
island from southern Florida.

There was a difference, however, between this ill-fated attempt
at intervention and those that had gone before. This one had
been planned with the full knowledge and cooperation of many
Cubans in Cuba. Had the force not been disarmed in Florida,
it might well have found massive support from the insular revolu-
tionaries. When word reached these latter insurgents that help
from outside could not be expected in the foreseeable future, they
shouldered the entire burden themselves. In a small village in
eastern Cuba—about as far away from the Spanish seat of power
in Havana as they could get—a band of patriots uttered the
grito, or shout of independence. This time it was not to be denied.
Like the *grito* sounded by Father Hidalgo, leader of the independence movement in Mexico long years before, this time
Cuba's appeal would bring freedom. That it did so only with the
intervention of armed troops under the American flag does not
really matter. It is another of the ironies that mark the forward
movement of civilization.

This insurrection born of the patriots' take-over after Martí's
death had been under way three years when the Spanish gunboat, captained by an officer who was either myopic or singularly
disinterested in international law on the high seas, chased the
Alliança through the Windward Passage and into the Atlantic.
The incident itself had little effect on the course of Spanish-
American relations, but it underscored for all persons in the
United States that there was in very truth an insurrection going
on in Cuba. From that day in March of 1895 there was no
longer any hope on the part of either Spanish diplomats or non-
interventionists in this country that the revolt against colonial
overlords in Cuba could be swept under the rug. It was not unlike a giant tree that falls across a highway. It could not be
ignored, particularly since the highway it straddled was America's path to world power.

When a member of the Foreign Relations Committee of the
United States Senate could bluster forth with words like "We
certainly ought to have that island in order to round out our
possessions as they should be, and if we cannot buy it, I for one

should like to have an opportunity to acquire it by conquest," there was no longer any reason to believe the insurrection in Cuba could be brushed aside.

Coincident with the rising pro-Cuban sentiment in the United States came realization on the part of the newspapers that, this time, revolution in Cuba was the real thing. A report from Madrid revealed that more Spanish troops were being sent to help cope with Máximo Gómez, leader of the patriots who had taken over when Martí was ambushed and killed. Concerning this report the New York *Tribune* editorialized: "It is difficult to believe that she [Spain] is sending eight thousand soldiers to Cuba merely for the benefit they may derive from the sea voyage."

A new premier, Antonio Canovas del Castillo, took office in Madrid and promptly sent the best military man in Spain to put down the revolt. General Martínez Campos sailed for Havana with terse but definitive orders in his dispatch case: "Put down the insurrection by any means at your disposal." If there had been any cause for doubt of the seriousness of the uprising, Campos' assignment ended it. The New York *World* said what every citizen was thinking: "We should never have thought of sending Grant to put down a railroad strike. When Spain sends its great general, Martínez Campos, to put down the uprising, it means that the trouble is serious."

A few statesmen and a few editors, studying the wild rumors quoting bloody battles and great victories by Gómez and his revolutionists, became aware that many of the most exciting dispatches were coming—not from the battlefields in eastern Cuba—but from the editorial rooms of Spanish-language papers in Florida or from Cuban émigré groups centered in the cigar factories.

The New York Times pointed out that "the most alarming Cuban revolutions have occurred in New York for many years— in speeches."

There was a modicum of truth in all this, but even the doubt- ers had to admit that this time the populace of eastern Cuba was rising in revolt, that agrarian provinces were no longer safe for Spanish troops in less than battalion strength, and that Spain herself—knowing the facts—was worried enough to be sending more and more troops across the Atlantic to quell a full-blown rebellion.

Then onto a stage already crowded with revolutionists, rapacious Spanish overlords, émigré politicians, gun-runners, American interventionists, Congressional hawks, and other assorted anglers who recognized troubled waters when they saw them, appeared a new cast of supporting actors—the war correspondents.

It is idle today to say that they should have played only a minor role in the international drama. Facts that are incontrovertible after more than seven decades leave no room for denial of the newspapermen's importance. Never before, and never since, have reporters with no responsibility for what they did and wrote had such power to alter the course of history. The Spanish-American War was many things—a revolt of the underprivileged and oppressed, a rung in America's ladder to world pre-eminence, a conflict to support the main thesis of the Monroe Doctrine, which held that the United States would not permit any intervention in western hemisphere affairs by European powers—but it was also a war in which newspaper headlines and reporters' dispatches had more explosive power than the artillery on both sides.

2 ★ ★ ★ ★ ★

"I Will Furnish the War"

THREE NEWSPAPER PUBLISHERS PROBABLY had more to do with making war between the United States and Spain inevitable than all the statesmen, legislators, or military figures of both sides. One of them showed how to make a paper into a puissant force —for either good or evil—and the other two, learning basic philosophy from the first, went on to make their own journals so powerful that when they called for war, a nation of ardent newspaper readers found itself swept into a conflict that should have been avoided.

James Gordon Bennett, Sr., established the New York *Herald* in 1835. Almost at once it began to feature the human interest approach so familiar to today's readers. Instead of long, often boring essays, bits of intelligence culled from European journals, and ponderous editorials, the *Herald* injected liveliness in massive doses. Murder was a subject that could be played up for readers avid for relief from a humdrum existence. Social scandal was another, and Bennett dealt with it in a saucy manner that won approval from a readership already chafing from straitlaced Victorian morality.

By the 1880's the *Herald* had altered journalism enough for Joseph Pulitzer to come into town with an even more exciting way of handling the news. Pulitzer transformed the *World* from a losing venture into a successful periodical devoted to the common man and his causes. He was a crusader who demanded breezy copy from his writers, clever headlines, and startling illustrations.

His men went off on expeditions bound to build circulation, exposing graft in high places, fighting municipal corruption, even rescuing a white girl captured by Indians. Nellie Bly's trip around the world was his idea, and proved a sensation.

The third publisher, who was to go even further, and who nearly converted the Spanish-American War into his own personal property, was William Randolph Hearst. A dropout from Harvard, young Hearst used money his father had made from the Comstock lode to create a bonanza out of the San Francisco *Examiner*. Then he invaded New York City, the journalistic capital of the New World.

Buying the *Journal*, he changed it into a rambunctious, sensational, often rowdy newspaper. Never as well-edited as the *World*, it was naughtier, more brazen in its headlines, and far less ethical.

Both Pulitzer and Hearst agreed on one point. If there wasn't enough exciting news to be written about, they manufactured their own with crusades, attacks on officials, drives against the white slave traffic, and similar exposés.

Had these two publishing titans not decided to slug it out toe-to-toe for circulation gains—and this is a sober commentary— the efforts of downtrodden Cubans to throw off the yoke of Spanish oppression might never have burgeoned into a war between Spain and the United States. Both Pulitzer and Hearst saw the rebellion as fodder for their printing presses. With single-minded purpose they moved to change a peasant revolt into an international conflict. They were not alone, of course, for other publishers saw the rich vein of news and wanted to mine it too, but the two giants in New York had the expertise and the desire so well developed that they led the pack in raising a hue and cry for our intervention.

Reporters for various American papers had been in and out of Cuba for years before the shelling of the *Alliança*, but their dispatches had not created unusual interest. Then the *Alliança* incident, plus growing evidence that the insurgents were causing real trouble in eastern Cuba, led editors and publishers to send correspondents to cover the rebellion.

These newspapermen found that Máximo Gómez had gathered several thousand men willing to die for freedom and put them under the command of José Maceo, José and Calixto García, and other lieutenants. His orders seemed both simple and attainable: burn the landowners' cane fields, wreck the railroads, and move westward toward Havana, picking up supporters on the way.

General Campos, borrowing from the military textbooks of the Chinese and the Romans, set up a barrier along a railroad running from Moron in the north to Jucaro in the south, in about the middle of the island. Called a *trocha*, the defensive line consisted of barbed wire and pillboxes, not a very effective device, particularly at night.

Maceo broke out of Camagüey province by leading a small detachment across under cover of dark, and Gómez himself with two thousand men crossed the *trocha* in a running skirmish unworthy of being designated an engagement. Meanwhile a small band of patriots was disrupting the harvesting of cane in the far western province of Pinar del Río.

To overenthusiastic war correspondents gathered in Havana these activities looked more significant than they were in fact. The reporters sent off cables grossly exaggerating the successes of the insurgents, placing them much closer to Havana than they really were, and indicating that the capital was facing a pincers movement.

Such careless reporting displeased the Spanish and a few honest newsmen who tried to correct the erroneous dispatches, but it was music to the ears of publishers eager for increased circulation. Headlines the size of bread pans were put above stories of battles where only a few men were killed or wounded.

Readers of the yellow journals—as the Hearst and Pulitzer papers were called—were entranced by the stories, and the interventionists in Congress used them to support flamboyant oratory calling on the administration to get tough with Spain.

A young British Army officer with a penchant for war and a

liking for writing appeared in Cuba about this time and put
things into better perspective. His name was Winston Churchill.
Attached to a column of Spanish regulars under General Saurez
Valdez, he was present when it met a body of Maceo's irregulars
in Puerto Príncipe province. The Spanish soldiery advanced in
tight formation across a clearing in heavy forest and undergrowth. Maceo's patriots fired and ran. Churchill wrote it as he
saw it, including this comment: "The insurgents are bad shots. It
appeared to me that tons of lead passed over the heads of General Valdez's staff, with whom I was. Three orderlies were
wounded."

The *World* printed the whole dispatch but later found fault
with it, having not the slightest concept of guerrilla warfare between poorly trained insurgents and European troops used to
fighting on open plains.

Insulted by the criticism, Churchill, who, even at twenty-one,
understood warfare better than many a general, wrote the editor
of the newspaper that what had come to be called the Battle of
La Reforma was in truth nothing but a skirmish between the
Valdez column and a rear guard of irregulars. To think that such
engagements could bring victory to either side, said Churchill,
was a mark of ignorance.

American reporters inflated such hit-and-run encounters into
gory battles, overlooking a much more important aspect of the
revolt. While Campos could win any real engagement, he could
not cope with mounted insurgents who moved almost at will
through the countryside, burning the cane fields, driving people
into cities, and threatening Cuba with starvation. Gómez was
fighting an early variation of the total war that emerged in the
twentieth century. It was not surprising, therefore, that old General Campos realized his own ineffectiveness and asked Madrid
to send a replacement.

The man Spain chose to replace Campos was General Valeri-
ano Weyler y Nicolau, a tough, cruel, realistic soldier who
thought wars should be won by any means, pleasant or unpleasant. His name would become well known in the United
States, as well as his reputation for ruthlessness.

It is a normal trait to consider what is done on your side in war to be necessary but to judge similar tactics by the enemy to be cruel, inhuman, or worse. Long before Weyler arrived in Havana on February 10, 1896, the headlines in the *World* and *Journal* were informing their readers of the Spaniard's "ferocity." When he issued an early statement that he would take drastic steps to put down the rebellion, Hearst ordered a personal vendetta initiated. Weyler was given the nickname of "Butcher" by the *Journal*, which pulled out all the stops to characterize him as "the most bloodthirsty general in the world."

Overnight the articles sent from Cuba became more gory and the cause of the insurgents almost a holy one. Spaniards were accused of barbarous treatment of prisoners and the general populace. Words like "torture," "rape," "atrocity," and "bestiality" were peppered through nearly every dispatch sent back to the more sensational papers, and they were invariably used to describe Spanish actions rather than Cuban.

Journalistic ethics were flouted day after day. Gunshots heard in the distance by a lady writing for one American journal became "volleys" fired by jailers as they "murdered" defenseless prisoners. She did not go to the fortress to check on the firing. It was enough that she imagined what had happened. Other correspondents broke the decent canons of objective reporting just as blatantly. It was all a part of the circulation and price wars being fought by newspapers in New York and other American cities, wars where anything was condoned that sold papers.

Sane men tried to stem the tide, and were excoriated for their pains. One veteran writer in Havana who had lived in Cuba long enough to know the language and the people wrote to his paper how the dishonest reporter functioned:

Filling his notebook with the stock stories of atrocities, battles, rapes and other horrors attributed to the Spanish troops by interested parties, and which every street gamin in Habana is thoroughly posted in, he returns to the United States, and in course of time drifts into Washington, there to offer his collection of "fakes" as evidence before the committees.

Towns no one had ever found in an atlas became the scenes of titanic battles, casualty lists grew longer by the day, but with-

out the bother of including names, and poorly armed bands of
roving insurrectionists suddenly assumed the stature of "columns"
and "battalions" of infantry locked in mortal struggle with
Spanish forces that refused to give quarter to man, woman, or
child.

One of the obvious reasons Weyler did not enjoy the esteem
of American correspondents was his refusal to let them go into
the field with his troops. The other was the rigidity of his censorship. When his assistants got through blue-penciling the articles
submitted at the cable office, they were shredded beyond all sense
and often altered to give a more favorable impression of Spanish
operations.

Then came a new situation that played into Hearst's hands as
successfully as though the publisher had planted the idea in
Weyler's mind. The authorities in Havana arrested several newspapermen. They were not too badly treated, although jailed for
varying periods, but their incarceration coincided with that of
several Cuban-American civilians. Then an American civilian
named Walter Grant Dygert, who was totally free of Cuban
blood or connections, was mistaken for a rebel army officer and
imprisoned without trial.

The *Journal* thundered that no American was safe in Cuba,
that justice had gone with "Butcher" Weyler's coming, and that
the American government must intervene to protect its na-
tionals. Hearst's henchmen trooped into Washington to win support for intervention and, to their surprise, found the climate
more salubrious than even they had hoped.

Many members of Congress, for many reasons, were urging
President Cleveland to aid the insurgents. The reasons included
pressure by Cuban-American constituents in Florida and New
York, the desire to embarrass an out-going chief executive, the
approaching election and, indubitably, a feeling that the people
of the country, running fevers because of the atrocity stories in
Cuba, wanted something done on behalf of the poor insurrectionists.

Into the breach stepped the Senate Foreign Relations Committee, all fire and brimstone because it imagined that the Spanish

ambassador to this country, Señor Dupuy de Lôme, had "interfered" with its duties by sending a message to the State Department stating what most honest men knew—that the insurgents were banking heavily on American intervention.

In the Senate hopper at the time were dozens of resolutions dealing with the crisis. They ranged from declarations of war all the way to mere requests for inquiries. The Foreign Relations Committee, acting with remarkable calm in the circumstances, opted for a resolution that the government should grant rights of belligerence to the insurrectionists "in the ports and territory of the United States."

It was one of those examples of zany tightrope walking for which the committee has been castigated on many occasions. Granting belligerent rights to the poorly armed rebels, with no ships larger than rowboats or fishing craft, was as meaningful as putting a seven-course dinner in sight of a man dying of hunger on the other rim of a canyon.

The resolution made no one happy. The interventionists wanted positive action—even military involvement—and this highly legalistic maneuver was mighty thin soup for hungry men. Business interests with investments in Cuba were equally unhappy. Their agents on the island told them of growing clouds of smoke by day and flickering flames of fire by night that destroyed one cane field after another.

It most assuredly did not please the insurgents. In their time of agony a diplomatic sidestepping of the issues meant nothing. It was no wonder that the old revolutionist Gómez, when next inspecting his tatterdemalion followers, lamented: "With these oxen we must plow."

In Washington the resolution was debated on the floor of the Senate with acrid intensity. President Cleveland exerted no special influence, not wishing to tie the hands of an administration soon to follow his own. Senator John Sherman of Ohio, chairman of the Foreign Relations Committee, was not as discreet. Charging that Spain's crimes were beyond description, Sherman offered supportive evidence from the columns of the *Journal*—a translation of a book by a rebel sympathizer named

Enrique Donderio. This text cited "barbarities" committed by
General Weyler in the Ten Years' War. The fact that Weyler had
not arrived in Cuba until years after the Pact of Zanjon had
ended that conflict mattered not a bit to Senator Sherman. He
used the evidence to back his demand that the United States aid
the insurgents, and if William Randolph Hearst went to bed that
night warmed by the words of the Ohio solon, it was no wonder.
Sherman called the *Journal* "one of the great journals of the
country."

Eventually the resolution, amended, altered, patched, and
repatched, was concurred in by the House and passed by that
chamber on April 6, 1896, by 247 to 27. It stated that "a condition of public war" existed in Cuba and that while the United
States should maintain strict neutrality, the nation's friendly offices should be offered by the President to the Spanish government
"for the recognition of the independence of Cuba."

The press reacted as was to be expected. The "yellow" journals
thought the resolution too weak-kneed; the conservative element
thought it might persuade Spain to grant more privileges to the
insurrectionists and thus make war unlikely. Had the latter group
thought enough about it, the realization would have come that
events had passed beyond the point of reasonableness. Cleveland
sent a new consul general to Havana—General Fitzhugh Lee,
a Confederate Army veteran and nephew of the Southern hero,
Robert E. Lee. Fitzhugh Lee was a politician, an old warhorse,
and a Virginian. He was hardly the man to pour oil on troubled
waters, if that had been Cleveland's purpose in naming him.

The Spanish Navy captured a gun-running schooner, the
Competitor, soon after General Lee took over his duties. There
was some legitimate doubt as to the true nationality of many of
the crew, but the skipper had good claims and a newspaper
correspondent who was on board was definitely an American.
The portly consul general moved swiftly to protect his countrymen, invoked various treaty guarantees, and saved them from
the firing squad. He could not keep them from a long and
arduous incarceration, but used the incident to keep a fire burning under the whole question of Spanish-American relations.

During the early part of 1896 the yellow journals persisted in working for intervention, but Cleveland thwarted their efforts. It was not pleasant for the President to stick to this position, as he was a humanitarian who knew how grievously mistreated the Cuban people had been under the Spanish yoke. He also realized that it was an election year, and everything pointed to a Republican victory. He saw no reason to embarrass the new incumbent of the White House just because he would probably be from the rival party.

When the political conventions were held, the country was given a preview of what to expect under a Republican President. Whereas the Democrats adopted a two-line plank in their platform expressing sympathy for the Cubans, the Republicans came out for a "firm, vigorous and dignified" foreign policy that would, among other goals, work for control of the Hawaiian Islands and use the nation's influence to "restore peace [in Cuba] and give independence to the island."

This appeared on the surface to indicate small interest in international affairs on the part of the Democrats, but in fact the party was so deeply involved in the question of parity between silver and gold in supporting the currency that foreign policy took a back seat. William Jennings Bryan's demand that a golden crown of thorns not be pressed down upon the brow of labor pushed the plight of the Cubans off the political stage, at least temporarily.

William McKinley, a kindly, well-intentioned, conservative man from Ohio, was elected President for many reasons, but the Cuban question played a singularly small role in the decision. Most voters liked him because he was a high-tariff advocate. Business liked him because he was "safe." Prominent men such as Senator Lodge and Theodore Roosevelt, thirsting for American take-over of various islands, areas, and parcels of territory not already nailed down by the great powers, liked him because they believed they could influence him to assume a stronger stance in international affairs than Cleveland had taken.

When election news petered out as front-page material, the American press went back to the problems of the Caribbean. The more sensational papers carried stories of Weyler's actions that were either untrue or grossly exaggerated. He was accused of removing women by the score from prison under cover of darkness and shooting them down in cold blood. He was vilified, unjustly defamed, and made into a symbol of Spanish oppression —a symbol that could not help inflaming millions of readers. Journalism as a profession, in too many instances, was degraded beyond belief. When stories without any foundation had Weyler's henchmen throwing Cuban rebels to the sharks, newspaper ethics touched bottom. That another generation would have to witness similar journalistic excesses, such as the charges that German soldiers were cutting the breasts off Belgian nuns, does not reduce the shame of the yellow press in the last half-decade of the nineteenth century.

It is true that American reporters, with few exceptions, have always supported the downtrodden. The plight of the Cuban insurrectionists, ragged, hungry, poorly armed, but heroically standing up against Spain's legions, worried the journalists as it did all decent men. But objectivity, the priceless, indispensable tool of the good reporter, was tossed aside too often. No other explanation is possible for the notorious affair of the naked lady on the *Olivette*.

Some months prior to the incident, the *Journal* had sent Frederic Remington, the famous artist and pictorial historian of the American frontier, to Cuba to wander around in the back country and sketch insurgent scenes. There were no skirmishes or battles of consequence, and the artist grew bored drawing scenes of burning cane fields and dejected families around their pathetic hovels. It was most natural that he wired home from Havana in a moment of low spirits:

> "W. R. Hearst
> Journal, New York
> Everything quiet. No trouble here. There will be no war. I wish to return.
>
> Remington"

Back went the reply that forever branded the publisher as an unethical, conscienceless meddler:

"Remington
Havana
Please remain. You furnish the pictures and I will furnish
the war.

Hearst"

Remington stayed on in Cuba and was soon joined by Richard
Harding Davis, then the most famous American war correspon-
dent. Davis traveled around the island, noting the same things
that had bored Remington, and wrote a few articles blaming
Weyler for most of the tragedy existing in the native villages.
After a few weeks Davis decided he had seen enough and left
for the United States, not bothering to get permission from the
Journal publisher.

He traveled on the mail steamer *Olivette*, luxuriating in the
pleasures of sea travel on a clean American ship after weeks
spent in crowded, dilapidated trains and on horseback. One of
his table companions was a pretty Cuban woman who introduced
herself as Señorita Clemencia Arango. The story she told Davis
became one of the most famous of the prewar days and a *cause
célèbre* that helped push America into the war that should not
have come.

The señorita, young and obviously of good breeding and better than average station, confided in the war correspondent, saying that General Weyler had ordered her expelled from the island
with two other young women because he believed they were giving aid and comfort to the rebels. Her brother was, in fact, serving with the Gómez forces at the time.

The señorita told Davis that on the day they were exiled,
Spanish detectives entered their homes, had them undressed and
searched for possible messages intended for the Cuban juntas in
Key West and Tampa. Then, as they passed through the custom
house, they were again disrobed and searched. Finally, said
Señorita Arango, they boarded the American mail steamer
Olivette, happy to be under the protection of the Stars and
Stripes flying from the stern.

But, Davis learned from the nearly hysterical young woman,
Spanish officials followed them to the deck, persuaded ship's officers to provide a stateroom for the purpose, and then forced

the women to undress for a third time while a search was made of their persons and luggage.

When the *Olivette* reached Florida, Davis wrote an account of the shameful incident, but strangely enough, did not "play it up" as other reporters would have done. In truth, he was a little casual about it, getting to the highlights of the story quite far down in the article. The editors in the *Journal* city room had none of Davis' phlegm. The wires hummed as orders went back and forth between New York and Florida. When they quieted down, Remington, who had drawn many a famous sketch of Indian scouts, mountain men, buffalo hunters, and cavalrymen, had drawn one of a young lady, intended to be Señorita Arango, stark naked, being searched by Spanish agents in the *Olivette* cabin. Those were somewhat Puritanical days when it came to sex, so Remington sketched the lady in such a way that her head and legs were visible but little else except a totally unclad and definitely feminine derriere. The story was splashed across the front page of the *Journal* on Lincoln's birthday under a headline which asked: "Does Our Flag Shield Women?"

What had gone before in the way of titillating news from Cuba was as nothing to this story. Americans were outraged. Millions agreed with the *Journal* when that paper, making the most of its position, and disregarding its own past excesses, editorialized about war being dreadful: "There are things more dreadful than even war, and one of them is dishonor."

One does not have to be a newspaperman to imagine the consternation that existed in the editorial rooms of the *World* and the inner sanctum where Joseph Pulitzer, nearly blind, listened to assistants reading the article on the rival front page.

Pulitzer and his men moved swiftly to counteract the impact of the Hearst scoop. It was fortuitous that they did, for their writers in Tampa interviewed the now famous Señorita Arango as she left ship after sailing there from Key West.

There was a different version this time. The lady disclosed that she and her companions had not in fact been undressed in the presence of men. Matrons had done the disrobing and the searching, and the Cuban beauties had never stood stark naked in the same cabin with male Spanish officials.

SPANIARDS SEARCH WOMEN ON AMERICAN STEAMER

DRAWN BY FREDERIC REMINGTON

This put matters in a different light. The *World* printed the truth, Hearst was red-faced and angry at being beaten at his own game, and Richard Harding Davis wrote to the rival paper, blaming the misconception on Remington's drawing, and asking it to print his note. It was bitter tea for the great war correspondent to drink in public.

As McKinley took office the situation in Cuba appeared to be changing. Weyler had instituted a policy of reconcentrating the people of some provinces in the cities and forbidding the large centers to supply the rural areas with food. He also ordered whatever cane fields had not been burned by the insurgents to be put to the torch by his soldiers, thus using economics to weaken the rebels. It was a strange twist. Gómez had ordered no food to go from the farms to the cities, hoping to force supporters to join his ranks. Weyler figured that a devastated countryside could ill support his enemies.

Famine became a reality in many provinces, and the apocalyptic horses, like the *reconcentrados* themselves, were now all together again in Cuba. A pall of smoke from the burning fields and peasant homes hung over the Pearl of the Antilles almost as thick as the political haze over Madrid and Washington.

Arch-conservatives in Spain wanted no part of the suggestions made by our ministers in Madrid. They saw no reason to give Cubans their freedom.

The interventionists in Washington were becoming more vociferous. Roosevelt, hanging on the fringes of officialdom, was busy writing letters to everyone he considered safe, urging a naval buildup, recommending stronger messages to Spain, even suggesting that our Asiatic Squadron steam to Manila, there to be ready to act if the insurrection in that Spanish possession gave it the opportunity. McKinley found that his pursuit of peace was a hard path to follow. Every time the skies seemed to brighten over Cuba, a new dark cloud appeared on the horizon. There was one there again.

And as had happened so often before, the trouble had its beginnings in the editorial sanctum of William Randolph Hearst. Hearst was bemoaning the lack of headline material on a hot

August day, when a cable from Havana was handed him. It had this message: "Evangelina Cisneros, pretty girl of seventeen years, related to President of Cuban Republic, is to be imprisoned for twenty years on African coast for having taken part in uprising Cuban political prisoners on Isle of Pines."

A cub reporter on his first day in the city room would have seen the potentialities in such a story. It had everything Hearst could desire: beauty, imprisonment, mistreatment, jungle heat in an African hell hole. Had he known it, there was even more drama locked in those few words of cable-ese: attempted seduction, incredible bravery, and unquestioned innocence.

The publisher of the *Journal* moved swiftly to turn those aspects of the case he knew into another crusade.

In the next day's paper a story emblazoned across the front page told of Evangelina's plight. She was facing a military tribunal on charges of inciting rebellion. Already word had passed that the verdict—inevitably one of guilt—would lead to her exile in a filthy prison somewhere in a Spanish colony on the malarial west coast of Africa. A three-column-wide drawing, done by an artist who had never been closer to Havana than Tampa, Florida, and had never seen Señorita Cisneros, portrayed a maiden with dark hair and piercing eyes. He was not far off target.

Years later George Clarke Musgrave, the British war correspondent, who claimed partial honors for discovering the girl in a Cuban jail, described the scene in this purple prose:

There suddenly appeared in their midst [a group of prostitutes from a reformatory] a white face, young, pure and beautiful; a maiden of perhaps seventeen was crossing the yard. With her pale features surmounted by masses of dark hair, her simple white dress and dignified bearing, all accentuated by the horrible surroundings, she resembled the Madonna of an old master, inspired with life but plunged into Hades.

Musgrave and another correspondent tried to spirit her out of jail, but the Britisher was left alone when his companion was expelled and never succeeded in freeing her. Then word of the

girl's danger reached a Hearst man, Marion Kendrick, and the
sensation that followed its publication in the *Journal* was all
Hearst could have wished for in his mad quest for circulation.

To make the most of the story, Hearst sent his men out to get
women to sign a petition to the Queen Regent of Spain demanding Evangelina's release. Mrs. Jefferson Davis, widow of the
Confederate President, wrote to the Spanish ruler in her own
shaky longhand, praying that the girl be saved from "a fate
worse than death." Julia Ward Howe, who had written the
"Battle Hymn of the Republic" when Mr. Davis' secessionist
armies threatened the Union, joined in the appeal. A few days
later the *Journal* could boast it had the signatures of more than
fifteen thousand American women. The name at the top of the
long list of petitioners was that of President McKinley's mother.

Meanwhile the *World*, hoping to expose another fraud, cabled
General Weyler for an official statement on the girl's trial. Aware
that the fires of passion were burning nearly out of control in the
United States and were sure to bring new demands for intervention, Weyler condescended to reply to Pulitzer's editors:

For judicial reasons there is on trial in the preliminary stages a
person named Evangelina Cossio y Cisneros, who, deceitfully luring
to her house the military commander of the Isle of Pines, had men
posted secretly, who tied him and attempted to assassinate him. This
case is in the preliminary stages and has not as yet been tried by a
competent tribunal, and consequently no sentence has been passed
by me.

The *World* published the general's cable, following the next
day with word from Fitzhugh Lee in Havana that the incident
had been badly exaggerated.

Lee did not know all the facts, nor did the *World*, the *Journal*,
or any official of the government. It was not until Musgrave
published his memoirs much later that the details were put on
record. According to the British journalist, Evangelina had been
allowed to accompany her father into exile when he was banished
for rebellious actions. While on the penal island, Musgrave
wrote, the girl came to the notice of Colonel José Berriz, the

military governor. Lusting after the beautiful Cuban, Berriz tried to rape the prisoner, but her cries for help brought three prisoners to her room just in time to save her from being ravished. Berriz claimed the whole thing was an enticement, and Weyler ordered the girl imprisoned in Havana in the jail where the lost women of Havana's streets paid their debts to a city to which, in truth, they owed nothing.

Absence of this information did nothing to cool the tempers of American women, but inaction on the part of the Queen Regent, General Weyler, and all other officials did have that effect. After a few weeks even Hearst could not figure out ways of keeping the story on page one.

But his reporters were not to be denied their own glory.

Karl Decker, one of the *Journal* men in Havana, turned the trick. He had been sent there specifically for that purpose, and nothing can really mitigate his daring or bravery. It was the sort of coup a million newspapermen have dreamed of pulling off.

Stories in the *Journal* explained it after it was all over. Decker had spent most of August and September effecting the rescue. He had studied the lay of the land for days as a first step. The prison was located in the midst of slums. Pathetic hovels of wood and adobe surrounded the jail on all sides. At one point only a narrow alley separated the prison walls from the nearest shanty.

Decker pondered the situation, first deciding the best technique would be to bribe the guards or get them drunk. Musgrave had tried this earlier but failed. Finally the *Journal* reporter decided on a bold rescue involving the use of a ladder to stretch across the alley and saws and files to cut Evangelina's cell bars. For this he needed assistance and won the help of two men, William McDonald, a shipping agent, and Carlos Carbonelle, a Cuban dentist. Carbonelle rented one of the hovels on the alley, and they secreted a ladder in the upper floor and collected tools for the jimmying of the iron bars.

On a dark night in late September Decker used the ladder to cross to the jail and went to work on the girl's window. The ladder shifted and knocked a piece of stone from the wall into the prison yard. Hurriedly the ladder was removed, just as a guard came by to see what had caused the noise. The labor

at the window was so difficult that the three conspirators gave
up to try again the next night.

On the second try a bar was sawed through, a wrench forced
it to one side and the slim prisoner wormed her way through
the opening. She was delivered from jail, but far from safe.
Decker, pleased with his success, knew enough to be patient.
He secreted her so well in Carbonelle's home that a house-to-
house search failed to reveal her hiding place.

Several nights later, dressed like a sailor, her cascades of
dark hair hidden under a soft fedora hat, Evangelina walked
through the streets of Havana to the waterfront with her three
rescuers tagging along behind, revolvers cocked in their pockets.
None of the Spanish gendarmes on the piers noticed her, and
she slipped up the gangway and to safety on the American
steamer *Seneca*, bound north to New York. President McKinley
welcomed her in a ceremony at Convention Hall in Washington,
millions of Americans felt prouder than they had in years, and
the pretty señorita fell in love with Carlos Carbonelle. After
the war which this incident and many others helped to bring
on, the heroine and hero, then long married, went home to a
free Cuba.

3

★ ★ ★ ★ ★ ★

Shadow over Havana

No HISTORIAN, *or* PSYCHIATRIST for that matter, has ever figured out why American Presidents, eager to have posterity think well of them, load down their cabinets with second- and third-rate men. It is easy to say that a cabinet post is a plum to be given for political services rendered during the election campaign, but even this is an oversimplification. No matter what the reason, the caliber of many cabinets did little to enhance a nation's stature.

William McKinley erred here too. He moved the aging, nearly senile Senator John Sherman of Ohio into the post of Secretary of State to make room for Mark Hanna, the Cleveland financier who had given McKinley his biggest leg up to the White House. Hanna, who was as astute as he was ruthless, wanted a post in the Senate rather than one in the cabinet because he thought it would look better.

Then the President selected Russell Alger for the post of Secretary of War. Alger was not so old as Sherman and certainly was more mentally alert, but he was in chronic ill health and poorly suited for such an important post. The third secretary in the top triumvirate was also a sick man. He was John D. Long of Massachusetts, a veteran from Congressional caucus

rooms and an old crony of McKinley. Long was so ill that he
could not even campaign to help the Republican nominee for
President, but that did not deter McKinley from naming him
to run the Navy.

So these three key cabinet positions were managed by a
superannuated Wynkyn'-Blynkyn'-and-Nod trio that should have
been put out to pasture years before.

These were the men McKinley had to rely upon at a time
when the press was pushing for intervention and the population
growing daily more disturbed by the tales of hunger and des-
peration resulting from the reconcentration decrees in Cuba.
There was exaggeration, no doubt, but the food problem was
actually critical and many peasants were dying of simple malnu-
trition resulting from gathering the population into centers
where they could not find food enough for urban or rural inhabitants.

The student of international affairs is aware that a vacuum
cannot last long in such delicate political areas. As the old men
could not or did not take active steps, Congressional leaders
moved in to exert their own brand of power. Consular authorities in Cuba, especially Lee, did all they could to force intervention. And behind these forces was the press, overwhelmingly
committed to a policy of belligerency, needling the President,
exhorting legislative leaders, titillating the public with stories
of horror and oppression, and the various Cuban juntas which
exploited every item of news for their own ends.

In a small way, the Spanish program was dangerously close
to being genocide. The *reconcentrados*, weakened by near
famine, came down with various diseases that took them off in
shocking numbers. Each repressive move by the government
was countered by reaction from the insurgents leading to the
burning of more farmland, the flight of agrarian workers loyal to
the government, and ever-diminishing harvests.

Diplomacy, at best, is a slow process, and McKinley's at-
tempts to keep the lid on by trying to win Spain over to a
milder policy in Cuba was no exception. Stewart L. Woodford,
his new minister to Madrid, bluntly told the Spanish govern-

ment that the United States could hardly be expected to go on playing an inactive role as hundreds were dying in the Cuban cities.

Finally in October a replacement for Weyler arrived in Havana, Captain General Ramón Blanco, and a few weeks later the Queen Regent issued decrees that softened some of the reconcentration measures instituted by his predecessor. But it was at best only half a loaf. Starvation continued in the provinces, and when McKinley sent his annual message to the Congress on December 6 even his patience had worn thin. He told the two houses that reconcentration was "not civilized warfare. It is extermination."

General Blanco bid farewell to "Butcher" Weyler and turned to the business of establishing some sort of autonomous government as outlined in the Queen Regent's decrees. He was essentially a humane man, seeking to execute orders, but the temper of the insurrectionists was beyond halfway measures. They wanted independence—or at the very least, American interference.

Spain, by now, had many of the feelings that were to rock the United States many years later because of involvement in Vietnam. She had sent scores of thousands of soldiers to the island to enforce peace and had spent millions in the same effort. Nothing seemed to work. Liberals in Spain used the failure as a weapon in seeking change in the government, and the treasury was becoming depleted.

All of this was not lost on Mr. McKinley, who, if not brilliant, had a certain strength that came from common sense. Pushing the niceties of diplomacy aside, he made a direct proposal to Spain that the United States be permitted to take steps to alleviate the tragic conditions in Cuba. Spain gladly gave her assent.

On the day before Christmas, 1897, the State Department issued a proclamation telling the American public that contributions of money for food and medicine for the Cubans would be welcomed. The response was magnificent—unquestionably fostered by the spirit of the season. McKinley himself donated

$5,000 but kept it a secret which was not revealed until after his death. Within a short time relief supplies were flowing into the island in a steady stream.

On the surface it looked as if the clouds were lifting, and Americans, in the main, began to hope that the tragedy on the island so close to their southern border would now be ameliorated.

While these events had been moving forward to what some thought would be a happy ending, other events had been taking place behind the scenes that helped to set the stage for far more serious trouble. They were not of immediate significance, but cannot be overlooked. Two in particular cast long dark shadows across the months ahead.

The lesser of the events was the appointment of Theodore Roosevelt as Assistant Secretary of the Navy. "Teddy" Roosevelt was a war hawk. His letters of the period between his appointment and the outbreak of the war reveal that he was almost as disenchanted with McKinley as he had been with Cleveland for keeping us out of war. He was given to writing bellicose notes to friends in Congress—especially Senator Lodge —in which he described intervention as a highly desirable maneuver that would eventually add various parts of the world to this country's territory. Among Spain's far-flung possessions at this time were the Philippines, far across the Pacific, but not far enough to be beyond the attention of the dynamic Assistant Secretary of the Navy.

Naval intelligence in the last decade of the nineteenth century was something less than well developed, but in the absence of any Spanish attempt to hide the facts, it was known that her Asiatic Squadron was normally based at Manila in the Philippines. Roosevelt, looking far ahead of the immediate situation, maneuvered the selection of Commodore George Dewey as commander of our own Asiatic fleet. Roosevelt callously used his influence, and not a little gall, to get the appointment at a time when Long was away from the Navy Department. The orders came through for Dewey to raise his flag over our squadron on October 21, 1897, and with them came more or less confidential instructions from Roosevelt to think in terms of attacking the Spanish fleet if events in Havana warranted it.

The public knew nothing of these steps except the appointment itself, which caused no stir because the background was not divulged. It seemed a routine change of command, something that went on in all navies at more or less frequent intervals.

The second chain of events that had been moving forward was of much more immediate import to America's course of destiny. It too involved the Navy.

All through the days when war correspondents were sending back dispatches from Cuba telling of Spanish oppression there had been demands by publishers and editors for the sending of American warships to Cuban ports to protect our investments and—after a few arrests were made—American lives.

Consul General Lee in Havana had been no less insistent on having a man-of-war close by if only to back his hand when dealing with Weyler and his subordinates. What was purported to be an anti-American demonstration in Matanzas played into Lee's hands. He blew it up out of all proportion to its real danger and asked his government to place units of the fleet at Key West so that they could steam to Cuba on a moment's notice. Up to that point he was acting well within his rights, even if not with excellent judgment, for he was undoubtedly seeing ghosts as he walked past the cemetery. But then he moved into higher levels of decision by arranging with Captain Charles Sigsbee, commander of the U.S.S. *Maine,* which had been sent to the Florida port, to sail to Cuba on a prearranged signal. According to their little "plot" the *Maine* would prepare to sail if Sigsbee received a message containing the code words "two dollars." If another, forgotten, code word arrived, the *Maine* would head for Havana.

Both the consul general and the captain worried about the possibility that at a critical moment the Spanish censors might cut the cable or stop the flow of mail. Behaving like students in a correspondence school for detectives, they wrote letters back and forth and cabled one another almost daily to test the communications. Sigsbee wrote a magazine article after the war, admitting that some of the messages were rather absurd. "In one

I inquired of General Lee the state of the weather on the south side of Cuba," wrote Sigsbee. "He promptly replied that he did not know—which was quite as gratifying as if he had been fully informed. At another time I cabled, 'What is the price of bull-fight fans?' to which he replied, giving me quotations."

There is no justification in Navy regulations for a ship's officer to execute orders from a consular official unless his superiors instruct him to do so. The whole scheme was a dangerous one when the two nations were little more than a whisker's width away from hostilities.

One evening Sigsbee did receive the preliminary signal, "two dollars," and ordered the *Maine* readied for sailing. No one higher up the chain of command knew anything about the cloak-and-dagger game, but fortunately the government took steps that made the clandestine plan unnecessary. Lee never did get to send the second message.

In January McKinley decided that a warship should "show the colors" as a sign of underlying friendliness with Spain while at the same time giving the worried consul general the military support the latter thought essential. Through diplomatic channels the administration informed Spain that it would send a naval vessel to visit Cuba and would at the same time welcome the appearance of Spanish warships in American harbors. McKinley was entirely honest about the proposal, having no sinister thoughts in the back of his head.

Spain was understandably less than excited about the prospect of the Stars and Stripes appearing in Cuban ports, but could hardly be discourteous enough to say no. She even sent the armored cruiser *Vizcaya* on a visit to New York.

At eleven o'clock on the morning of January 25, 1898, the *Maine* steamed majestically past the guns of the Morro and into Havana harbor. An observer wrote that it was "a beautiful sight and one long to be remembered." Consul General Lee, still afraid something was under his bed, but too frightened to look to verify his fears, sent off a message to Washington, "No demonstration so far."

If there was hidden tension it rarely surfaced. Official calls were exchanged between Captain Sigsbee and the acting Spanish captain general. The weather was beautiful, as it can be in the Caribbean in midwinter, and the American sailors went ashore on liberty, strolled about the city, bought souvenirs, and flirted with the pretty Cuban girls. The Spanish official sent the naval captain and his officers a case of fine sherry, and Sigsbee—more of the Puritan—sent the captain general a copy of his own work, *Deep Sea Sounding and Dredging*.

Accompanied by several officers and Consul General Lee, Sigsbee even went to a bullfight on a Sunday, which irked him a little. On the way back across the harbor to the *Maine* the Americans passed a crowded ferryboat, and perhaps fifty of the latter's passengers whistled derisively and catcalled at the naval party. Yet, on the whole, the atmosphere was less than electric, and life was but little changed in Havana because of the *Maine's* visit. It was the lull that so often comes before a storm.

4

★　★　★　★　★　★

The Bugle Sounded Taps

Millions of americans opened their Saint Valentine's cards on February 14, 1898, looked at the little cupids, floral wreaths, and pierced hearts honoring the patron of love, and did little more than think fondly of those who had sent the missives. A few may have let their fancy roam afield far enough for them to hope that with the war fever somewhat abated international amity might reflect the spirit of the day.

On the same day the carnival season opened in Havana. All day long the streets of the city were filled with celebrants, masked grotesquely, dancing to the frenetic rhythms of drums and horns. The horror of starvation in the distant provinces, even the fear of American intervention, were pushed into the deepest recesses of the maskers' minds. Today, they seemed to be shouting to one another, is carnival! Let tomorrow take care of itself.

"Tomorrow" was February 15, a day Americans would ultimately have to place alongside another at Concord Bridge and still another in Charleston harbor. As a nation grows older the list of these tragic beginnings grows longer and longer. Lessons that should be learned are too often forgotten under the emotional hammering of national pride.

The day dawned with warm breezes blowing across the island from the south, pushing thick clouds toward the tip of Florida. Dancers still flocked into the streets, and as darkness approached their numbers increased. The wind died down and the stars came out in all their tropic glory. A correspondent for the *Journal* wrote that they "seemed to give assurance of eternal peace."

On the dark waters of the harbor Spanish men-of-war, passenger steamers, freighters, and ferries lay quietly in their moorings or shuttled about on their errands like jeweled toys. On board the *Maine* Captain Sigsbee, using the admiral's cabin since no senior officer is normally assigned a ship on detached duty, was writing a letter to his wife. Through the portholes he heard the bugler blowing taps.

"I laid the pen down to listen to the notes of the bugle which were singularly beautiful in the oppressive stillness of the night," he wrote much later, but at the time he had no feeling of approaching tragedy.

He apologized in the letter for having carried a note to his wife from one of her friends around in an unused coat for ten months. He put the paper in the envelope and started to seal it when the quiet of the evening was shattered by a thundering explosion. The *Maine* lurched, listed to one side, and trembled from end to end. The explosion was followed by the rending, tearing noises of the superstructure falling to the deck. The lights went out and black, acrid smoke poured up from the engine room.

Sigsbee made his way to the poop deck, accompanied by the Marine guard who had dutifully reported that the *Maine* had been blown up. The executive officer, Lieutenant Commander Richard Wainwright, several other officers, and a few enlisted men joined the captain, but it was a pitifully small complement of men. Most of the others, asleep on the berth deck or on duty below, were killed by the explosion, scalded to death in the steam from the shattered boilers or drowned by water rushing in through fractured hull plates.

Nearby, small-arms ammunition was exploding in a locker near the officers' wardroom. It was almost the only sound. Sigs-

"Destruction of the Battleship *Maine,* at Havana, February 15, 1898" by
W. Louis Sonntag, Jr.

bee realized that the main magazines, one forward and one aft, had gone up in the initial explosion and that the guncotton magazine in the after part of the battleship either had exploded or was flooded with water.

The captain posted sentries about the rail, thinking for a moment that enemy boarding parties might appear. Instead, small boats from the Spanish cruiser *Alfonso XII,* moored at the next buoy, and the *City of Washington,* a Ward Line steamer, started to arrive alongside.

Many months later, writing of his first impressions, Sigsbee said he "heard the sound of many voices from the shore, suggestive of cheers." Within minutes, however, there was no opportunity for speculation. His men were picked up by the small craft, and the wounded sailors were lifted over the side into the boats from the *Alfonso* and the *City of Washington.* It was made easy by the settling of the *Maine.* Sigsbee looked about his crippled ship, saw there was nothing anyone could do, and stepped directly from the deck into a lifeboat from the Ward Line steamer. He did not even get his feet wet.

Consul General Lee, who had so eagerly insisted that an American naval vessel be sent to Cuba, saw a great column of smoke rising from the harbor after the echoes of the explosion died away. He hurried by horse cab to the palace of Captain General Blanco and discovered the latter in tears. Driving on, Lee reached the waterfront, crowded with onlookers, and was rowed out to the *City of Washington.* In a cabin he found Captain Sigsbee, using the official stationery of the New York and Cuba Mail Steamship Company (the correct name of the Ward Line) to compose a message to the Secretary of the Navy.

The letter, with many lines crossed out and others substituted, was a masterpiece of succinctness and honest concern:

Maine blown up in Havana harbor at nine-forty tonight and destroyed. Many wounded and doubtless more killed or drowned. Wounded and others on board Spanish Man-of-War and Ward Line steamer. Send Light House tenders from Key West for crew and the few pieces of equipment above water. No one has clothing other than that upon him. Public opinion should be suspended until further report. All officers believed to be saved. Jenkins and Merritt not yet accounted for. Many Spanish officers including representative of General Blanco now with me to express sympathy.

Sigsbee

When the sun came up the scene was disarmingly peaceful. Small boats by the dozens moved about the waters of the harbor, where a few twisted sections of the mainmast and tangled segments of the superstructure were all that showed above the surface to reveal the *Maine's* burial place.

A count of survivors showed that 252 officers and men were killed by the explosion or drowned. Eight others died soon after. Jenkins and Merritt, engineering officers, were the only officers lost. The enlisted men, whose quarters were below, suffered the worst, only 16 surviving. Of the 350 men and officers who had sailed into Havana a few short weeks before, only 90 were alive.

Far away, in the city of Washington, President McKinley had gone to bed early, confessing to a servant that he was more tired than usual. A short time after two o'clock the next morning a night watchman awoke him, saying the Navy Secretary, Mr. Long, was on the telephone. McKinley, still barely in command of his faculties, listened in dismay as Long read him Sigsbee's terse message, which had been transmitted by Consul General Lee.

For a time McKinley just paced the floor, the night watchman remembered, muttering, "The *Maine* blown up! The *Maine* blown up!" Then he dressed and summoned his cabinet.

The Spanish *chargé d'affaires* received early notification of the disaster and went to the State Department, his driver whipping the horses through the silent city streets. Whatever the official learned made him feel that the Americans believed the explosion was accidental.

Telegraph wires hummed as correspondents in Havana and Washington detailed the tragedy and its possible meaning. Americans awoke to find that newspapers had used their largest type and darkest ink to spread the news. Headlines ran across most front pages, and reproductions of the *Maine* filled three and four columns. It was bitterly cold in the northern states, but readers feverishly read the news and sensed that war was very close.

William Randolph Hearst was more certain. He phoned the night editor to ask how the story was being played. Told it was on the front page, Hearst asked if any other news shared that page. The editor, aware that several other important articles had been "dummied" into place on the first page replied:

"Only the other big news."

"There is not any other big news," roared Hearst. "Spread the story all over the page. This means war."

McKinley knew some sort of intervention was now inevitable. Looking aged and tired, he sought to calm his more militant associates. Secretary Long thought the President looked "more oppressed and careworn than at any time since I have been in the cabinet." No wonder McKinley's voice quavered as he told the cabinet there must be no war because "the country was not ready for war." Ready or not, angry members of the Congress and most of the men in the street demanded some action, and the French ambassador told his government that "a sort of bellicose fury has seized the American people."

Mr. Hearst and Mr. Pulitzer did nothing to dampen this anger. Their papers took it for granted that the *Maine* had been blown up by the Spaniards, and the *Journal* even ran a diagram of what it called a secret "infernal machine" and showed precisely where it had struck the warship. Where this information came from must have puzzled some readers, as the *Maine* was now deep in the silt of Havana harbor and no diver had yet made an inspection. But evidence was the last thing needed to convince most Americans that the man-of-war had been the victim of a dastardly plot.

For a time Congress behaved surprisingly well, not wishing to provoke the situation. McKinley ordered a naval board of inquiry to make an investigation and hoped secretly that the storm might pass over. He did not stop there, but used every diplomatic power he possessed to get Spain to take steps that would ease the tension. Spain was told that if she granted autonomous rights to the Cubans, the Americans might be persuaded that war was no longer necessary.

It was all futile. Maria Christina, the Austrian-born Queen Regent of Spain, was absolutely adamant. She told Woodford "that she wished to hand over his patrimony unimpaired to her son when he should reach his majority; and that she would prefer to abdicate her regency and return to her Austrian home rather than be the instrument of ceding or parting with any of Spain's colonies."

McKinley had little left with which to fight the war hawks. A Spanish naval court reported that the *Maire* was destroyed by an internal explosion. The American naval commission submitted its findings that an external explosion had been the cause, although it did not assign guilt. In all the United States there could not have been more than a handful of persons who doubted that the external explosion had been the work of Spanish saboteurs.

McKinley teetered at the center of the seesaw, with the yellow press urging immediate armed intervention and a few legislators and diplomats holding out for a delay that might give the Spanish government time to make some amends in Cuba that could be used to quiet the jingoists.

Behind his back, in the highest councils of his Republican administration, the war party was hard to work. Secretary Long left the Navy Department for a needed rest, and within hours Senator Lodge and the Assistant Secretary, Mr. Roosevelt, managed to push the nation very close to the abyss.

"Teddy" Roosevelt, never happier than when exercising virtually unlimited power, ordered ships shifted closer to Cuba, let bids for the purchase of ammunition, and even urged members of Congress to enact laws at once that would lead to the enlistment of thousands of sailors. But this was not the worst. Preempting powers that McKinley should have wielded, Roosevelt and Lodge, enjoying their usurped privileges, sent a wire to Commodore Dewey in Hong Kong.

Secret and confidential. Order the squadron, except *Monocacy,* to Hong Kong. Keep full of coal. In the event of declaration of war Spain, your duty will be to see that the Spanish squadron does not leave the Asiatic coast, and then offensive operations in Philippine Islands. Keep *Olympia* until further orders.

Roosevelt

About this time the Navy Department decided that although the Spanish fleet was divided between the Atlantic and Pacific oceans, the squadron reported in the Cape Verde islands represented the greater power for evil. With our Atlantic forces obliged to defend the east coast, maintain a blockade of Cuba if war came, and defeat the Spanish fleet for mastery of the seas, reinforcements were needed.

Dewey needed every vessel he had off the China coast if he was to challenge the Spaniards in Manila. But there was the battleship *Oregon,* one of the newest in the Navy, lying off the Washington shore. Secretary Long ordered her to steam at full draft down the coast of Central and South America, around Cape Horn, and to a rendezvous somewhere in the West Indies. As the threads of peace wore thin, the American populace watched the *Oregon*'s race as if the nation's survival hung in the balance.

Other, less warlike events were going forward, of course. Woodford, whom history should honor as a fine ambassador, pleaded, begged, cajoled, threatened, and explained. He took message after message from McKinley to the Spanish government, showing that Congress was tugging at its halter, eager to declare war, but that the President thought real independence for the Cubans would suffice to turn the American legislators away from armed conflict.

He was understating the feelings in Washington. Roosevelt told a friend that McKinley was a "white livered cur," a Senator told Long that Congress would "run over" the President and declare war itself, and Senator Chandler, urging intervention, pompously declared that any war with Spain would last from fifteen minutes to three months at the most.

Then Congress passed a bill raising $50 million for the Army and Navy, without a single negative vote.

The Pope offered his good offices to mediate the dispute, but the Americans were beyond this point. New York State appropriated $1 million for defense, and even Iowa, about as far away from any danger from the Spanish fleet as it is possible to be in the United States, appropriated half that sum.

Impelled by the knowledge that the Republican Party would suffer badly in the November elections if he did not take a firmer stand, McKinley finally began to prepare a message to Congress that would, in effect, permit it to vote on a war declaration.

While he was at work the Spanish capitulated. They agreed that Captain General Blanco should declare an end of hostilities in Cuba. McKinley went on composing the message, making it clear that regardless of the sinking of the *Maine,* the United States could not sit back and do nothing about the injustice being meted out to the Cuban people.

He asked Congress to give him powers to secure a final termination of hostilities in Cuba, to establish a stable government there, and to use the military and naval forces in achieving these ends. Then, at the very end of his message, he revealed that the Spanish government had acceded to most of his demands. He went on:

This fact, with every other pertinent consideration, will, I am sure, have your just and careful attention in the solemn deliberations upon which you are about to enter. If this measure (the end of hostilities in Cuba) attains a successful result, then our aspirations as a Christian, peace-loving people will be realized. If it fails, it will be only another justification for our contemplated action.

McKinley did not actually ask for a declaration of war. But in view of the temper of the legislature and the people, it was the same thing. The House voted overwhelmingly for a resolution authorizing the President to intervene in Cuba and set up a stable government on the island. The Senate was more bellicose. It urged military intervention and recognition of the Cuban "republic." Hours of debate in committees finally worked out a compromise which dropped the recognition of the phantom government but kept an amendment disclaiming any wish to maintain sovereignty over the island and promising to hand such control back to the Cubans when peace was restored. On the morning of April 20, 1898, a little more than two months after the sinking of the *Maine,* McKinley signed the joint resolution. It was not, in truth, a declaration of war, but it amounted to the same thing.

Woodford, who had labored so incessantly to preserve a shaky peace, was instructed to inform the Spanish government that it must relinquish all control over Cuba and withdraw its military and naval forces from the island. The Spanish foreign minister outfoxed him at the last moment, stating that the resolution was the same as a war declaration and handing the American diplomat his passport. The ultimatum was never delivered, and it was just about the last time Spain could claim it had saved face.

Men like Roosevelt, Lodge, Chandler, Pulitzer, and Hearst were consummately happy. So were millions of Americans, sure of their strength and righteousness. McKinley was far from pleased over the prospect of bloodshed. He had fought manfully to prevent intervention but had come to realize at the end that a democratic, freedom-loving nation like the United States could not sit by forever while tyranny and stupidity destroyed the Cuban people.

Even the saber-rattling "Teddy" Roosevelt was aware that behind the jingoism were motives of sincerity and decency. He wrote to Elihu Root a fortnight before the final vote was taken in Congress revealing this: "I quite agree with you as to the distinction between fighting for the destruction of the *Maine,* and fighting for the freedom of the Cubans."

Whether war could have been avoided is highly doubtful. Spain was living out her final days as a ruling power of great influence. Her royal leaders could not change their ways after centuries of absolutism. It became evident toward the end that although they realized they could not hope to defeat a younger, powerful nation only sixty miles away from the scene of conflict, as compared to their own position far across the Atlantic, they would prefer a military defeat to a surrender of colonial interests.

Very few Americans wanted peace. They were only a hundred years away from their own war of independence and felt strong kinship with the Cuban patriots. There had been a long fuse, burning slowly, and the sinking of the *Maine* carried a spark directly to the powder magazine.

Crowds milled noisily around the government buildings in Washington and in front of the newspaper offices of the nation's cities for the next few days, aware that war had come, yet confused by events. McKinley ordered a blockade of Cuba's ports and called for 125,000 volunteers for the Army. Yet there had been no formal declaration of war.

The day after Congress acted, the American squadron at Key West moved from its anchorage and headed for Cuba. At dawn on April 22 the flotilla assigned to Havana could just make out the gray battlements of Morro Castle.

Three days after that, in response to a message from the President that seemed unduly late, the Congress adopted a joint resolution establishing that a state of war with Spain actually existed.

In the old days, more often than not, this was how wars began.

5

★ ★ ★ ★ ★ ★

Machining an Army

AMERICA WENT TO WAR with flags waving. A joyous spirit was abroad in the land after the months of waiting. For every voice hushed by caution there were a hundred shouting for the guns to start firing. Men eager to do battle with the Spaniards formed long queues outside enlistment offices. The few arsenals and armories that had supplied arms and ammunition needed to quell a few rambunctious Indian tribes found themselves with huge orders for shells, powder, and guns. They hired more workers and labored around the clock. If all the war correspondents who asked to sail aboard units of the fleet had been counted, there would have been enough to man a cruiser.

At first, it appeared that the Navy would be the only service deeply involved. Blockading is not as dangerous as assaults on enemy beaches, but it exerts a powerful force, particularly against an insular foe. With this in mind, some of McKinley's advisers foolishly thought the bulk of the fighting could be left to the Cuban insurrectionists while our ships quarantined the island.

With a pitifully small regular Army, every burden that could be shouldered by the Navy became important. This, and the desire to keep the Spanish fleets from joining forces, led to the sending of new orders to Dewey at Hong Kong. The day before

Congress made war an actual, legal fact, Secretary Long, with McKinley's approval, sent a coded message to the Commodore showing that they, at least, knew war had come. It read: "War has commenced between the United States and Spain. Proceed at once to Philippine Islands. Commence operations at once, particularly against the Spanish fleet. You must capture vessels or destroy. Use utmost endeavors."

Long also sent a cable to Captain William T. Sampson on the cruiser *New York* giving him command of all ships in the North Atlantic fleet and the rank of rear admiral. A few hours later came the orders to blockade the northern coast of Cuba. With hardly enough time to have new braid sewn on his uniform, Sampson led his fleet out of the Key West roads and headed for Havana.

For a time at least, he would have to rely upon the ships he had at hand. Other components of the North Atlantic fleet under Commodore Winfield S. Schley were ordered to remain in and near Hampton Roads, Virginia, and to form themselves into what became known as the Flying Squadron. This decision was not based on naval strategy, but on public pressure.

Word had reached the Navy Department earlier in April that Admiral Pascual Cervera had started across the Atlantic from Spain. Soon this information seeped down to the general public, and overnight a spasm of fear gripped the entire Atlantic coast of the United States. Mayors wired Washington for naval protection. Coastal guns that had not been fired for decades were unwrapped and oiled. Parents wondered if they should send their children to relatives living in the hinterland.

For some reason New Englanders ran the highest fevers, so the Navy put guns on merchantmen and sent them to patrol the waters off Maine, Massachusetts, Rhode Island, and Long Island.

The Spanish fleet that evoked this panic consisted of four armored cruisers—the *Infanta María Teresa, Almirante Oquendo, Cristóbal Colon,* and *Vizcaya*—escorted by six ships classed variously as torpedo boats and destroyers. Three of the latter had to be towed and all were ready for the shipbreakers. The *Colon,* newest of the cruisers, did not even have her main battery installed. It was a woefully inadequate force with which to start a war, and Admiral Cervera knew it. He had pleaded for ammunition, for repairs, and for men. None of these had been granted him when he was ordered to sea. It was no wonder he told his friends and fellow officers that he had no idea what he could do with such a decrepit squadron.

Nonetheless he sailed to the Cape Verde islands, first stop on the way to the West Indies, where he held a council of war with his captains. They were as pessimistic as the Admiral, and he cabled the Spanish Ministry of Marine that he was convinced it would be "disastrous" to continue on to Puerto Rico. That he did, finally, leaving three of the small ships behind, was at least proof that he was patriotic and courageous. On April 29, four days after Congress voted for war, Cervera's fleet steamed slowly—very slowly—into the vast wastes of the Atlantic.

Sampson, by then on patrol off Havana and other ports on the northern coast of Cuba, had instituted a tight blockade and issued the order that led to the firing of the war's first shot. On his way to Cuba, when seventeen miles off Key West, his escorts spotted a plume of smoke on the horizon. He sent the little gunboat *Nashville* to investigate, and she found the smoke came from a small steamer, the *Buena Ventura,* flying the Spanish flag.

The *Nashville* fired a blank shot which did nothing but incite the steamer to greater speed. A solid shot fired across her bows, which went skipping over the waves like a waterbug, changed the fugitive skipper's mind. He surrendered, not knowing that this was the first expression of anger voiced by the military might of the United States.

Admiral Sampson commanded a fleet so far superior to the Spanish force that any test of strength could have resulted only in an American victory. His flag flew from the new and heavily armored cruiser *New York.* The battleships *Iowa* and *Indiana,* the protected cruiser *Cincinnati,* the unprotected cruisers *Detroit, Marblehead,* and *Montgomery* and the monitors *Puritan, Terror,* and *Amphitrite* gave the American force a better than 4 to 1 edge in firepower over Cervera's antiquated squadron. These men-of-war and the gunboats, torpedo boats, and colliers seemed to fill the whole Strait of Florida when they quit Key West.

The fleet was inexperienced in maneuvers and combined operations but it was manned by many veterans, and what was lacking in skill was offset by martial spirit. Few fleets have gone to sea with more enthusiastic crews on board.

Enthusiasm, as a matter of fact, was the order of the day all over the United States. Most males, from boys to graybeards, offered their services. Civil War veterans, most of them arthritic and short of wind, volunteered on both sides of the Mason-Dixon line. Half the cowboys of the West wanted to "jine the cavalry," and the mills making bunting for American flags went on night shifts and still could not keep up with the demand.

Enthusiasm bordered on lunacy at times One Southern governor announced he would lead his own state's militia into battle, and William "Buffalo Bill" Cody, the old Indian fighter and frontiersman, penned an article for a newspaper describing how he could run the Spanish Army out of Cuba with thirty thousand Indian warriors. Mr. Hearst, never at a loss for headline material, proposed that men like Jim Corbett, Bob Fitzsimmons, "Cap" Anson, and other famous athletes of the time be inducted into a regiment that would so overawe the Spanish that they would lay down their guns.

The fretful, dynamic Assistant Secretary of the Navy, Mr. Roosevelt, had made up his mind very soon after the sinking of the *Maine* that he would not sit out a war at a desk in Washington. He was going to fight. In a letter to Charles Dana, editor of the New York *Sun,* he explained his position, already firm, on April 18:

I want to go because I wouldn't feel that I had been entirely true to my beliefs and convictions, and to the ideal I had set for myself if I didn't go. . . . I am entirely certain that I don't expect any military glory out of this Cuban war, more than is implied in the honorable performance of duty. . . . For two years I have been urging that we put Spain out of Cuba, and if there ever was a righteous war it will be this; and if, owing to the unfortunate delay in beginning it, we see our men dying of yellow fever in Cuba I should hate to be comfortably at home in Washington, although I have as much dislike of death as anyone could have, and take as keen enjoyment in life.

"Teddy" Roosevelt had directed his efforts astutely. Congress authorized the raising of three volunteer cavalry regiments even before the war began, and Secretary of War Alger had promptly offered a colonelcy to the Assistant Navy Secretary. Conscious of his inexperience, he had chosen the next post, as lieutenant colonel, in a regiment to be headed by Colonel Leonard Wood.

Before the first shot had been fired—indeed before Congress had acted to make war inevitable—Roosevelt was on the way to that "military glory" he had told Dana didn't interest him.

Captain Alfred T. Mahan, the brilliant strategist and advocate of seapower as an adjunct to international policy, had been writing for years about naval influence on history. Some of his thinking governed the development of long-range, powerful cruisers for the American Navy, as well as many other changes.

Fortunately or unfortunately, depending upon one's attitude toward Mahan, no one was doing this type of planning for the Army. After the huge levies of manpower needed to win the Civil War were sent home, the regular Army had been allowed to shrivel until, when the Cuban crisis arose, there were fewer than thirty thousand officers and men in uniform. Many of these had been engaged on the frontier with Indian uprisings, which gave them personal experience but in extremely limited spheres of activity.

Indian fighters learn many of the techniques applicable to guerrilla warfare, but very little that helps them when they become part of vast forces working in more or less concentrated maneuvers.

Captain General Blanco, on the other hand, had eighty thousand Spanish regulars who had picked up from one to three years of hard experience fighting in the subtropical climate of Cuba. The noisy but nonmilitary exponents of American strategy assumed that these Spaniards would fade away the minute an American force won lodgment on Cuban soil. The men running the War Department and most of the higher officers had either fought in the Civil War or studied it closely and knew better. They wanted no rabble in arms dumped in Cuba just because the Navy appeared able to protect the lines of supply.

As in most wars involving this country, the leaders must seek men to fill out the ranks of a small regular army and inevitably

they turn to the National Guard. If they do so in despair, it is
not entirely the Guard's fault. The man in uniform during a war
is a hero. In peacetime he is something much less. He gets as
little training and actual support from the War Department as
he does acclaim as a citizen soldier from his neighbors. The les-
son learned when the South seceded in 1861 was forgotten
within a few years after Appomattox, and as a result the state
militia was weak in technical training, had almost no artillery,
and did little but participate in close order drill and parades.

But when McKinley signed the war resolution there were
about 100,000 men in such militia units, and Secretary Alger
knew that such aptitudes as they possessed were far more valuable than those of the men waiting in line to enlist. General
Nelson A. Miles, commanding the nation's armed forces, would
have liked to enlist the guardsmen in a new volunteer army,
officered and led by West Pointers. He never had a chance of
getting his way. State militiamen owed their allegiance to their
respective governors, not the federal government, and they
elected their own officers. There were two sides to this sticky
situation. While the system provided the perfect culture for
breeding political favoritism and high social status in most states,
it did tend to support the thesis, dear to most Americans' hearts,
that every man had the right to bear arms. There was an analogy
to all this, moreover. These men abhorred the idea of a huge
standing army under federal control. Many of them were from
European countries whose militarism had been a prime factor in
their decision to seek freedom in a new land. Or they were the
descendants of such men.

Another troublesome facet of the problem involved what to
do with the men of wealth and influence who were raising their
own regiments of volunteers. The financiers and brokers of Wall
Street were calling for the right to form their own company. So
were wealthy cattlemen, socialites, and others who had access to
the ears of Congressmen. The last thing these individuals wanted
was induction into a regular army where their regional or professional identity would be lost or where their own chosen officers
would be replaced by men trained at the military academy.

Confronted with this state of affairs, the government in Washington was forced to fashion compromises. It devised a bill for the enlistment of volunteers by National Guard units if the various governors desired it that way, with their own officers, but under federal control. In New York the democratic process was invoked to mollify many of the guardsmen. They voted on whether to join the federal Army or not. Most regiments did, but the famous socialite Seventh Regiment of New York City voted against it. Its officers announced it would go to war to defend the country if needed—but not as a component of the regular federal Army. It was this prideful reasoning that led to the regiment sitting out the war in its posh armory.

Between the enlistment of new men and the induction of state militia units, Alger and Miles at least had the makings of a good force for the task at hand. Whatever these young volunteers' differences, they were all enthusiastic, and next to good training nothing makes a better soldier.

It was beginning to warm up in the northern states. Summer was close at hand and the formation of the Army—even if still only on paper—assured the people that all was going well. They wanted to be assured or they would have tossed and turned in their beds, knowing in their hearts that an army of men without equipment was no army.

There were not enough guns, tentage, field artillery, or vehicles to serve a force of even 100,000 men. There were not enough horses and mules to move what there was to be moved. We had laughed at the inability of the Spanish regulars to flush out the insurrectionists in Cuba, but they at least used smokeless powder in their field guns. Our gunners were supplied with black powder which could give an enemy spotter an easy fix on any of our long-range pieces. Although the Army was expected to total a quarter of a million men within a year, there were exactly fifty-seven experts in the Quartermaster Corps to handle the supplies.

The warm weather, just mentioned, did more than arouse hopes in the breasts of American patriots. It had an evil portent too. In the swamps and river valleys of Cuba the *aedes aegypti* mosquitoes were emerging from their watery incubation, many of them infected with the virus of yellow fever. If troops landed on the island before October there would be a worse enemy awaiting them than the Spanish soldiers. So, perhaps, it was a minor blessing that confusion reigned wherever Army affairs were handled. Although there were plenty of little old ladies—and some fussbudgets among the other sex—who hated to witness the damage, it was fortunate indeed that the first men mustered into service found their encampments to be the lawns of state capitols, county courthouses, and village greens. They were much healthier than a Cuban swamp or salt marsh.

McKinley was the last President who had seen service in the Civil War. Perhaps he remembered the inefficiency of the early days when Lincoln was trying to fight a war with poor generals. Whatever the reason, he strove to choose the best men for the job of leading his new, enlarged Army. It was not easy. Every influential man in the country who was able to walk without a cane seemed to think of himself as a natural choice for general's rank. By the hundreds these petitioners waited outside the President's door, or connived with legislators from their home states. The pressure was almost as hard to endure as that of purveyors and suppliers who wanted to get rich in a hurry—at the taxpayers' expense.

Considering everything, McKinley did well to appoint 19 regulars as major generals out of a total of 26, and 66 regulars as brigadier generals out of 102. And he managed, against the importunings of many politicians, to place the best-trained men he could find in the technical and supply services, where mistakes are as troublesome as those on the battlefield.

This does not mean that the men were always the best for the job. There were situations where a stronger chief executive might have moved more adroitly or brutally, but McKinley was a politician himself, and often found himself boxed in because of it.

He saw no way to avoid continuing Major General Miles as commander. Miles was one of the last of the "boy generals" of the War between the States, had won fame as an Indian fighter later, and had powerful friends in Congress and the military establishment.

As field commander, McKinley chose General William R. Shafter, an *opéra bouffe* figure of a soldier who weighed three hundred pounds and tucked all this poundage into a uniform that was always much too tight for him. The rule of seniority made Shafter the choice, and the President did not buck the rule.

There was one more selection that showed that McKinley, even if weighed down by the duties of office and the worries of war, was still a man with a full allotment of noble motives. For some time the President had been thinking of how to show the old rebel guard in Congress and high-spirited Southerners in general that he held no grudges from the bitter days of the Civil War. He decided that one of the key field generals should be from Dixie and summoned Joseph "Fighting Joe" Wheeler to the White House from the halls of Congress, where he had been among the most active of the war hawks. But Wheeler had been one of Robert E. Lee's best cavalry leaders in an army that boasted many of the world's greatest generals of the mounted arm. Grasping the old Confederate's hand, the President said: "There must be a high ranking officer from the South. There must be a symbol that the old days are gone. You are needed."

To most Americans, lacking any inside knowledge, these appointments were pleasing. To tell the truth, though, those who were inhabitants of the populous east coast were much more concerned with the threat of attack and bombardment by the Spanish squadron that rumors had put all the way from Eastport, Maine, to Key West.

Hysteria grew apace as the newspapers hinted that death and destruction were possibly only hours away. The final, crushing evidence that war—as General Sherman had said a little more than three decades before—was hell came when society editors warned the beautiful people of that era not to open their mansions at Newport.

6

★ ★ ★ ★ ★ ★

"You May Fire When Ready, Gridley"

WITH THAT WELL-MANNERED ADHERENCE to protocol for which British diplomacy is famous, the Englishman serving as consul in Hong Kong took note of the fact that the American Congress had voted for war, and promptly had himself rowed out to Commodore Dewey's flagship. Apologetically he informed the naval officer that, as America was now a belligerent, his fleet would have to leave the neutral port within twenty-four hours. Dewey indicated that he knew the rules too, and had the consul piped over the side.

Dewey was as eager to leave the British crown colony as the diplomat was to have him leave, but not for reasons of international comity. He had the decoded message in his cabin ordering him to steam to Manila posthaste, and he could almost taste the sweet fruits of victory.

The American fleet moved along the China coast to Mirs Bay, where the men-of-war took aboard every pound of coal for which there was space. Then the collier replenished its supply and the whole squadron waited impatiently to start for the Philippines.

What delayed the fleet was Dewey's desire to get a report on Spanish strength and dispositions from Oscar F. Williams, American consul at Manila. The Commodore had asked the consul to come to Hong Kong with the latest information, but that official had been slow in finding a ship for the passage. Two days after the squadron reached Mirs Bay, Williams arrived at the anchorage and hurried into consultation. His story of the situation in Manila was incorrect, in that he supposed the harbor had been mined, but he could tick off the ships Dewey would have to fight.

Under the command of Rear Admiral Don Patricio Montojo were the *Reina Cristina,* which was called both a battleship and a protected cruiser, the *Castilla,* a wooden man-of-war without engines; two protected cruisers, the *Isla de Cuba* and the *Isla de Luzon*; two gunboats, the *Don Juan de Austria* and the *Don Antonio de Ulloa*; and a five-hundred-ton vessel, the *Marques del Duero,* a picket boat.

Some of the approaches to the city of Manila were fortified, Williams reported, but the chief danger lay in the seven 6.3 inch guns scattered through the Spanish squadron and four relics of 5.9 inch caliber on the wooden *Castilla.* Dewey looked over his seven vessels, smiled to himself, and sailed for the Philippines at 2 P.M. on April 27, 1898. Williams went along and so did three war correspondents, one of whom behaved as if he were a Spanish patriot instead of an American journalist.

His name was Edwin W. Harden and he was there because Frank Vanderlip, his brother-in-law, was Assistant Secretary of the Treasury and had invited him to sail on the new revenue cutter *Hugh McCullough,* ordered to join Dewey's squadron. Although Dewey had asked the three correspondents not to file any dispatches that would reveal his plans, Harden sent off a cable to the New York *World* before the fleet left Mirs Bay, revealing that Williams had told Dewey Phillipine insurgents were preparing to cooperate with the Americans and that the fleet would sail at once for Manila. This story was published in the *World* while Dewey's force steamed across the China Sea.

It was no wonder Captain Mahan warned that American

commanders should be reluctant to let the press know vital information.

Their hulls and top hamper hastily painted a dull gray instead of the shimmering white so familiar along the China coast and in Japan, Dewey's ships formed two columns and steamed east for a landfall on Luzon. His flagship, the new protected cruiser *Olympia,* led the battle line, ahead of the protected cruisers *Baltimore, Raleigh,* and *Boston.* Next came the unprotected cruiser *Concord* and the gunboat *Petrel,* bringing up the rear. In the other column were the revenue cutter *McCullough,* the collier *Nanshan,* and a supply ship, the *Zafiro.* On the first night out they did not even extinguish their lights. It seemed as if the Americans had nothing but contempt for the enemy. This feeling was surely justified by events, but it was a mighty strange way to head into battle.

Even stranger, however, was the Navy's attitude toward the three newspapermen. Two, on the *McCullough,* were assigned duties with a gun crew and, when not engaged in dummy firing practice, pranced about the deck learning how to use a cutlass. Another, on the flagship, was invited by Dewey to serve as his aide on the bridge when the officer normally performing that duty went off to serve the main battery.

On Friday morning, April 30, the squadron sighted the shore of Luzon Island, more than a hundred miles north of Manila. The *Boston* and *Concord* hurried ahead to discover that the coast was clear, and the squadron turned south for Subic Bay. There were no ships in that anchorage either. Dewey ordered "dead slow ahead," not wishing to reach Manila in the daylight. His captains joined him on the *Olympia* for a final conference. The Commodore, who thirty-six years before had first tasted the smoke of battle under Farragut on the Mississippi River, did not bother with fancy orders, written or verbal. "Follow the motions and movements of the flagship," he said. For well-trained subordinates, that seemed enough.

Picking up speed after nightfall, the American fleet turned into Manila Bay just before midnight, steaming between Corregidor Island on the north and an islet called El Fraile to the south. The night was dark but not entirely so. Great masses of fluffy clouds hid the moon most of the time, but at infrequent intervals the ghostly column of warships was illuminated by its soft light breaking through the cover.

At almost the moment the *McCullough,* last ship in the line, came abreast of Corregidor, her stack belched forth a great plume of fire and sparks. Soot had caught fire, and to the men on the warships ahead it looked as if the little revenue cutter was putting on a fireworks display to celebrate the coming battle. A rocket from Corregidor went up in a great, red, parabolic arc and guns on El Fraile barked three times. Gunners on the revenue cutter fired back, if only to sound a noisy requiem for their chief engineer, who died in the pulsating 170-degree heat of the boiler room just as the fleet turned into the bay.

The fire in the *McCullough's* stack died down, the firing from the harbor forts ceased, and Dewey's column moved relentlessly on in the oppressive stillness of the subtropic night. A fireman on one of the American cruisers emerged topside and uttered one of those deathless comments that mark battles: "We people don't have to worry, for Hell ain't no hotter than this."

The heat did not keep Admiral Montojo from attending a party in Manila. Having convinced himself that there was no hope of a Spanish victory, he had decided to do battle at anchor under the shore batteries of Cavite naval base. He enjoyed himself at the celebration but was careful to leave in plenty of time to share the fortunes of war with his men. He was on the bridge of the *Reina Cristina* when lookouts saw the silhouette of the *Olympia* emerging from the morning mists. Behind her came the American squadron in silent Indian file.

Dewey thought the enemy ships might be lying off Manila, where Consul Williams had said several batteries of modern artillery were emplaced, but he found none. Montojo was no Horatio Nelson but he was a gentleman and did not want to fight where stray projectiles might plunge into the city. So Dewey turned to the south toward Cavite, spotted the Spanish men-of-war, and turned again, this time toward the west. At 5:06 A.M. one of the land batteries opened fire. Standing down in column, with the *Baltimore, Raleigh, Petrel, Concord,* and *Boston* following the *Olympia* at four-hundred-yard intervals in that order, the American Asiatic Squadron steamed straight for the enemy. Shells from the land batteries and from the Spanish ships splashed closer to the column, but Dewey waited until he was five thousand yards off the light at the entrance to Cavite. Somewhere between 5:41 and 6:19 A.M. (no witnesses agreed on the precise moment) Dewey left the open bridge and went to the conning tower, where Captain Charles V. Gridley of the *Olympia* had repaired in order to lessen the chance that all officers would be killed by a single shell's explosion.

"You may fire when ready, Gridley," said the Commodore, and the flagship's eight-inch guns roared out from the forward turret.

Soon all the American ships were firing as the column stood westward, the port batteries hurling a steady curtain of shells into the immobile Spanish squadron.

When all the ships had passed the naval base, Dewey turned to starboard and stood back, using his starboard batteries this time and steadily closing the distance to two thousand yards. Like ducks following their mother, the other American ships followed the *Olympia* in one pass after another, their guns firing without cessation. Through the pall of smoke created by the black powder, which both the Americans and Spanish were using, men on the Yankee cruisers could see some of the enemy ships blazing furiously and others, their cables severed, aimlessly moving about the anchorage. Despite this evidence of damage, the Spanish fire held up well, but the shells fell short or straddled the American ships. Only a few hits were counted and they did surprisingly little damage. Montojo sallied out toward his attackers with his flagship in flames, but the American fire was so heavy that he had to turn back. It was the Spaniards' last gasp.

Just as victory seemed assured, Dewey inquired of his captains how much ammunition they had left. In the turmoil of battle the reply indicated that the ships were down to fifteen rounds per battery. The Commodore ordered the squadron to retire so that the men could have breakfast, but this was only a blind. They could have gone on for another five hours, so delighted were they at the pounding they were giving the enemy.

But a check on the messages revealed that instead of being down to fifteen rounds, the various commanders had reported that they had expended only fifteen rounds. That made breakfast taste better for everyone.

At 11:16 A.M. Dewey re-engaged the Spanish fleet—what was left of it afloat—and the Cavite batteries. By then the *Cristina* and the *Castilla* were engulfed in flames. Montojo had taken his flag to the *Isla de Cuba,* leaving the captain and scores of men on his flagship dead and more wounded. The damage done by the American shells was incredible to the Spaniards. Decks were slippery from blood, magazines had exploded, one hospital room on the *Cristina,* filled with wounded, suffered a direct hit from a five-inch shell and everyone, wounded and medical men alike, was killed. Another well-aimed shell went plunging into the main magazine of the *Don Antonio de Ulloa* and she sank at once. The open decks of the remaining ships in Montojo's out-gunned force looked like slaughterhouses.

The history of wars is replete with evidence of administrative callousness, of unpreparedness, even of total disregard for the welfare of those who fight wars. It is also replete with stories of heroism—blind, senseless heroism for a cause already lost. Admiral Montojo's bravery was such an example. Although his largest ships were lost, he ordered those still able to fight to withdraw to the bottom of the roads at Bacoor and to resist to the end. Ships were to be sunk rather than surrendered. It was a noble gesture, but his men were far more realistic.

Dewey signaled to the *Petrel,* shallowest of his vessels, to enter the naval basin and destroy the remaining Spanish ships. The little gunboat went in, guns belching, at noon. Within moments not a single red and yellow ensign was left waving over the hulks. Lieutenant Hughes sent a boat off from the *Petrel,* and the crew set fire to the *Don Juan de Austria,* the *Isla de Cuba,* and the *Marques del Duero* when the Americans found them abandoned by the Spanish sailors. Supply ships and transports were put to the torch as well, and a white flag fluttered above the batteries of Cavite. In seven hours Dewey had utterly destroyed the entire Spanish squadron and the naval base and made the anchorage useless. It is not often that orders like those cabled by "Teddy" Roosevelt and Secretary Long are obeyed so explicitly in time of war.

Withdrawing his ships to deep water off the city of Manila, the Commodore called for a casualty report, knowing that his ships had been hit several times during the first attack. One after another the warships signaled "no casualties," until the *Baltimore* reported that a shell had hit a box filled with three-pounder ammunition and that two officers and six men had been wounded "very slightly." Those minor injuries and the death of the *McCullough*'s chief engineer from a heart attack induced by the engine room's high temperatures were the only American casualties among the 1,748 men who had gone into battle that muggy Sunday morning.

On the enemy side, it was a different story. Of the 1,875 Spanish officers and men who had tried to uphold their nation's honor with the tools at hand—an antiquated, unprepared, broken-down squadron—a count showed 167 dead and 214 wounded. With the war less than a week old, Spain had lost almost half her fleet and had been swept off the Pacific Ocean as if a typhoon had struck.

No one summed it up better than Lieutenant Fiske, one of the officers on the doughty little *Petrel*, when he wrote: "When the battle was over we did not feel that we had done anything wonderful; and I do not believe that anybody in the fleet appreciated the fact that the Battle of Manila was one of the most important battles that had ever been fought in any country or in any age."

It is entirely possible that Commodore Dewey sensed the importance of his victory although he voiced no such flowery comments. This could explain his very strange action in ordering that the submarine cable from Manila to Hong Kong be pulled up from the silt of the bay and cut. He must have known that the Spanish authorities had sent reports off during the battle and in the quiet hours between its cessation and the severing of the cable that evening. Perhaps he wished no American version of the event to reach the United States until he himself had time to write out a full and accurate account. The Commodore was not a man who hurried—except into battle.

Thus it happened that the Sunday that fell on the first day of

May in the United States—long hours after the smoke had blown away over Manila Bay—dawned with no word from the American fleet in the Philippines. The *World* had carried Harden's dispatch virtually setting the date for the engagement between the two fleets, but this was thin gruel for a populace hungry for the red meat of conflict.

Late in the afternoon a few official dispatches reached government offices in Washington from diplomatic sources in Europe. There had been a battle in Manila Bay; that was certain, but details were missing. Other bits of information trickled out of Madrid to London and Paris, and so into American newspaper offices. Patched together, they indicated that there had been a fleet engagement of major proportions. Few papers went to press with the information because it was Sunday evening, but the news went up on bulletin boards in the front windows of the publishing houses. Crowds gathered and cheered, certain as crowds always are, in such circumstances, that the victory was ours. What the dribs and drabs of news did not reveal, the joyous throngs made up out of whole cloth. The Americans had won! The victory was complete! Long live Commodore Dewey!

Mr. McKinley and his cabinet were less sure. They studied the few official messages, read the news stories handed in by White House correspondents, but still had no clear picture of what had happened across the far Pacific.

An item from Madrid via London told of an American "landing," but another hinted at a later "retirement." To the officials this was maddening, particularly because by now crowds had gathered near the White House and rumors were spreading of a victory that would rank with Trafalgar. It was just as tantalizing for the newspaper editors who stormed up and down their offices growling, "Why doesn't Dewey send some word?"

Before the next morning, however, enough news had been collected in Europe to justify the belief that Dewey had indeed won a handsome victory. And with this conviction, all the idealistic babbling that had echoed through Congressional halls about our disinterest in using the war with Spain as a lever to pry territory out of the enemy's hands and into our own was forgotten. The legal-minded men in Washington saw an escape hatch that would allow them to circumvent the Teller Amendment. That clause had forbidden acquisition of Cuba, but the Philippines were another story. The islands were up for grabs, and within four days after Dewey's defeat of the Spanish squadron McKinley had authorized the sending of an expeditionary force to wrest the islands from Spanish hands.

What was the justification for this bald scheme? Technically it rested on two shaky bases. In war victory brings in its train the power of seizure. In 1898 the theory of self-determination of peoples had few backers in high places. The second argument was more oblique. Dewey had reported to his superiors, and the various consuls in Asia had told theirs that there was a growing insurrectionist movement under way in the Philippines. The leader of this effort was a Filipino, Emilio Aguinaldo, then in exile.

Aguinaldo sent agents to Hong Kong to keep Dewey informed of conditions and Dewey had, in fact, taken two of these agents along with him when he sailed to Manila. They were put ashore after the battle.

If the insurrection succeeded, Washington philosophized, Spain would lose the islands anyway. If an American army of occupation seized them before the insurgents could solidify their hold, then the United States would have a toehold on the edge of the Asian continent, a trading point near China, and a naval base seven thousand miles nearer that part of the world than the ones on the west coast.

Long before Dewey's own report on the battle had been received by the Navy Department, McKinley ordered General Wesley Merritt to head a force to be gathered at San Francisco with the utmost speed. We were not going to wait. There were, it was said in Washington, too many other nations looking greedily at the big archipelago. We would have to work fast to beat them to the prize. Fortunately we had Dewey on the scene, and Dewey was not a man who scared easily.

Without waiting for orders from his superiors—after all, he had cut the only cable himself—the Commodore entered into a compact with the Spanish authorities in Manila. If they refrained from firing at his ships, he told them, he would not attack the

city. In justice to the naval officer it should be said that he himself had not the slightest desire to occupy the islands or even
Manila. He was without any troops and the fleet marine guard
numbered only a few score. Supreme while on his ships, his men
would have been helpless in the narrow Old-World streets of
the Filipino capital. A tight naval blockade was the obvious
ploy, and Dewey put one into effect at once.

Probably the happiest man back home was "Teddy" Roosevelt. He had been the one who put Dewey in command of the
Asiatic Squadron, and he had messaged the Commodore not
only to sink the enemy fleet but to undertake offensive operations
in the Philippines, in the event of war. War had come and the
Commodore had followed the first instructions to the letter. If
he was hesitant about the latter, that could be corrected easily,
once communications were restored.

At any rate, on the day after Dewey's victory, Roosevelt put
in a very busy session with his secretary. The first result was a
message to the hero of the hour: "Let me congratulate you with
all my heart upon your magnificent work. You have made a
name for the nation, and the Navy, and yourself; and I can't
say how pleased I am to think that I had any share in getting
you the opportunity which you have used so well."

The week before, the Assistant Secretary of the Navy had
written various close friends telling them that he was leaving the
government to serve with a volunteer regiment. After dashing
off the congratulatory cable to Dewey he dictated a telegram to
Brooks Brothers, the posh outfitters in New York: "Ordinary
cavalry lieutenant colonel's uniform in blue cravenette."

Another note went to a friend urging him to help enlist eastern blue bloods to fill out the ranks of the regiment. It had been
intended at first that all the volunteers would be mountain men
and cowboys from the West, but socialites along the Atlantic
coast won their point and enlistments were opened for some of
them. To one of the latter, Guy Murchie, Roosevelt sent a third
note on that busy May 2. It read: "Bring on your men so that
we can enlist them . . . at ten Thursday morning, May fifth
without fail."

Ah, what a glorious war it was! A naval victory within the

first week, a handsome new uniform for a dashing volunteer, fine companions flocking to the colors, a joyous populace, fireworks in the streets, new lands to conquer. . . .

Two days later Roosevelt was still exultant. He wrote to another friend: "Didn't Admiral Dewey do wonderfully well? I got him the position out there in Asia last year, and I had to beg hard to do it; and the reason I gave was that we might have to send him to Manila. And we sent him—and he went!"

Far off in the suffocating heat that gripped Manila, Dewey was still composing his message on the battle. How was he to know that a devoted administration and a thankful chief executive had made him a rear admiral?

Five days after he had blasted the Spanish squadron into masses of twisted ironwork and gutted hulls, Admiral Dewey signed his last dispatches, put them on board the *Hugh McCullough,* and sent the cutter to Hong Kong. The three war correspondents, who had fretfully put in their time polishing and repolishing their stories of the great sea battle, went along too. At long last the world would know what a fabulous victory it had been.

When their dispatches finally were set in type and the papers hawked by a thousand newsboys all over the United States, it was just a week from the time Dewey had told Captain Gridley to fire when ready.

The full description of the battle was not in the least anticlimactic. The public hung on every word, the statesmen gloried in this new sign that the United States was well along the road to world eminence, and the newspapers went typographically insane.

Having literally pushed the country into war, the yellow press now screamed for annexation. The Philippines, the editors argued, were essential as an outpost. The islands faced the vast, rich continent of Asia and would be a bulwark as we expanded both our trade and our naval strength. Hawaii too should come under the Stars and Stripes, most expansionists held. The people of the Sandwich Islands wanted it, and we should grant their request. Finally Puerto Rico joined the places that an exultant nation saw as necessary to its own safety, and to its commercial betterment.

Librarians were kept busy helping their fellow Americans leaf through geographies, maps, and gazetteers to find where places like Subic Bay, Cavite, San Juan, Oahu, and other romantic-sounding towns and islands were located. Staid senators and representatives rose to speak of the country's "manifest destiny" and the golden opportunity that history was presenting a Christian nation to take under its wing the weak, the oppressed, and the Godless natives of distant islands. "The fear I have about this war," said Senator Frye, "is that peace will be declared before we can get full occupation of the Philippines and Porto Rico."

The Baltimore *American* was equally blunt: "Common sense tells us to keep what has cost us so much to wrest from an unworthy foe. Back of that is the solid, irresistible sentiment of the people."

Nothing is more pleasant to a politician than to be sure that his wishes are supported by the "solid, irresistible sentiment of the people."

If the solons in Washington saw a "solid" sentiment on the part of the populace, it was limited to such grandiose projects as acquiring real estate in far places. There was no such solid sentiment when it came to opinions about the way things were going around Cuba.

Admiral William T. Sampson was fighting his naval war on a stage, whereas Commodore Dewey had carried his on in a news vacuum. Dewey had three correspondents with him and nearly succeeded in bottling up all their dispatches. Sampson's fleet was accompanied by steamers, tugs, sailboats, even foreign flag ships, all chartered by newspapers and carrying scores of eager reporters. His every change of course was the subject matter of articles published back home. Considering the very real danger that he might run into Cervera's fleet at any time, the presence of this potpourri of auxiliaries took on most of the aspects of a comic opera.

As a result of the stories born of this extensive coverage, the general public became both naval strategists and craven cowards. It "knew" what Sampson and the Navy Department should do in the West Indies, and it "knew" they were not doing enough to protect the Atlantic coast from death and destruction at the hands of the new Spanish armada. If the people had had their way every port would have had a warship anchored offshore. When some of the state militia units ordered into active service were withheld by frightened governors eager to withstand landing parties, the Washington government could not help realizing how serious the apprehension had become.

Armed merchantmen were sent to a few of the larger cities and Schley's Flying Squadron was kept at Hampton Roads, but the Navy Department held firm against any further dilution of its forces. It did send its heavy, awkward monitors down to join Sampson, knowing they would be nearly worthless by themselves in a fleet action. These monitors were little more than floating gun platforms for heavy guns. Used at the entrance to a harbor, they could inflict heavy damage with their powerful rifles, but they could move only a short distance without refueling and were barely seaworthy, pitching and yawing in the mildest of seas. Sampson, or any other commander, would have traded all of them for a couple of fast armored cruisers.

Captain Mahan, writing after the war, agreed that the Navy had been wise to keep Schley's ships bunched off Cape Henry, where they could move swiftly north or south to protect any point if the Spanish fleet appeared. Mahan was a relentless foe of dispersing naval forces, knowing that single ships can never do the chore a large squadron can.

With so much ocean to cover, the Navy did its best to fill all requirements. It requisitioned two swift steamers of the American Transatlantic Line—the *St. Louis* and *Harvard*—and sent them to the Windward islands with instructions to steam north and south along a line about eighty miles east of the French islands of Guadeloupe and Martinique. These neutral points were about as close to Cervera's last known position off the Cape Verde islands as any land in the western hemisphere, and it was thought the Spanish squadron might seek to coal in one of the ports. The auxiliary cruisers could not have engaged the enemy, but their speed would have allowed them to maintain surveillance while staying out of gunshot range.

Each day at noon they met at the center of the picket line and then headed back to the extremities. This patrol was carefully figured out to keep the merchant cruisers on station until such time as the Spaniards would have made a landfall somewhere in the New World. The entire assignment proved valueless through no fault of the scouting ships. No one, either at the Navy Department, on board Sampson's flagship, or on the auxiliaries themselves knew that Cervera's squadron was moving at a snail's pace, towing the three torpedo boats. Just after the *St. Louis* and *Harvard* were ordered to relinquish their search, Cervera's fleet showed up off Martinique. The Admiral sent one of his torpedo destroyers to St. Pierre, where the *Harvard* was coaling. As the former passenger ship had been supplied with only a few guns it was a ticklish situation, but the Spanish vessel, her engines in wretched shape, decided against staying on the scene on the chance of doing battle once the *Harvard* was outside neutral waters. Even if outgunned, the American ship could have shown her heels to the enemy easily.

All through the days that the two auxiliaries had been on patrol, rumors of the Spanish fleet's whereabouts had been springing up everywhere from the rocky headlands of Newfoundland to the palm-shaded sands of Trinidad. It did not matter whether the enemy could physically be where it was rumored to be. Little factors like logistics meant nothing. Cervera would have had to fly to be anywhere near Newfoundland, but the public seldom worries about such small details. If it wishes to worry it will worry without any basis of fact, and even do a better job of it that way.

Secretary Long and his advisers and the admirals were doing a little worrying of their own, although on much sounder principles. They were concerned with Cervera, true, but also were troubled by the difficulties involved in blockading the coast of Cuba, an island with a very long coastline.

On May 11 the torpedo boat *Winslow* was sent to scout in the harbor of Cardenas and found itself enveloped in withering fire from shore batteries. One shell tore through the hull, disabling one of the main engines, and others wounded the commanding officer, put guns out of action, and wrecked part of the bridge. A tug, the revenue cutter *Hudson,* went in to tow the *Winslow* out of range and was herself hit repeatedly. As hawsers were being strung between the vessels another shell exploded on the torpedo boat's deck, killing an ensign and wounding five other men.

On the same day the cruiser *Marblehead* and the gunboats *Nashville* and *Eagle* steamed into the outer roads of Cienfuegos under orders to cut the cables that connected that city with Spain. Commander B. H. McCalla of the cruiser asked Lieutenant Cameron Winslow, navigating officer of the *Nashville,* to lead the cable-cutting party.

The approaches to the port sliced through a shoreline that was most unusual, in that the land on the eastern side was hilly while that on the western side was marshy and low. The cables came out from a blockhouse on Colorado Point, behind a lighthouse that guarded the eastern entrance to the channel. High chaparral ridges reared up behind the point, which itself was a low extension of coral reefs, and in the thick brush rifle pits had been dug by the Spanish soldiers.

Winslow had had some experience laying submarine cables and knew what to expect. They were copper wires covered with layers of tarred rope and all armored with an outer sheath of wire, manufactured to withstand the friction and chafing common to shallow waters. He described the cables later as two inches in diameter and weighing six pounds to the linear foot. "So far as cutting the cable was concerned," he wrote, "it was equivalent to cutting through a bar of iron about as thick as a man's wrist."

The party used two steam cutters and two sailing launches with the working crews in the launches and seven marine sharpshooters in each steam cutter. The crews carried grapnels on heavy ropes to lift the cables, heavy sledges, cold chisels, a block of hard wood faced with iron plating, axes, and cutting pliers. While they waited to go in, McCalla sent the *Eagle* to destroy the lightship at Diego Perez Island as a revenue steamer, the

Windom, and the collier *Saturn* had come up to aid in the blockade.

Soon after daylight on May 11 the *Marblehead* took station where she could watch the harbor, and the *Nashville* moved in to a point off the lighthouse. Each opened fire on the shore installations, demolishing the cable house, as the steam cutters towed the sailing launches into the surf. A steady fire by the Marines kept the enemy in their rifle pits.

The water was so translucent that Winslow could see the bottom clearly, and it did not take long to spot two cables. One was grappled and lifted with great difficulty and the men went to work severing it. It took nearly a half hour of back-breaking labor to saw through this line, but it had to be cut again two hundred feet farther out to prevent easy repairs.

Winslow figured that the severed cable led to Santiago, and assumed the other led toward the Yucatán channel. To cut the second one the small boats moved to within sixty feet of the land and less than a hundred feet from the rifle pits on the chaparral ridge. Realizing that the work party was in grave danger, the *Marblehead* and *Nashville* opened fire on the Spanish positions. Some of the shells barely cleared the boats and Winslow and his men wondered if they would be killed by their own friends, but this did not stop them from their task.

The second cable was even more taut than the first and it was with great trouble that it was snagged and lifted. The rough water set the boats to bouncing, knocking them together so hard that wooden planks and gunwales were splintered and broken.

The men hacking and sawing at the cable grew tired, but Winslow urged them to continue as by now the Spanish riflemen were shooting at them whenever the warships slackened their firing. Each time the Marines opened up with their guns—a one-pounder Hotchkiss in the *Marblehead*'s steam cutter and a Colt machine gun in the *Nashville*'s—the big ships opened up to support them. An hour later the second cable was severed in two places and the party thought its work was done.

As the men were preparing to go back to their ships, Winslow spotted a third, smaller cable that apparently connected the cable house with the city of Cienfuegos inside the harbor. He grappled for it and got it to the surface just as enemy reinforcements swarmed through the chaparral and opened heavy fire. The new arrivals had at least one machine gun.

Winslow saw a man in his boat go down, shot through the head. A second later a man in another boat dropped, hit by a Mauser bullet. Then a seaman, Robert Volz, standing in the stern sheets of the sailing launch, was struck down, struggled to rise, and fell again, a gaping wound in his head, two bullet holes in his body, and a bullet in his shoulder.

It became apparent to Winslow that he would lose all his men if he continued in the attempt to cut the last cable, so he ordered a withdrawal. The steam cutters moved in fearlessly, gathered in the towing lines and started offshore, but not before five men in one of them were wounded and a Mauser bullet went through Winslow's hand.

Getting away in the heavy surf was slow work, and the towing lines broke twice, but the men behaved with incredible intrepidity. Halfway along on their return to their ships, the four small boats were raked by fire from the lighthouse on Colorado Point, where a nest of snipers had the advantage of height and protection from the shots the Marines poured at them.

The entire operation took three hours and, as Admiral French E. Chadwick wrote, took greater courage than a cavalry charge:

To sit calmly within a few hundred feet of an entrenched enemy and saw an iron bar is another matter. . . . If the brilliant hurrah of the cavalry charge deserves a poem, we cannot do less than do the best we can for this courageous band in cold but most appreciative prose. America has never lacked the poet of heroism. There has been many a field for his effort, but none finer than this, though the dramatic sabre must be exchanged for the unpoetic cold chisel and hacksaw. The courage, however, which keeps cool and steady for three long hours, unrelieved by movement, is of far finer sort than that of the brilliant charge, and should have its meed of praise and the highest that can be given.

It was a little flowery perhaps, but these were brave men and deserved high praise. The two men who died were the first victims of the war, as the engagement took place a few hours before the one in Cardenas Bay. Once the working parties were back aboard their ships, McCalla called the *Windom* to join the *Marblehead* and *Nashville* in a bombardment of the lighthouse, knocking it to rubble in vengeance for what the snipers had done.

There was an amazing final chapter to the saga of the valorous engagement off Cienfuegos. Seaman Volz, with the four wounds his companions thought would be fatal, was taken to a Key West hospital, but ten days after he was wounded, he ran away from the institution, rejoined his mates on the *Nashville,* and made a full recovery on the gunboat.

The attempt to cut the cables failed. It was discovered much later that several others had been undetected and messages could still go through from Havana to Spain. What was more important, psychologically, was the death of men in the two actions on the same day.

Dewey had sunk an entire squadron of Spanish warships in Manila Bay without losing a man to enemy gunfire. Now American seamen had been killed and others wounded. Overnight the public back home sensed that war is never a pleasant enterprise. What had seemed to be such an exciting venture a few days before was now a bloody, serious business, and the faces in the crowds reading the bulletins in front of newspaper offices showed it.

7

★　　★　　★　　★　　★　　★

The Bottle Is Corked

THE FIRST CASUALTY LISTS did nothing to diminish the patriotic fever of a nation aware it was on the highroad to international eminence. In fact, coming just after the news of victory at Manila, they spurred enlistments and stirred the hearts of even the most conservative of citizens.

Home-grown poets were busy penning odes and couplets to the glory of Dewey, the new hero, and everything from postcards, celluloid buttons, and flags to children's uniforms did him honor. A young woman walked down the streets of Washington wearing a coat and skirt designed to resemble a volunteer's uniform, even to stripes down the sides of the skirt. When she threw back her coat, her ample bosom was found to be clothed in a silken blouse of red, white, and blue stripes. All across the land boys and older gay blades strung similar striped bunting through the spokes of their bicycles.

Mr. Roosevelt shipped his personal belongings home from the Navy Department after a frenetic week spent rounding up as many Ivy League graduates, wealthy stock brokers and bankers, and exclusive club members as he could lure into joining his volunteer regiment. The best tailors in New York, Washington, and along the Main Line outside Philadelphia were busy whipping up uniforms, and hatters scoured their stock for wide-brimmed sombreros suitable for warding off the hot rays of a subtropical sun.

Then Roosevelt took the train with many of his fellow volunteers to San Antonio, there to help wield everyone into shape. The excitement of the camp, glamorous as it seemed, did not keep him from seeing the virtues of continuing his avocation as a writer. To Robert Bridges, editor of *Scribner's Magazine,* he wrote:

I think I understand about that invitation. The *Century* people and the *Atlantic Monthly* have also been writing to me. If I do this job at all, I am going to do it thoroughly. Possibly I could make some such arrangement (provided neither the yellow fever nor a Mauser bullet catches me) as I have made before, namely, to have the thing appear in magazine form, that is, in popular form, yet when it comes out as a book to be in shape as a permanent historical work.

President McKinley was aware of the patriotic feelings of his countrymen, whether shown by simple manifestations or the garish behavior of the lady with the Stars and Stripes on her bosom and the boyish enthusiasm of the gung-ho ex-Assistant Secretary of the Navy. But he was sobered by the problems war had brought. There was the menace implicit in Cervera's fleet—growing more formidable with each day it was undiscovered—and there was the unexpected opportunity to move into the Philippines with an eye to annexation. And always there was Cuba and the eighty thousand Spanish regulars waiting there.

The President was also discovering what other American Presidents have discovered before and after a term in office. The Congress—egged on by the people—has a way of leading the country into war at times when it is least prepared. McKinley wanted desperately to put a force ashore in Cuba to attack Havana. Having called thousands to the colors, he seemed to think that they could be formed into an expeditionary force overnight. General Miles, who knew the true state of affairs, told him it would take months to train the men, manufacture guns and ammunition, get Army transport, Navy transport, and field rations.

Fear of yellow fever was another deterrent. Miles wanted to

wait until the worst of the summer was over, but the American people were demanding the capture of Havana. Finally a compromise was worked out. The Army Chief of Staff agreed to allow some small-scale assaults to lend support to the insurgents but won a delay—which proved only temporary—in planning a large-scale landing.

With all the shortages, the Army and Navy started purchasing supplies with an almost reckless abandon. The Navy bought or leased steamers and yachts, tugs and freighters—anything that could carry men or supplies. Meat packers were ordered to step up production of tinned as well as fresh meats, and manufacturers spurred to produce arms, tentage, uniforms, and other supplies.

Confusion existed everywhere. Plans to gather an invading force at Key West had to be abandoned when it was found that there was not enough fresh water. New Orleans and Mobile were suggested as embarkation ports, but Tampa was chosen as the closest point to Cuba where there was room for a big encampment. It was a bad choice. A single railroad line ran into the city, and a lack of marshaling yards and spurs left trains backed up for days in the broiling heat. If cars with meat and other perishables were at the rear of a train, the boxcars ahead of them had to be emptied before workers could reach the refrigerator cars. There was spoilage, breakage, and bad stowage. Guns went on one ship while the ammunition for those guns often went on another.

General Shafter set up his headquarters in the Tampa Bay Hotel, where scores of war correspondents, purveyors, politicians, and the curious gathered, adding to his other worries. Troops were sent to train in southern states so as to become acclimated, and slowly, very slowly, the process of machining an army went forward. For the most part the state militiamen settled down to the business of becoming good soldiers without complaining, although the headlines dealt less frequently with the regular army and militia units than they did with those volunteer regiments in bivouac at San Antonio. Colonel Wood, who had been McKinley's physician, found himself playing second fiddle to the publicity-conscious Lieutenant Colonel Roosevelt. Wood did not even get his name in the picture. The regiment he headed had several popular titles—the Western Regiment, the Rustler Regiment, the Cowboy Regiment—but it was not long before it was known as Teddy's Terrors, and finally as the Roosevelt Rough Riders. A casual perusal of the newspapers of the era would have led the reader to believe that the war with Spain was to be fought only with this one volunteer regiment.

Shafter was a good army man, despite his tremendous avoirdupois. As he saw the recruits coming in by the trainload, he must have felt much as Wellington did in the Peninsular Campaign. Looking over a new batch of English levies, the man who would defeat Napoleon at Waterloo said: "They may not frighten the enemy, but by God, they frighten me." But Shafter went ahead, trying to build order from disorder.

Newspaper stories that did not deal with the Army reported the progress of the *Oregon,* now racing up the east coast of South America after her fast voyage down the Pacific from Seattle. And with these reports there arose a growing concern, both in official quarters and in the public mind, lest she run into Cervera's squadron and have to fight alone.

This fear, added to the Navy's eagerness to hunt out and destroy the Spanish fleet, finally goaded the Navy Department into granting Admiral Sampson's request that he head eastward with his main force in hope of intercepting Cervera.

It was decided to order the American fleet to San Juan. This harbor in Puerto Rico was the closest fortified port to Spain. If Cervera was running low on coal it would be a natural destination for him, and if he went elsewhere there was always the prospect of reducing the fortifications there. Moreover, if the Spanish flotilla was heading for the south coast of Cuba, as seemed likely, it might try to enter the Caribbean through the Mona Passage, between Puerto Rico and Santo Domingo, or the Windward Passage, between Haiti and Cuba. Both could stand watching.

So, early in May, Sampson set a course for San Juan, taking with him all of his big ships—the battleships *Iowa* and *Indiana,* and the flagship, the armored cruiser *New York*—plus assorted lighter vessels. Seeking a preponderance of firepower, he also took along the monitors *Amphitrite* and *Terror*.

The top speed of which these two "ugly ducklings" were capable was a maddening six knots. They had to be refueled at frequent intervals. They bobbed like huge corks in the most ordinary of ground swells. They had gone but a short distance before Sampson realized that towing was the only expedient. From then on they yawed at the end of hawsers like reluctant truants being dragged to school. The *Indiana*, one of the four battleships that were the pride of the Navy, developed boiler trouble and her speed dropped to seven knots.

Steaming in and out of the columns of fighting vessels were more than a dozen ships and steam-powered yachts chartered by newspapermen. One troublesome day followed another as the flotilla steamed along north of Cuba, and sober men on the bridges of the men-of-war looked about them and wondered if they were a fleet of warships headed toward battle or a Sunday rendezvous of pleasure craft. The reporters' vessels carried messages between ships, served as couriers, and brought rumors from the four corners of the earth pinpointing Cervera's force at a dozen places.

From May 4 to May 11 this motley potpourri of men-of-war and accompanying craft toiled eastward, making a landfall off El Morro at the entrance of San Juan's magnificent harbor before dawn of the twelfth. From the open sea nothing can be seen of the sheltered anchorage, so high are the walls of the fort, and Sampson was unable to tell whether Cervera's fleet lay inside. He decided to gamble and at 5:30 A.M. opened fire on Morro Castle, the fortifications stretching eastward toward Santurce, and the small emplacements on Palo Seco across the harbor entrance to the east. For two hours and fifteen minutes the fleet lobbed shells into enemy positions. Desultory fire answered from El Morro while the Americans steamed back and forth as Dewey had done before Cavite. The monitors, pitching in the surf, proved almost valueless. Their heavy rifles thundered and barked, but all the spotters in the *New York*'s superstructure could see was the eruption of dirt and sand near the enemy guns.

At 7:45 A.M. Sampson made two decisions: to end the bombardment, which had made it clear no enemy ships were in the harbor, and to return to the Florida Straits off Havana. There was some natural disappointment in his failure to find Cervera's force, and there was the obvious realization that, even if he reduced the forts at San Juan, he would not be able to do more without troops for an occupying force. Without hesitation, therefore, Sampson turned back and started the slow voyage westward. He had no way of knowing, although the Navy Department received reliable notice late that very night, that Cervera had passed by Martinique and had himself headed west on a line roughly parallel, but much farther to the south. Only sailors who have spent years at sea can know how easily ships or fleets can miss one another in the ocean wastes. Without any of the modern electronic devices now available, a vessel just over the horizon was as well hidden as though it were on another ocean. When it was hundreds of miles away, as in this case, discovery was dependent upon chance.

It was not until the small hours of Sunday morning, May 15, while his ungainly flotilla was crawling toward Havana to support the small ships maintaining the blockade, that Sampson received definite word of Cervera's whereabouts. A dispatch boat steamed up with official messages from the Navy Department disclosing that the Spaniards had been at Martinique but were now at Curaçao, taking on coal. The same dispatches ordered him to push at full speed toward Key West. What must have pleased him even more was word that Commodore Schley's Flying Squadron had been instructed to proceed from Hampton Roads at top speed for a rendezvous in the Florida Straits.

Sampson, Secretary Long, and the President were all relieved to learn that Cervera was in the Dutch Antilles. The *Oregon* had last reported in at Bahia, on the northern coast of Brazil, on May 9. She had left on the same day, abandoning slower escorts, and navigators poring over charts with dividers and pencils estimated that there was now little chance of a meeting between the battleship and the Spanish squadron.

Yet there had been a nagging fear in many of the Navy men's

minds. Cervera had been seen heading west from Fort-de-France
in Martinique, but that meant nothing, since he could have
altered course once he was out of sight. They knew that the
Spanish admiral was aware of the approach of the *Oregon*. Her
every move, her every stop for refueling, was proudly announced
in the American press, which was more excited about her race
with the clock than it had been by most of the other incidents
of the naval blockade. To have thought that this information
would not have reached Madrid would have been idiotic.

Writing of this problem a few months later, Captain Mahan
voiced the typical military man's thinking about censorship, and
even those who despise censorship cannot fail to see some
justice in his words:

It was feared that even so vital and evident a necessity as that of
concealing her [the *Oregon*'s] movements would not avail against the
desire of some newspapers to manifest enterprise, at whatever cost to
national interests. If we ever again get into a serious war, a close
supervision of the Press, punitive as well as preventive, will be one
of the first military necessities, unless the tone and disposition, not
of the best, but of the worst, of its members shall have become
sensibly improved; for occasional unintentional leakage, by well-
meaning officials possessing more information than native secretive-
ness, cannot be wholly obviated, and must be accepted, practically,
as one of the inevitable difficulties of conducting war.

Mahan was a purist. Sampson and the President were more
realistic and at first made little effort to keep confidential news
away from the press. American interests actually suffered little
because of this open-handed policy, but it was because of the
lack of wireless communication, rather than any wisdom in high
places. In later wars, when news could travel around the world
in minutes and when no ship moved in a news vacuum, censorship became a necessity, just as Mahan predicted.

When Captain Charles E. Clark of the *Oregon* reached American waters much later, it became evident that he and his officers were far less concerned than their superiors or the general
public about the possibility of an encounter with Cervera. Clark
had, from the time he rounded Cape Horn, devoted much

thought to what he would do if he ran into that particular segment of the Spanish fleet or any other enemy squadron.

He had made up his mind that he would not seek to escape battle but would invite it on his own terms. The *Oregon* had a powerful stern battery and a speed not greatly at variance from that of the enemy men-of-war. Clark intended to draw away from the foe and hoped to overcome the ships one by one, assuming that they would have difficulty in maintaining the same speed. His only fear, really, was that the Spaniards could keep together and could come close enough to use their rapid-fire batteries, and then mount a torpedo attack with their small ships. This would have been a ticklish situation, as Captain Clark admitted. "The torpedo boat," he wrote Mahan much later, "was a rattlesnake to me, that I feared would get in his work while I was fighting the tiger."

In order to steam faster, he had left the torpedo boat *Marietta* behind off the coast of Brazil, and felt a little naked at the thought of a fleet action without such support. If he had known the full story of the poor condition of Cervera's squadron, he would have welcomed battle. As it turned out, the *Oregon* was not sighted by the Spanish force. Clark stopped at Barbados for coal and learned that Cervera was supposed to be at Martinique. Acting on this news, he refueled hastily, left Bridgetown after dark, sailing west for a time but later making a wide arc until he was east of Barbados by a wide margin. Then the *Oregon* sped northward to a safe haven at Jupiter Inlet, Florida.

Her safe arrival after steaming fifteen thousand miles from Puget Sound, Washington, all the way around South America, in eighty days, electrified the nation. Headlines blazed across the length and breadth of the land, and the stories under them made Clark almost as great a hero as Dewey had been a few days before. There was considerable justification for the nation's elation. Although events that followed did not actually require the battleship's presence, the fast voyage of the *Oregon* was one thing that had gone off perfectly in the midst of many mistakes, near failures, and a general inability to get on with the business of preparing for war.

Now, with the exception of Dewey's squadron in the far

eastern reaches of the Pacific, virtually every major warship in
the United States Navy was near or approaching Cuba. Sampson's flotilla was still plodding westward along the northern
coast of Cuba, Schley's was rushing down the Carolina coast
to meet Sampson at Key West, and the *Oregon* was loading
coal near Palm Beach.

This gathering of naval forces had been ordered by the Navy
Department as soon as Cervera had been positively located at
Martinique. From that instant it became apparent that the danger
of a sudden appearance of the enemy off Boston, New York,
Charleston, or any other continental port had disappeared.
Tension eased in these places, politicians stopped their bleating
for protection of their constituencies, and the theater of war
shifted definitely to the West Indies, and Cuba in particular.

Commodore Schley led the Flying Squadron out of Hampton
Roads on the afternoon of May 13, the day after Sampson
shelled San Juan, Puerto Rico. He flew his flag in the armored
cruiser *Brooklyn*, and with him went the first-class battleship
Massachusetts, the second-class battleship *Texas*, the smaller
cruisers *Columbia* and *Minneapolis*, and the ram *Katahdin*, together with auxiliaries and supply ships.

Sampson's fleet was traversing the approaches of the Mona
Passage at this time. It lumbered on until May 17, when it was
in the Old Bahama Passage between Cuba and the Bahama
Banks. There Sampson decided he was needed more urgently
off Havana than where he was, nursing the wayward monitors.
He turned over command to Captain Robley Evans of the *Iowa*
and pushed ahead in his flagship, the *New York*, which was the
fastest of his armored vessels. He had been alone for less than
six hours when he raised the torpedo boat *Dupont* coming
toward him at full tilt. It bore orders instructing him to do
exactly what he was doing—send his fastest armored ship to
join the Flying Squadron, now nearing Key West. It must have
pleased the Admiral to know that his concept of strategy was
so perfect a reflection of the Navy Department's. But Sampson
was not the only officer on the high seas who sensed that power,
and lots of it, was essential somewhere on the southern coast of
Cuba to which Cervera was obviously headed. Captain Evans

steamed along with the rest of the flotilla for a time until he too decided to break away. So the *Iowa* followed on Sampson's heels, steaming along San Nicolas Channel to Key West.

Like actors appearing from the wings for the climactic moment of a play, the ships bore down on the tip of Florida. Schley's Flying Squadron arrived first and refueled. Sampson reached Key West on the afternoon of May 18 and he too took on coal. Then the two commanders conferred on strategy. A reporter later wrote that Schley told him the meeting had been a very friendly one, although there were rumors that the Commodore was grumpy because Sampson had been picked over him to take command in the Atlantic.

As a result of the conference Sampson gave Schley one of his armored cruisers, three battleships, and some smaller warships, retaining only one armored cruiser, one battleship, and the awkward monitors with which to maintain the blockade off Havana and patrol the coast north of Cuba. The next morning, May 19, the Flying Squadron sailed westward and around the tip of Cuba through the Yucatán Channel on a new search for Cervera. The armed merchantman *St. Paul* sailed east to take up a station off Cape Haitien. Finally, thirty-six hours later, the *Iowa*, without waiting to take on coal since she was a vessel of very great fuel endurance, followed in Schley's tracks, taking along the collier *Merrimac* to supply the force that had gone on ahead.

Captain Clark on the *Oregon* was given no opportunity to rest on his laurels as the naval forces gathered for their search-and-destroy operation. He told his chief engineer to make a thorough inspection of the engines and boilers, and when that officer reported that they were in as good shape as when the ship quit Puget Sound, the *Oregon* steamed off to beef up the blockade of Havana.

Most Americans took no note of this last incident, unaware of its significance. Those who had to fight and sail on the sea, however, realized that the battleship's excellent condition and seaworthiness constituted a rousing tribute to the men who built and fitted out our newer men-of-war. Whereas earlier battleships and cruisers had been less than perfect, those that followed the *Oregon* down the ways of American shipyards would be an-

other breed—built beautifully for sustained high speeds, able
to endure damage, and possessed of great firepower.

Schley and the Flying Squadron were sent to scout at Cienfuegos because rumors in Spain had been picked up indicating
that Cervera was bringing arms and ammunition to strengthen
the defenses of Havana. Cienfuegos was the closest port to the
capital on the southern coast of Cuba and was connected by a
railroad. There was no reason to support a theory that Cervera
might go elsewhere, so the squadron headed for that port. When
still thirty or forty miles from Cienfuegos, officers on the bridge
of the *Brooklyn* heard bursts of heavy gunfire, and most of them
assumed this was a welcome salute fired to Cervera as he entered
the port. Because they believed this, they were preconditioned to
the assumption that the fleet from Cape Verde was inside the
harbor when they reached it in the middle of the night of May
21–22. When daylight came they looked into the harbor as well
as they could past headlands that prevented a clear view and saw
a few smokestacks and the masts of sailing ships. Were the
stacks those of fighting ships or freighters? No one agreed. A
reporter on the *Texas* later wrote that most officers were "firmly
convinced" Cervera's fleet was not inside but that Schley was
just as "firmly convinced that they were." The next day the Commodore received a dispatch from Sampson by the torpedo boat
Dupont instructing him to stay on guard off Cienfuegos even
though rumors had Cervera already in Santiago. This pleased
Schley because it gave him an opportunity to delay departure
while determining if the enemy was in fact in Cienfuegos.

The next day he received another message from Sampson
mentioning further confirmation that the Spanish fleet was at
Santiago. It ordered Schley to move to Santiago "with all dispatch" unless he was sure Cervera was at Cienfuegos.

This put the Commodore back in the stew pot. While he was
trying to find a way out of his quandary, the cruiser *Marblehead*
raced up with a copy of the message sent earlier on the *Hawk*.
Sampson had used two vessels as courier boats for fear one
would be delayed. The captain of the larger ship had been on
patrol off Cuba for many days and knew of a signal that had
been devised to inform American vessels when Cuban insurgents

on shore wished to communicate with them. The signal was three white lights flashed from the same spot on the beach. When he told Commodore Schley about this, the senior officer became furious. For each of the three nights the *Brooklyn* had been maintaining station off Cienfuegos, the lookouts and officer of the deck had noticed the three white lights. Schley sent the *Marblehead* up the coast a few miles, the lights flashed on again, and a boat was sent in to contact the Cubans. There were no Spanish ships in the harbor, the insurgents said, and if Schley had known about the signal he could have left for Santiago three days earlier. He did leave within thirty minutes of the cruiser's return from the rendezvous.

Lack of swift communication between Sampson and Schley created serious problems. All messages had to go by dispatch boat and some of the distances were great. Thus Sampson received one from an American agent at Môle Saint Nicolas in Haiti which had come from Schley on May 22, but it was May 25 when the Admiral received it. It said that Schley could not tell whether Cervera was at Cienfuegos or not. By then, naturally, Sampson had received almost infallible information that Cervera was at Santiago.

Schley set a leisurely pace for the Flying Squadron because of heavy seas and engine room breakdowns on the *Merrimac*. On the evening of May 26 he met the *Minneapolis, Yale,* and *St. Paul*, which reported they had not seen the Spanish flotilla. Not bothering to make a search himself, although he was by then very near Santiago, Schley turned and headed for Key West, towing the *Merrimac*, because he feared he would run out of coal. He had been on the return voyage only a short time when the *Harvard* overtook the squadron with orders from the Navy Department to see to it that the Spanish fleet did not leave Santiago.

It was at this juncture that Commodore Schley sent off a message that has been the subject matter of discussion in Navy wardrooms for more than seventy years. He told the Navy Department he could not take on coal in the high seas that were pounding his flotilla. Then he added these sentences: "It is also regretted that the department's orders cannot be obeyed, earnestly as we have all striven to that end. I am forced to return to Key West via Yucatán passage for coal. Can ascertain nothing certain concerning enemy."

The *Harvard* steamed off to put the dispatch on the cable in Haiti, and soon after the seas moderated. Conditions changed drastically as the *Texas* and *Marblehead* refueled and the *Merrimac* effected repairs to her engines. Schley, thinking perhaps that he had been precipitate, ordered a 180-degree change in course and headed straight for Santiago. The next day, when the sun dispelled the mists along the shore, the Flying Squadron steamed past the harbor entrance. There, for all to see, were the *María Teresa* and the *Cristóbal Colon*. Behind them could be made out the top hamper of a third-man-of-war. There was no longer any doubt. Cervera was at Santiago. It was the morning of May 28, and he had been there more than a week.

This was determined later by a perusal of the *St. Paul's* log. On May 17 the armed merchantman, which had just a short time before missed Cervera at Fort-de-France, Martinique, steamed into the harbor of Santiago with the armed tug *Wompatuck* under orders to cut the cable leading from that city to Jamaica. The former transatlantic liner, still armed with only a few guns, went bravely to work with the tug. Scattered gunfire started up from shore, but the two Navy vessels stayed at the job until the cable was dredged up and severed after two days during which, constantly under fire, the American ships luckily suffered no hits. Then they steamed fifty miles east to Guantánamo Bay. The next morning Cervera's fleet entered the harbor of Santiago.

Sampson had grown impatient at Schley's strange reluctance to move to Santiago. On May 23 he decided that he should remain in the narrow waters between Key West and Havana no longer. He gathered together his armored cruiser, his battleship, a monitor or two, and some unprotected cruisers and steamed eastward to be closer to Santiago while still guarding the Bahama Channel and the Windward Passage. Jokers in the flotilla dubbed it the "Bargain Counter Squadron" because many of the ships were in a sad state of disrepair, but Sampson knew it had enough fire power to handle Cervera if he ran into the Spanish fleet, and he also was sure, from Cuban reports, that Cervera was actually in Santiago.

There was one final evidence that Schley was less than the ideal man for the task at Santiago. As his squadron patrolled back and forth off the mouth of the harbor, the *Cristóbal Colon* continued to lie well within view just inside the entrance. It was a challenge many a fleet commander would have reacted to with instant pleasure. Schley, however, pondered the matter for two entire days. Finally, on the last day of May, he took three of his ships in close and formed a line at right angles to the throat of the harbor. As each warship steamed by, it fired at the *Colon*, which replied with a desultory fire herself. No hits registered on either side. Schley withdrew to deeper water, and the next morning the *Colon* weighed anchor and went deeper inside the protected anchorage. She was barely out of sight when Sampson and the Bargain Counter Squadron came up to reinforce the Flying Squadron.

It had all been a little like a comedy of errors or the children's game of pin the tail on the donkey, which must be played while blindfolded. It had also come close to being a fiasco, but it was finished now—for the time being, of course. The Americans had finally put the cork in the bottle.

8

★   ★   ★   ★   ★   ★

Gussie Goes to War

For the navy, May had been both a busy and a most successful month. Dewey had sunk the Spanish fleet at Manila and opened the door to our eventual annexation of the Philippines. The *Oregon* had completed her magnificent fifteen-thousand-mile voyage from Puget Sound to Florida, and Sampson and Schley had succeeded in trapping Cervera at Santiago.

For the Army, May had been considerably less than noteworthy.

Regular troops from all over the country had been funneled into Camp Thomas at Chickamauga National Park in Georgia. They had drilled for a short time and then entrained for Tampa. State militia units followed them into the bivouac at Chickamauga and discovered that almost nothing was ready for them. At one time 44,000 recruits were left to mill about with insufficient tentage, food, or arms. Some of the new enlistees had no changes of underwear, some had neither shoes nor socks, and many had no breadstuffs other than hardtack because no one had thought to assign bakers to their regiments. Equipment issued years before to National Guard units had deteriorated until it was almost useless. Haversacks had rotted, leather articles had decayed, cartridges would not fire because the powder had become wet, and when ordnance men did have ammunition they discovered that many of the cartridges would not fit in the odd assortment of old issue rifles brought into camp by the militiamen.

There were not enough horses, or mules, or wagons, or medicine. Although our involvement in the Cuban insurrection had been under urgent discussion for years, the only uniform cloth on hand was of winter weight because it had never occurred to the War Department that our soldiers might have to fight in the Tropics.

What had happened was to be expected, if not liked, in a democracy. From the end of the Civil War to the start of the new war with Spain the military force had been allowed to dwindle until it was little more than a small frontier body suitable for fighting Indians. General Miles, who took office as Chief of Staff in 1895, did not get along well with Secretary Alger.

Alger himself was not a man for his job once war was declared. He shifted responsibility for many important matters to subordinates and often spent almost his entire day seeing politicians and businessmen who wanted favors granted. A queue of these men lined up outside his door every morning, and instead of throwing them out, he frittered away hours and days dealing with them. Favoritism was rampant everywhere. At a time when the regular Army was still using black powder and the state militiamen were forced to use old Springfield rifles, Colonel Roosevelt succeeded in getting new rifles, smokeless powder, tropical uniforms, and other niceties for his Rough Riders. The three regiments of United States Volunteer Cavalry authorized by special legislation, making them separate and apart from the regular Army and the National Guard, attracted college athletes, the socially elite, and prominent businessmen. It was a thoroughly undemocratic situation, but so great was Roosevelt's charisma that the newspapers could not print enough about him and his regiment, and the public seldom criticized him for his high-handedness.

Somehow, however, McKinley and Miles succeeded in getting enough troops to Tampa to entertain the idea of an invasion. The existence of armed men, fretting for battle, is a temptation

to any commander. Shafter was already bitter at all the headlines acclaiming the Navy's many victories or activities. Therefore, with full backing from Washington, he set out to mount
a small landing for the purpose of delivering guns and ammunition to Cuban irregulars. This decision led to what must go down
in history as one of the most hilarious expeditions in all military
undertakings. Even its name, affixed by more than a score of
news-hungry correspondents, was ridiculous—the *Gussie* expedition.

When it was decided to send arms to the Cubans, Sampson's
flotilla was hunting for Cervera and the Navy had little to offer
in the way of suitable vessels. Thus it happened that an old
side-wheeler, the *Gussie*, painted fire-engine red from her walking beams to the water line, was chosen for this gesture of
goodwill to the insurgents. Two tugs, the *Triton* and the *Dewey*,
chartered by newspaper reporters, served as the *Gussie's* escort
when the old side-wheeler sortied from Key West on May 10,
bound for Mariel. By then, if any world capital, or any newspaper not printed in a trackless jungle, did not know that the
Gussie was bound for the Cuban coast, it was not the fault of
the newspapermen. They had filed dozens of stories telling of
the expedition, the probable place of landing, the purpose, and
how many troops were on board. It was another of the incidents
that sent poor Captain Mahan's blood pressure skyrocketing.

The *Gussie*, with walking-beam threshing noisily, sailed with
all her lights ablaze. She was barely out of the Key West outer
roads when she was accosted by naval vessels on patrol. One
reporter wrote that at least one officer had demanded to know
"what in Hades kind of lunatic asylum had gone adrift."

Eventually the old riverboat reached Cuba and decided to
put ashore three Cuban agents and their horses to make contact
with the insurgents so that they could come down to the shore
to receive the arms and ammunition. The *Gussie* spent three
hours getting her anchor to hold on the rocky bottom of Cabañas Bay. Then the horses were dropped overboard. One tried
to swim toward Florida, apparently smarter than the Army
officers who thought a landing could be made in broad daylight
from such a craft without detection. Events moved very swiftly.

Forty American soldiers went ashore and ran into scattered rifle fire immediately. The leader of this small detachment divided his force and, disregarding lessons learned, or not learned, at West Point as well as international conventions about the use of noncombatants in battle, assigned James F. J. Archibald, a reporter for the San Francisco *Post*, to command one of the groups.

The soldiers advanced in a line of skirmishers and again ran into heavy fire. Archibald took a bullet through his arm above the elbow and thus achieved fame as the first American injured on Cuban soil. Outnumbered, the invaders retreated to the beach and fortunately discovered that several small American naval vessels had come up to investigate the sound of firing. These ships lobbed a few shells over the heads of the Americans, and the Spanish soldiers disappeared into the jungle. The *Gussie* herself had been under attack, her wooden decks and superstructure peppered with small arms fire, but no one on the dauntless riverboat was wounded. It was decided that the invasion should be called off, but even in her final moment confronting the enemy the *Gussie* suffered addtiional humiliation. The anchor that would not hold at first now would not come up at all. There was nothing to do but cut the hawser with an axe.

When wars end victoriously it is commonplace for famous ships to be sought for display in various ports. Nelson's flagship, the *Victory, Old Ironsides,* the *Constellation,* and others before and since have been thus honored. But no city asked for the *Gussie.*

It was during *Gussie*'s expedition that Mr. Roosevelt became Lieutenant Colonel Roosevelt at a ceremony in his Navy Department office. He had spent the last week or so enlisting those men of the "gilded gang" he deemed worthy to fight alongside Arizona, Wyoming, Montana, and Dakota horsemen in his regiment. These easterners were put in K Troop, and whoever served as company clerk must have been amazed at the names.

Taken more or less at random, these men are typical of the K Troop volunteers: William Tiffany, nephew of Mrs. August Belmont; "Reggie" Ronalds, son of Pierre Lorillard Ronalds, a friend of the Prince of Wales; Dudley Dean, former captain of the Harvard football team; Henry Bull, a member of the *Crimson* crew; Horace Devereaux, who led a famous Princeton football team; Guy Murchie, Harvard coach; Woodbury Kane, polo player, hunter, and football player at Harvard; J. C. Clagett and L. M. Montgomery, both Maryland gentleman farmers, who offered to pay their own transportation and to supply their own mounts; and Craig Wadsworth, of whom the Rough Riders' historian, Edward Marshall, wrote, "He had led the Genesee Valley hunts for some years, and at other times had led many a german in New York ballrooms."

Roosevelt took these and other men to San Antonio, where the bronzed riders from Arizona, Indian Territory, and other western states soon found that "easterner" was not always synonymous with "tenderfoot." The "dude warriors," as K Troop was known, may have had money in the bank, but on the dusty salt flats of Texas they stood up with the toughest cowboys and asked no favors. Colonel Roosevelt was in a private seventh heaven whipping these troopers into shape. A photograph taken at the time shows him with his superior, Colonel Wood, and other officers at mess under a tree, the table well supplied with food, what appear to be china dishes, and a fine selection of bottled sauces for their meat. A white tablecloth flaps idly in the breeze. The new lieutenant colonel looks very stern, nowhere near as ebullient as he would seem from a letter he sent a few days later to President McKinley:

My dear Mr. President,

This is just a line to tell you that we are in fine shape. Wood is a dandy Colonel, and I really think that the rank and file of this regiment are better than you would find in any other regiment anywhere. In fact, in all the world there is not a regiment I would so soon belong to. The men are picking up the drill wonderfully. They are very intelligent, and, rather to my surprise, they are very orderly— and they mean business. We are now ready to leave at any moment, and we earnestly hope we will be put into Cuba with the very first troops; the sooner the better; at any rate, we do want to see active service against the enemy.

Pray present my warm regards to Mrs. McKinley and tell her that she will never have cause to fear being ashamed of the First Volunteer Cavalry, which is, in a peculiar sense, her regiment.

The Rough Riders had been in camp about fifteen days at the most, but Colonel Roosevelt had not the slightest doubt that they were ready for the crucial test of battle. His letter to Mr. McKinley was penned on May 25. On June 7 he wrote from Tampa to a relative that he was expecting to sail for Cuba that evening. Less than a month had elapsed between his swearing in and his appearance on the docks at Tampa. It may well have been one of the shortest training periods in the long history of soldiering.

To the future President's amazement, Tampa was a madhouse. He said so in a letter to Senator Lodge which must stand as a classic denunciation of inefficiency, stupidity, and lack of ability on the part of his superiors and the War Department in general. He told of arriving with his men and being unable to find food for them for twenty-four hours, of needing twelve hours to go nine miles on the one rail line running to the port of embarkation, of having to "seize" his transport and hold it against all comers, and of being jammed like sardines on transports tied up under a broiling sun. He called the canal near the docks an open sewer, the below-deck areas of the ship "a Black Hole of Calcutta," and lamented the fact that the command staff had decided to leave the cavalry horses in Florida and have the troopers fight dismounted.

There was no need for exaggeration. Everything Roosevelt described was gospel truth. An army that its leaders did not want to go to Cuba in the heat of summer was being readied for just that purpose. The public was yammering "on to Havana," and there was no ignoring the pressure.

On the wide front porch of the Tampa Bay Hotel dozens of newspaper correspondents kept the rattan rockers going as they guessed when Shafter would leave, how many men he would take with him, and where he would put them ashore in Cuba. Their stories did nothing to allay the suspicions of millions of Americans that Tampa was the focal point of one of the worst mix-ups in our military history.

If there had not been such thorough coverage of events in Florida by the press, more attention might have been paid to a similar, if smaller, evidence of disorganization, confusion, and lack of guidance far across the continent. General Merritt, instructed to prepare an expeditionary force to help Admiral Dewey hold Manila, was having the same trouble Shafter was experiencing. At first he had too few men, then untrained volunteers, and only after repeated remonstrances was he sent five companies of regulars. On May 25 three transports steamed out of the Golden Gate bound for what seemed a destination in another world. America's road to empire had become an exceedingly long one.

Colonel Roosevelt, who had played such an important role in getting the nation involved in the Philippines, was champing at the bit to see action in Cuba. Dewey, whom he had hand-picked for fame, fumed at Cavite, waiting for troops to do what he could not—capture and hold Manila. Alger in Washington was unhappy under the whiplash of public opinion for not having captured Havana within a few days. Shafter was equally unhappy at the thought of fighting a campaign in Cuba with an army short of regulars, poor in officer material, and deficient in supplies. At the White House the President was as discontented as anyone in the administration, wanting a victory in Cuba, hoping for a defeat of Cervera's fleet, nettled over charges of graft and favoritism at home, and unsure of how to handle the Philippines. June was bursting out all over, but there seemed to be no prospect of joy anywhere. All over the country the flags were becoming frayed and the bunting had started to fade.

The American press was also unhappy, and when this condition exists the American people become unhappy. What bothered the correspondents was Shafter's invocation of a rather rigid censorship. Ever since the Cuban insurrection had reached the boiling point, reporters had been going in and out of Cuba without any hindrance from the United States. They had made themselves unofficial couriers to take messages from their publishers to Gómez and bring back pronunciamentos from the guerrilla leader for Americans to read. They had operated under the noses of "Butcher" Weyler and General Blanco as though they enjoyed special dispensation from heaven itself. Once we declared war, they swarmed over the ships of the fleets or chartered boats to go to sea with the various expeditions.

Newspapermen have always exercised initiative in such situations and have been applauded for it. But some of the more ambitious ones had crossed the boundary between initiative and carelessness. These men had sent dispatches to their papers revealing troop and fleet movements, numbers of troops assigned to specific operations, and other highly sensitive information of great value to an alert enemy.

It was obvious in the aborted effort of the *Gussie* to put arms ashore for the insurgents that the Spaniards on the island had been alerted to the steamer's purpose. The destination first decided upon was Mariel, and this information was sent to the hometown newspapers from Tampa and Key West. When the *Gussie* appeared off this coastal town, it was evident that the Spanish were ready and waiting. So the side-wheeler worked its way up the coast to Cabañas. There too were apparently plenty of enemy soldiers who had been kept informed of the approach of the American vessel.

Shafter reacted strongly to the debacle. He ordered that no dispatches be sent from Tampa without first being cleared and stamped by a censor. President McKinley instructed Brigadier General A. W. Greely, chief of the Signal Corps, to put censors in cable offices in New York and other key cities. Lieutenant Colonel George O. Squier, in charge at New York, issued an order in mid-May spelling out the new rules: "The United States authorities declare that all messages containing information of prospective naval movements and current military operations are inimical to the United States, and are consequently forbidden."

Censorship, anathema though it was to the press, brought almost immediate, and successful, results in at least one instance. The War Department, eager to help the insurgents help themselves, prepared another small expedition—this time on the steamer *Florida*. One reporter was allowed to go on the voyage, but his messages were held up until after the mission was accomplished. The failure of the *Gussie* at least led to smarter methods, and the captain of the *Florida*, instead of wandering along the coast of Cuba in plain sight, steamed up the Florida Strait until darkness gave him cover and then made his landfall direct from sea. The *Florida* landed at Puerto de Banes, on the eastern end of Cuba, sent agents into the interior to gather up insurrectionists, and unloaded food, arms, and ammunition before the Spanish officials had any inkling of the expedition.

The crackdown on what reporters could send to their papers had another, less salubrious effect. It muzzled many of them sufficiently to keep the public from knowing what a shambles the military installation at Tampa really was. But it did not muzzle all of them. Poultney Bigelow, writing in *Harper's Weekly,* criticized the Army for drilling men in heavy woolen uniforms in ninety-eight-degree heat and for supplying "greasy pork" which sent a large number of soldiers on sick call each morning. He cited a growing rate of dysentery as proof of poor rations.

Richard Harding Davis, the Beau Brummel of correspondents, attacked Bigelow, whitewashing the authorities in prose that endeared him to generals and politicians alike. The dispute became a running fight in the press, with other reporters taking sides, until the New York *World* felt it had to editorialize on the squabble. The editorial itself had little effect on anyone, but it did give a pen portrait of Mr. Davis that belongs in the annals of war reporting, and this particular war most of all:

But Mr. Davis has had his portrait published as a war correspondent, attired in a Norfolk jacket with twenty-four pockets, golf trousers, cavalry boots, hat and gauntlets, a field g'ass, a notebook, a revolver, a cartridge belt, and a practicable flask. In fact no war correspondent on the stage has ever surpassed the equipment of Mr. Davis when facing the camera.

The press of foreign nations, where wars were more common, had many bitter things to say about this country's preparations for invading Cuba. The German periodicals lambasted the Navy for permitting press boats to accompany fighting forces, and the London *Times* bluntly accused the higher officers and the War

Department of misfeasance, while giving many American reporters the back of its hand by saying they knew little of war and would be more at home covering divorce scandals and lynchings.

Behind this unfortunate washing of dirty linen in public lay serious mistakes, many of which did not come out until after the war was over. There was, in truth, ample evidence that many officers had never had any experience beyond drills in armories or on parade, that the inefficiency and fumbling of which Colonel Roosevelt complained was a way of life at Tampa, and that the food served many of the men was bad or at least badly balanced.

There were brighter aspects to the situation. For the first time since the Civil War the regular Army of the United States had been gathered together in one spot. About 26,000 of them were actually available, and most of these men had had enough experience in the field to make them a most valuable nucleus for an expeditionary force. Their officers were West Pointers for the most part and had been loyal to the Army through many lean years. Such men have a quality that cannot be found in the ranks of volunteers.

Good as the regulars were, however, they had a wretched time trying to unravel the snarls at Tampa. Quartermaster Corps officers had what seemed a strange system for getting supplies to the port of embarkation. Anything that was needed—food, ammunition, uniforms, vehicles, coal, or draft animals—was put on the nearest train at the point of origin and sent steaming off to southern Florida. Often a train could get no closer than twenty-five miles to the encampment. One reporter said supplies for the invasion were scattered from one end of the peninsula to the other. It was no exaggeration.

Decoration Day on the Gulf coast was hot and humid. Dust swirled up from crowded roads and parade grounds, and the rocking chair brigade at the Tampa Bay Hotel waved their palmetto leaf fans and consumed great quantities of iced tea in a futile effort to be comfortable. The three-hundred-pound Shafter rode up in a buckboard, eased himself slowly to the ground, and went in to see what the evening mail had brought.

On top, where a dutiful orderly had placed it, was a telegram from Secretary Alger in Washington. As he read it, the general found that the good dinner he had just eaten and the rich, dark coffee that had topped it off suddenly became bitter in his mouth. The last line of the wire asked bluntly, "When will you sail?"

Shafter stayed up half the night issuing orders to regiments to stand at the ready to board transports, to find critical supplies strung along miles of single-track railroad, and to load what was available at once. Sweating men tried to carry out the orders the next day but could not break the logjam. On the day after that—June 1—General Miles arrived on the scene, and where there had been confusion before there was now utter chaos. Two generals issuing orders in the same place guarantee a lamentable lack of order. But at least the newcomer had the perspicacity to see what was plaguing Shafter and to wire Alger that everyone was doing the best possible under the circumstances.

Poor Mr. McKinley, although a very patient man, found it increasingly hard to get to sleep at night.

9

Hobson Scuttles the
Merrimac

ALL THINGS CONSIDERED, Admiral Sampson was fairly content
with events at sea. He knew Cervera was in a bag and that he
and Schley held the string tightly. He knew that Dewey's victory
had eliminated the bulk of the remainder of the Spanish fleet
except for a few vessels in Spain. The international picture was
not too worrisome, thanks to Britain's stand in favor of the
United States. Most continental nations in Europe tended to
side with the enemy, but with Britain on our side they did
nothing more menacing than to issue disgruntled statements
favorable to Spain.

One might have expected Sampson, therefore, to take it easy,
but he was too good a sailor for that. He knew that neither
firepower nor diplomacy could be relied upon if nature herself
acted up. In the Caribbean it was getting close to hurricane
season, and the Admiral feared that a storm might disperse his
ships outside Santiago and provide Cervera with an opportunity,
albeit a slim one, to escape to the open sea.

He had been thinking of this even before all doubt that the
Spanish squadron had been bottled up had been dispelled. It

was only natural, then, that while steaming east through the
Bahama Channel to add his ships to Schley's, he would make
an effort to temper the danger if a hurricane struck. He called to
his cabin a young lieutenant, Richmond Pearson Hobson, a
naval constructor who had been teaching engineering recently at
the Naval Academy. To him he confided that he was thinking
of sinking a ship in the channel at Santiago in an attempt to
prevent the Spanish squadron from escaping no matter what
happened to the American ships outside. He asked Hobson how
a metal ship could be scuttled and made to sink quickly. From
then on throughout the voyage to Santiago the young engineer
and Sampson had their heads together most of the daylight
hours. Between them they decided that the ship to be used
should be the collier *Merrimac*, the troublesome old tub that had
caused Commodore Schley so many unhappy hours.

Hobson went off to his cabin and started drawing sketches and
figuring out things like stress and strain of explosions on hull
plates and bulkheads, the rate at which water enters certain
sized openings, and how to stop a ship at a precise point when
tides and currents in a narrow channel are unpredictable.

The first plan was a real harum-scarum idea. It was proposed
that the collier would behave like a foreign freighter coming to
supply the Spanish squadron. The American ships had caught
several of them and others were known to be somewhere on the
high seas hoping to evade the watch off Santiago. Hobson filled
in the details: how the ship would approach from the east,
hugging the shore while the American ships fired rapidly—but
carefully—to avoid hitting her. Having given the impression
that she was fleeing from the enemy, the *Merrimac* would then
turn into the harbor mouth and there scuttle herself under the
guns of Morro Castle and Estrella Point.

This project was abandoned when it was learned that the
turbulence in the channel was so great that tugs had been used
by the Spaniards to aid those colliers which had reached Santiago before it was blockaded. Any ship coming in at night,
then, would be suspect under any circumstances.

Hobson went back to his stateroom and devised another plan.
He proposed to Sampson that he, with a minimal number of

men, would take the *Merrimac* into the harbor in the small hours
of the morning just as the moon was starting to sink behind the
hills west of the city. The waning moon would give him enough
light to steer by but would be gone by the time the collier was
at the spot where Hobson wanted to sink her. Hobson agreed
that a flood tide was necessary for handling the collier, and the
almanac suggested that June 2 would be ideal. There would be a
flood tide running at 3:30 A.M., just as the moon was setting.
Their own estimated time of arrival off Santiago would be early
on June 1, Sampson's navigators said, which would give Hobson
and his men most of that day and night to prepare the collier
for its errand.

How best to sink the ship in a hurry was a debatable point.
With the equipment then available, it was decided, there were
really only two feasible techniques: either to place explosives
inside the hull and blow out sections of the bottom plates, or
to place them outside and blow the hull plates inward.

In the former method the rivets would have to be loosened in
advance and pipes filled with powder rigged to simulate cannon.
When they were fired the blast would drive the loosened plates
out. But Hobson told Sampson it might take a couple of days
to free the rivets in the *Merrimac* because of their position and
their rusted condition. So it was decided to use torpedoes on
the outside to do the damage. These would have to be held in
place by a fore-and-aft cable strung around the ship which
would be kept from shifting position by hogging lines strung
around the ship at right angles to the main cable.

The chief gunner and his mates on the *New York* were put
to work making the torpedoes out of tanks, sacks of brown
prismatic powder, a smaller sack of quick-firing black powder,
and an electric primer. Hobson wanted ten of these home-made
torpedoes, one to be placed abreast each bulkhead and cargo
hatch for maximum impact. Wires from each of the devices
would be strung up to the bridge so all could be fired simultaneously. The young naval constructor hoped that some sort of
electric generating "machine" could be found to fire the torpedoes, but there was none to be had in the Bargain Counter
Squadron so he drew plans to substitute batteries for the gen-

erator. Hobson was a careful, precise officer. He wanted to leave nothing to chance. Knowing that batteries were a fragile substitute for an electric generator and that enemy gunfire might damage the torpedoes prematurely, he asked Sampson for the warheads of two torpedoes from the *New York*. These he planned to install inside the center hold of the *Merrimac* as a backup means of sinking the collier. Sampson turned the proposal down cold. "Two hundred pounds of guncotton on the inside," he growled, "would blow everything to the devil."

When the Admiral's flotilla poined the main force at Santiago, word of the impending plan spread like wildfire through the combined fleets. Hobson had said he wanted six volunteers to accompany him on the dangerous mission.

Captain "Fighting Bob" Evans of the *Iowa* signaled Sampson, "Every man on the ship wants to go." Captain J. W. Philip of the *Texas* sent word he had 250 volunteers, and the *Brooklyn* signalmen wigwagged that two-thirds of that battleship's crew was eager to serve. Even Captain J. M. Miller of the *Merrimac* volunteered, claiming it was his right to go because it was his ship.

That was the era before draft cards were burned. If every volunteer had been allowed to go on the *Merrimac* the collier would have sunk in the open seas before nearing the channel. Hobson believed he could do nicely with six aides. He wanted two anchors slung over the sides, chains on deck, and lashed with rope in a simple manner so the men could let go the anchors by cutting the rope with an axe. One man was needed in the boiler room, another in the engine room, a third at the wheel, and the fourth to assist with torpedoes.

It was planned to steam swiftly to the entrance of the harbor, there slow down to about five knots, port the helm and then, as the collier started to swing, let go the starboard stern anchor with forty fathoms of chain. This should cause the ship to swing broadside to the narrow channel, effectively blocking it. The *Merrimac* was 333 feet long and the channel about 350 to 400 feet in the narrower sections.

On paper it looked fail-safe. But the next day, while Sampson's squadron maneuvered with Schley's off Santiago, Hobson learned that the deed is never as easy as the wish. First the *Merrimac* had to be stripped of valuables and the crew's belongings. Then the torpedoes, lines, wiring, and other controls had to be arranged, the anchors lifted to the deck, and coal shifted to free those hull plates to be blown inward. New Manila rope was secured for the torpedo fore-and-aft lines and the anchors and put aside in a safe place. Then Hobson went off to confer with Admiral Sampson. When he returned to the *Merrimac* everything had been fouled up. The stripping parties, thinking to save everything valuable, had made off with the new hawsers. The anchors had not been freed and the coal-heavers, misunderstanding their assignment, had shoveled tons of coal from one side to the other but not away from the all-important sections of the hull.

Gangways were jammed with supplies and personal gear. Even a beer barrel had gone adrift. The anchor windlass could not lift the chains from the lockers, and even with the help of scores of volunteers the stubborn links refused to budge. Then the forward stream anchor was slung from the cargo boom to the deck of the *Massachusetts*, which dropped aft, where it was picked up by the stern cargo boom of the *Merrimac*. Night fell and the crew went on working by the light of kerosene lanterns. Down in the bowels of the old collier, men opened every manhole cover, hatch, and other opening so water could rush in more easily. Then seven hundred tons of water were pumped into the ship's double bottom to make her heavier.

Hobson had picked his crew by the time he went to dinner and a final conference with Sampson on the *New York*. John P. Phillips, a machinist; Francis Kelly, a water-tender; and a quartermaster named Oscar Deignan—all from the *Merrimac*—were chosen because they knew their own vessel well. James Mullen, boatswain on the collier, was accepted as a volunteer because the handling of the anchors would be an exceedingly dangerous operation and no one knows more about such things than a ship's boatswain. A crew member named George Charette from the *New York* who had served with Hobson on the *Chicago* years before, asked to go and was taken. Then Daniel Montague, the chief master-at-arms on the flagship, was picked as the last of the daredevil volunteers.

Long after midnight on the morning of June 2, the Admiral, who was almost as excited as Hobson, left the *New York* and steamed across to inspect the *Merrimac*. He went all through the collier, discussing the plans and devices for sinking her, making suggestions and alterations. Calling the crew together on the deck, he thanked each one personally for volunteering, told them the nation would be proud of their actions, and wished them well.

As the *New York*'s steam launch moved away from the *Merrimac* the propellers of the small boat fouled a line hanging from the collier. It took more than a half hour to free them, at a time when a half hour was critically important. Hobson waved and the launch put-putted back to the flagship.

All lights doused, the *Merrimac* stood in toward the entrance of the channel, Hobson guiding her along an imaginary line formed by two of the warships anchored in tandem for that very purpose. A thousand feet ahead the skipper and Deignan saw a strange craft flashing a white light. Hobson approached the mystery vessel, not knowing whether she was friend or foe, but it turned out that she was a press boat that had lost her bearings while scouting off Morro Castle. Directions were supplied and once again the *Merrimac*'s engines throbbed wide open.

False dawn was brightening the sky to the east when Hobson set his course straight and true for the mouth of the channel. He knew in his heart that too much time had been lost and, in obedience to instructions, he kept a lookout to the rear where the *New York* lay at anchor. In a few minutes he saw a light on Sampson's ship, signaling him to return. The Admiral feared that daylight would break before the collier could reach her position for scuttling. Hobson backed his engines reluctantly, put the helm over and rejoined the fleet, dejected at the thought of waiting another twenty-four hours.

Hobson and his six volunteers went aboard the *New York* and a relief crew took over the *Merrimac* for the time being. Mullen, who had worked two days without sleep, was so exhausted that the surgeon ordered him replaced by another volunteer. The new man turned out to be a coxswain named J. E. Murphy from the battleship *Iowa,* picked by his mates as the ablest man for the purpose.

During the long, enervating wait on the flagship the scuttling crew was babied and petted by everyone. The captain asked Hobson to have late afternoon lunch with him since the lieutenant would be leaving for his ship about dinner time. The volunteers were offered fresh oranges which had just come on board, and at least one bottle of spirits was handed Hobson for the run into the channel that evening. Still another officer tried to get Hobson to take an expensive brace of pistols. All were made to lie down and rest in preparation for their hour of peril later on.

Meanwhile, on the *Merrimac,* the various gunner's mates had found that the batteries would not fire the torpedoes from a central location. So it was necessary to wire a set to each torpedo, necessitating the individual firing of each of the explosive containers.

Hobson told his men of the change. Instead of his firing them from the bridge, they would all have to handle one or more themselves. They were to be fired in succession, starting forward so the first damage to the hull would cause the collier to sink by the bow. Murphy was to let go the anchor and then fire torpedo No. 1 without further orders from the bridge. Charette was to explode No. 2 and No. 3. Deignan, after putting the helm hard aport, was to dash onto the deck and fire No. 4 as soon as the third one had gone. A new volunteer would have to do the same for No. 5.

Phillips and Kelly were to stop the engines, open the seacocks, flooding the holds, and then climb briskly to the deck, there to fire No. 6 and No. 8. The other torpedoes had been found inoperable.

About midnight the *Merrimac's* scuttling crew went aboard her and tried to sleep while a relief crew took her closer to Morro Castle, guarding the channel mouth. Hobson could not

get to sleep and went on deck to find his ship idle in the water.
In the weird moonlight he could see the other ships of the fleet,
the *Brooklyn* looking almost white in the reflected glow of the
moon but the *Texas* dark and sinister because he could see only
her unlighted side. The other men-of-war looked like phantom
ships.

Hobson went to the bridge and found at the wheel a young
coxswain from the *New York,* whose looks he liked even before
the young sailor asked to accompany him. So in this fashion
was Rudolph Clausen selected to handle the extra torpedo. He
was not, as some newspaper stories told it later, a stowaway.

Between midnight and 2 A.M. the various members of the
relief crew left the *Merrimac* by launches, and finally the last
man was gone, leaving Hobson and his seven volunteers. They
had fired the boilers, built up a full head of steam, and left
things so the scuttlers would have little to do but run the collier
straight into the channel.

Hobson ordered his men to strip to their shorts, to strap on
their revolvers and life belts, and to lie down when not performing essential duties to reduce the chance of being struck by
small arms fire. Charette put a bucket of coffee against the
boiler to heat it and then carried it up to the deck.

The *Merrimac* stood on, straight toward the narrow throat of
the channel that gives access to Santiago harbor. Her anchors,
hanging over the side, dragged just below the surface of the sea,
setting the water to foaming.

At nine knots the collier moved briskly almost straight north.
Off the two-fathom banks under Morro the bow swung a little
to the northwestward.

"Meet her," ordered Hobson.

"Meet her, sir," replied Deignan, checking the swing.

"Steady."

"Steady, sir."

The old tub, Hobson recalled later, moved like a sleek yacht
with Deignan's light touch on the wheel. Minutes later the
shadow of Morro Castle was hard on the starboard bow. Except
for the noise of the collier's bow wave and the low humming of
her engines far below, the men on deck could hear nothing in

the darkness. Were they going to pass this dangerous point without being seen, they wondered?

It was now exactly 3 A.M. and Hobson thought he could see a white spot beyond Morro, a spot where the light shining through a cleft in the hills justifies the name Punta Estrella— Star Point. Then out of the black night on the port side came a flash of light and a blast from a small gun. The shell must have gone astern. Another flash and the shell also went off a hundred yards behind the collier. The Spaniards were firing at the rudder, the most vulnerable single spot on the ship. Looking through his night glasses, Hobson could see that the firing was coming from a small picket boat lying just under Canones Point. If only he had a rapid-fire gun of his own, thought the commander, he would not be a sitting duck in a mill pond.

The picket boat's opening gun was the signal the Spanish forts were awaiting. From far above on the starboard side the heavy cannon of Morro Castle bellowed and flamed, answered immediately by other batteries on Canones Point and somewhere ahead across the channel from Punta Estrella.

A shell burst near the *Merrimac*'s bridge but Hobson and Deignan were untouched. The captain stepped to the engine room telegraph and signaled the order "Stop engines!" Even in the midst of the heavy firing he heard from far below the sound of seacocks being broken off as Phillips and Kelly swung their axes. Charette left the bridge to stand by his torpedo.

As the *Merrimac* passed the bluff on which Morro Castle stands, she was making four and a half knots and a following tide added another knot and a half. Nothing, it seemed, could keep the collier from reaching the narrow throat of the channel where she was to be scuttled. Just then Hobson noticed the bow was turning.

"Hard aport," he ordered.

"Hard aport, sir," answered Deignan.

There was no response to the rudder.

"Hard aport, I say," roared Hobson.

Deignan looked at the skipper, his face white with anxiety.

"The helm is hard aport, sir, and lashed."

The rudder was gone. At the last, crucial instant, a heavy shell from one of the big guns had wrecked the stern structure, cut away the lashings of one of the anchors, and destroyed the rudder head. Like a riderless horse the collier was heading straight up the narrow channel.

Hobson pulled at the line looped around Montague's wrist to alert him, then he pulled again, three times. Before he could wonder if the signal arranged so many hours before had been received, he heard the bow anchor let go and slide into the water. A second later there was a dull roar and torpedo No. 1 had gone off.

Other torpedoes should have been fired after the first, but there was no sound other than the increasing shriek of shells whistling around the *Merrimac*. Charette came running to the bridge to report that No. 2 and No. 3 could not be fired because shells had wrecked the battery packs. Hobson told him to see that any left intact be fired. A minute later he heard No. 5 explode.

Fire from the shore—especially rifle fire—was increasing. Bullets struck the deck and sides of the ship like hailstones. Weeks later the scuttling party learned, while in prison, that an entire regiment was shooting at them from one side and another regiment from the opposite side of the channel.

Hobson, seeing that there was little he could do on the bridge with the rudder gone, went to the deck to see what could be done about firing more torpedoes. It was futile. Nos. 2, 3, 4, 6, and 8 would never go off as their battery packs had been smashed and riddled by bullets and flying shell fragments. This was when he could have used the two warheads that Sampson had denied him.

Still under considerable way, the *Merrimac* moved inexorably up the channel. Charette thought the stern would go aground and said so, but Hobson, looking through a chock that served as a peephole, saw that the collier's momentum seemed unabated.

Two torpedoes had gone off and the *Merrimac* was taking water but at far too slow a rate to sink her where the crew wished. Anchors had been dropped, but they too failed to hold, the chains having been shot away by the heavy guns at Morro Castle. There was not a thing Hobson and his men could do to stop the stubborn collier from riding the breast of the tide into the harbor.

Mustering his men at the base of the bridge housing, Hobson counted and all seemed accounted for. Then he saw a nearly naked man, revolver in his shaky hand, coming up the main deck from the mainmast. There was blood on his face and Hobson leveled his own revolver at the intruder, thinking the Spaniards had sent a boarding party out from shore. Then he recognized Kelly, the boilerman.

Kelly had helped Phillips smash the seacocks and had followed him topside. Standing near the mast and strapping on his lifebelt preparatory to going to his assigned station at one of the torpedoes, he was knocked down by a tremendous explosion that dashed him against a winch. A shell had hit close by the mainmast.

When the boilerman came to, still groggy, with his lip cut away on one side, his instinct directed him to go below. He started down the engine room hatch and found water rising near the top of the ladder. This sight apparently restored his memory, and he dutifully turned to crawl toward the torpedo, but found the batteries shattered, cells strewn about the deck as if by an angry giant's hand. Then he followed instructions and started for the mustering point, only to find he was mistaken for a boarder. Recognition brought help and his companions gave him first aid.

Just as Hobson holstered his revolver, they all felt a thunderous shock beneath their feet and the boat seemed to lift straight up. A series of shocks followed and then the *Merrimac* settled again. Hobson cheered with glee. A mine had ripped the collier and she might yet sink in the narrow waterway. Soon, however, it dawned on the men that they were nursing a false hope. The sinking rate increased hardly at all. Tons of coal must have absorbed the shock and could even be plugging the hole.

It was nothing less than a miracle that the eight men were not hit by the hail of bullets. Repeating rifles were firing straight

down upon the deck from the bluffs above the channel on the
eastern side, and what seemed like hundreds of soldiers were
shooting from both banks.

As the collier was carried up channel she came within range
of batteries on Socapa Point. Nordenfelt rapid-fire guns and
Hotchkiss revolving cannon added their unmistakable noise to
the deeper-throated roar of the old nine-inch mortars. From the
trajectory of some of the shells, Hobson sensed that some guns
were being fired from shipboard—almost level with the deck of
the collier. Writing of the event a year later, he described what
it was like to be at the vortex of this heavy gunfire:

A deadly fire came from ahead, apparently from shipboard. These
larger projectiles would enter, explode, and rake us; those passing
over the spar-deck would apparently pass through the deck-house,
far enough away to cause them to explode just in front of us. All
firing was at point-blank range, at a target that could hardly be
missed, the Socapa batteries with plunging fire, the ships' batteries
with horizontal fire. The striking projectiles and flying fragments produced a grinding sound, with a fine ring in it of steel on steel.

They all became aware of a strange physical and psychological reaction to the drumfire of the shells. They became parched
by thirst and, lying belly down on the deck, drank from their
canteens as if they were on a desert under the rays of a tropic
sun.

Hobson found himself wondering what the sensation would
be if a shell tore into his body but, being a brave man, he pushed
such morbid thoughts away and again peered through the claws
of the chock. The Merrimac had apparently gone aground near
Estrella Point, but then he noticed the bow swinging, and he
knew the tide was straightening her out. This action by the
current pulled her off and sent her on up the channel toward
where it debouched into the wide harbor.

Enemy fire fell off momentarily and they looked ahead, only
to see the cruiser Reina Mercedes and the torpedo boat Pluton
moving into position so their torpedo tubes would bear on the
collier. For the last time Hobson enjoyed the luxury of a forlorn
hope. Perhaps torpedoes would strike the Merrimac and sink

her before she emerged from the narrow passage. But he realized his error when the battered ship beneath him plowed on even though lurching to port in a shuddering movement. The *Merrimac* swung still further to port, her bow went down, and the stern rose steeply. Water rushed along the deck and then the ship went under, righting herself as she sank.

Some of the men were washed over the bulwarks but were washed back aboard at the inrush of water when the vessel was going under. Kelly, who had suffered most of all, was sucked below into a coal bunker by receding water, but a sudden lurch brought the water back and he was ejected through the same opening into which he had been dragged and found himself once more on deck.

Their lifeboat had been shattered by shellfire or torn away when the collier went down, but a second craft, a sort of catamaran, was still floating above the wreckage, tied by a line to a cargo boom. The men swam to it and held on while enemy boats patrolled the waters near Socapa Point looking for survivors. Time went by and while they waited, tired and forlorn, Hobson could see that the entire enterprise had been a complete failure. The *Merrimac* lay inside the harbor off to the west from the channel, leaving plenty of room for the Spanish men-of-war to pass in and out without danger.

The moon went down behind Socapa Point, the water grew chilly, and the men wondered what would happen when dawn revealed their plight. No one complained except that the mission for which they had held such high hopes had failed.

They had been in the water about an hour and a half when daylight disclosed a steam launch bearing down on them. A squad of riflemen on the tiny forecastle aimed their guns but held fire. An officer came to the rail and helped Hobson climb aboard as others assisted his men to the deck. Shivering and numb with cold, they lay below and warmed themselves beside the boiler as the launch took them to the *Reina Mercedes*. Only when they boarded the man-of-war did Hobson learn the identity of the officer who had helped pull him from the water. It was Admiral Cervera himself.

The Americans were given clothing, questioned amicably by

their captors, and then sent off to incarceration in Morro Castle. Everything was done with punctilious correctness, and there seemed to be a complete lack of animosity on the part of the Spaniards. After all, they had every right to feel elated. Their escape route to the open sea was still open.

Out on the ships of the blockading fleet there was deep anxiety. Watchers had seen the shell bursts and heard the heavy firing, aware from the virulence of the cannonading that the *Merrimac* was in trouble. When things quieted down they waited for word from the *New York*'s steam launch, which, under command of naval Cadet J. W. Powell, had been stationed almost in the shadow of Morro Castle to help in a rescue attempt if Hobson and the crew had escaped on their catamaran. But daylight brought no sign of the launch, and everyone became concerned lest that small craft had been sunk. Finally the lookouts made out a plume of black smoke and beneath it the little launch emerging from the channel, hugging the western shore. The tide was against her and the seas made her bounce like a cork, but she kept plugging along for another half hour before the artillerists high above spotted her. Shells burst all around her as she wallowed in the troughs, but none struck her and she made her way to safety. Powell had risked all to stay within easy gunshot of the shore until the last minute but had no word of the scuttling crew. He did reveal, however, that he could see the masts of the *Merrimac* sticking out of the water at a spot where it offered no obstacle. Every American from Sampson down to the newest cadet shared a common disappointment.

What they did not know did not stop many of the correspondents from filing stories back home indicating that the attempt had been a success. Using the fanciest adjectives in their vocabularies, they told of the heroism of the formerly unsung naval constructor, and before the day was over the people of the United States had a new hero—Richmond Pearson Hobson.

The Associated Press unequivocally announced that the *Merrimac* had blocked the channel, and the New York *Journal*'s lead article said that "the name of Hobson has gone on the list of American heroes, with Lawrence, Paul Jones, Perry, Cushing and the rest."

It was the sort of news Americans had been waiting to hear. Dewey's victory had grown a little stale, and nothing is more desirable than a hero in war time. Now there was a new one.

But this feeling was not reflected in the fleet off Santiago. All through the day they waited for some accurate word of Hobson's fate. It came from a most unexpected source and in a most unusual manner. About 4 P.M. a Spanish gunboat, flying a flag of truce, came out of the channel—itself tacit proof the mission had failed—and an officer asked to confer with the fleet commander. Taken on board the *New York,* the officer, who was Cervera's chief-of-staff, Captain Bustamente, informed Admiral Sampson that Hobson and his seven men were unharmed. It was bad news to hear about the failure of the gallant attempt, but the correctness of the Spanish Navy's behavior was not to be denied. As in any war, there were many gentlemen on both sides of this conflict.

Signal flags went up on the *New York*, and the entire fleet learned that not one of the volunteers on the *Merrimac* had been lost or hurt. Admiral Cervera had told Hobson on the *Mercedes* that his deed was "*valiente*," and every American sailor felt the same way.

The excitement over, and the Spanish gunboat back in port, the fleet picked up the dull routine of maintaining its blockade. The large vessels formed a semicircle three or four miles off the mouth of the channel and smaller ones took station closer in. As soon as darkness fell a warship moved to the center of the arc with her searchlights turned on to illuminate the scene if the Spaniards attempted a sortie. Four hours later another man-of-war took her place, and so it went all through the night, night after night after night.

10

★ ★ ★ ★ ★ ★

Landing at Daiquirí

"ONE MAN SHOULD BE in absolute control here."

Those words were written June 10 to Senator Henry Cabot Lodge by Lieutenant Colonel Roosevelt, who was finding the confusion at Port Tampa almost more than he could stomach.

What bothered him most was his enforced inaction. On the evening of June 6 men began to board the many transports under the urging of everyone from Shafter to President McKinley. Roosevelt received orders to go aboard the *Yucatan* on June 8 and discovered that two other regiments had also been assigned to the same ship. This was just the sort of situation where the colonel was at his best. Rounding up a number of his Rough Riders, he headed for the pier at the double. No sooner had the lines been made fast and a gangway thrown over than Roosevelt and his men went on board and took possession. As if all other units were the enemy, they refused to allow anyone to board but members of the First Volunteer Cavalry.

This was a pyrrhic victory for Colonel Roosevelt because the *Yucatan* steamed away from the pier a mile or so and dropped anchor, there to wait for the rest of the convoy. What had happened was another of the comic incidents so common to the business of waging war.

Just as Shafter was hoping delays were over, a converted

yacht, the *Eagle*, on patrol north of Cuba, reported sighting what it believed to be a Spanish cruiser and a torpedo boat. Consternation swept from San Nicolas Channel all the way to the Navy Department and the White House. Could it be, everyone wondered, that all of Cervera's fleet was not bottled up in Santiago? Or had other units crossed from Spain? Secretary Alger dispatched a frantic telegram to Shafter forbidding any transports to sail. Sampson sent a young Navy lieutenant, Victor Blue, ashore with Cuban guides to make an actual count of the ships in Santiago and while awaiting his report ordered the men-of-war which were to have guarded the Army convoy to scout the waters between Cuba and the Bahamas.

Quartermaster Colonels Humphrey and Weston had managed by dint of long hours and legerdemain to get fewer than ten thousand soldiers on board the various transports when their escorts steamed off on their wild goose chase after what the Army called "the phantom fleet." It did not seem like a very big landing force but it was big enough to cause trouble, cooped up in crowded transports under the blazing sun. Horses of the one regiment of regular cavalry that was destined to go with Shafter started dying in the holds of the ships. Officers gave up their quarters to men weakened by fever and dysentery and slept on deck. Some units were disembarked and had to be got aboard again when the Navy sent word that it had found no enemy warships. Those who did not go ashore were packed in tighter than sardines. As the men sweltered, rumors became common that sharks had been attracted to the vicinity by discarded food, but this did not keep many officers from permitting their troops to swim near the transports.

Roosevelt wrote another letter to Lodge saying that the Senator should inform the President of the horrible chaos and —most indiscreetly for an Army officer—that while he had been hesitant to believe that he was fitted to be a colonel before he was sworn in, he now believed he would make a better brigadier general than those who were running the operations at Tampa.

There was no denying that the colonel knew what was best for his men and his own image. Just before the *Yucatan* had left the dock, two men with motion picture cameras had asked permission to sail. They were the first newsreel cameramen ever to cover a war. Roosevelt, who had turned away two regiments, saw no reason to turn away the two men.

While the colonel was penning his red-hot letters of protest, Shafter was patiently building up the number of men on the transports until by the evening of June 13 his assistant adjutant general, Colonel E. J. McClernand, was able to report that the full capacity of the ships had been made use of and that 815 officers and 16,072 men were embarked. The next morning, June 14, the heavily loaded transports stood down the channel and headed for the Dry Tortugas. Sampson, way off on the *New York*, had sent word that if the Army could send ten thousand men at once, Santiago could be captured handily. Now he was getting his wish, in double portions.

Sometime on June 15, passing the Tortugas, Shafter's thirty-two awkward, barnacle-encrusted ships were joined by the Navy escort, a force powerful enough to handle almost any imaginable enemy force in the vicinity. There were the battleship *Indiana*, the unprotected cruiser *Detroit,* the gunboat *Castine,* and other smaller ships including the *Manning*, the *Eagle*, the *Wasp*, the *Wompatuck*, and the *Osceola*. The torpedo boats *Ericson* and *Rodgers* rendezvoused with the convoy after it rounded Key West.

Speaking at a dinner twenty-four years later in Washington, General McClernand told how fine the convoy looked, with Navy ships on the flanks and ahead and astern of the transports. But reporters on the various vessels wrote at the time that it straggled over fifteen miles of ocean, that the *Yucatan* nearly ran down the *Matteawan*, and that the *Olivette* was nearly struck by a water barge that broke away from the ship that was towing it. The weather was unusually hot and the sun beat down from a brassy sky, but most of the soldiers found the voyage infinitely preferable to the long waiting in Port Tampa and in the channel outside.

On board the *Segurança,* Shafter's headquarters ship, the high command of the expedition knew where it was heading, but the rank and file of the men, and all of the reporters, could only guess where the landing would take place. A shortage of true facts deterred no one from guessing, from planning strategy for imaginary landings, or from that most ancient pastime of all armed men—grousing. There was plenty of justification for the last activity. On the *Miami* there were exactly twelve toilets for twelve thousand men. The food was horrible. Canned beef, upon which the Army had relied heavily as a staple of the field rations, seemed to be spoiled when the cans were opened or to spoil almost immediately afterwards. Beans were a poor item for shipboard cookery and certainly too heavy for men doing little but loafing in the tropical sunlight.

There was not enough water for the men to bathe and not too much for drinking and cooking. Even so, the soldiers were better off than the crew of that ill-fated tub, the *Gussie*, loaded down with three hundred thirsty, irascible mules. Time had to be taken out from the serious business of convoying to permit a stop at the Bahamian island of Inagua to refill the old side-wheeler's tanks.

The water schooner broke its towing hawser again. The *City of Washington* was sent back for her. A few hours later the *Leona*, carrying two cavalry regiments, disappeared, and the fleet had to wait until the two wayward craft caught up.

If the weather had been bad, men would have suffered much more than they did. These transports had been picked up wherever available and some were barely seaworthy. The *Yucatan*, for one, had been a freighter before the Army commissioned a civilian contractor to install bunks. He and his men had used the cheapest and greenest lumber at hand and very few nails. On the very first night many of the berths collapsed when the men got into them, and the unfortunate soldiers spent the balance of the trip sleeping on the deck.

The convoy crawled across the steel-colored bosom of the sea at seven knots, a speed adjusted to the slowest tug and a schooner filled with what all hoped would remain fresh water. The transports were still commanded by their civilian skippers, and every last one was a rugged individualist. They seemed united only in their dislike for Navy orders and convoy regulations. At night every ship sailed with all her lights on as if in defiance of the enemy, while the evening hours were made noisy as regimental bands vied with each other playing popular music.

What the foreign military observers who accompanied Shafter's Fifth Corps thought of the strange behavior of the convoy is not known. Either they were all fine gentlemen not wishing to be discourteous to their hosts, or they found it to their liking. Later they had a few unkind things to say about tactics and strategy on the battlefield, but that was something else again. Among the foreign officers were: Captain Arthur H. Lee of the British Royal Artillery; Major Clément de Grandpré, French Legation; Count von Goetzen of the German Imperial Army; Colonel Yermeloff of the Russian Imperial Legation; Lieutenant Rodler of the Austro-Hungarian Navy; Lieutenant Saneyuki Akiyama of the Imperial Japanese Navy; Captain Abildgaard of the Royal Norwegian General Staff; and Commander Dahlgren, Naval attaché for Norway and Sweden.

Whether the men of the Fifth Corps would have been as nonchalant had they known what was going on at Guantánamo Bay is one of those questions no one can answer easily. Fortunately for the morale of all, the events taking place on the southeastern tip of Cuba might have been going on somewhere on Mars.

A battalion of American Marines numbering about 650 men had been sent from Key West on June 6 to aid in gaining control of the fine harbor formed by Guantánamo Bay. Their transport, the auxiliary cruiser *Panther*, dropped anchor off the harbor on June 10 and found that the unprotected cruiser *Marblehead* and the gunboat *Yankee* had reduced the forts at the entrance and driven the only Spanish vessel, the small gunboat *Sandoval*, deep inside the bay. The next day the Marines went ashore under cover of a light bombardment, made camp, and dug trenches. That night and the next day all seemed quiet, but on the second night the Marines found themselves under heavy fire that seemed to come from every quarter of the perimeter. Large numbers of the men were bathing on the beach when the staccato bark of the rifles shattered the stillness. Naked as jaybirds, they picked up their rifles and started a charge through the brush to dislodge the enemy. The Americans drove off their attackers, but the same thing kept happening time after time. The heavy guns of the warships would disperse the Spanish massing in the chaparral, but when the cannonading ceased the enemy drifted back to the edge of the encampment and started firing again.

Stephen Crane, the famous correspondent and novelist, was with the Marines and wrote many times of their valor and efficiency. His description of one foray, entitled "The Red Badge of Courage Was His Wig-wag Flag" described how two-hundred Marines and fifty Cuban fighters conducted an offensive to clear a hill overlooking the detachment's encampment.

It was on June 14, the fourth day of the battle for Guantánamo, and the day Shafter's expeditionary force left Port Tampa, that Captain G. F. Elliott led off to capture a ridgeback. The sun was so hot that Crane thought it would "melt the earth." Together, the Americans and Cubans made it to the top of the hill only to find themselves under heavy fire from a thicket on the far side. Crane wrote of the scene:

Along our line the rifle locks were clicking incessantly, as if some giant loom was running wildly, and on the ground among the stones and weeds came a dropping, dropping rain of rolling brass shells. . . . Two hundred yards down the hill there was a thicket—a thicket whose predominant bush wore large, oily, green leaves. It was about an acre in extent and on level ground. . . . This thicket was alive with the loud popping of the Mausers. From end to end and from side to side it was alive. . . .

The battle for Cusco Hill lasted five hours and was the key to the seizure of Guantánamo Bay. Sporadic guerrilla warfare continued for a time but virtually ended when Sampson ordered the battleship *Texas*, the *Marblehead*, and the gunboat *Suwanee* into the bay to bombard the city of Caimanera.

A few Americans were killed and wounded in the more than a week of fighting, but the most significant aspects of the battle were the seizure of a harbor of limitless value to the American Navy and the fact that this was the first real land fighting of the war with Spain.

As the Fifth Corps steamed around Cuba, no one on board knew that the Marines had landed first and had won their beachhead.

The ever-watchful Colonel Roosevelt, writing another letter on the *Yucatan*, expressed amazement that the Spaniards were not enterprising enough to attempt to interfere with the straggling convoy. By now, on June 15, some of the slower vessels were tagging along far behind, left more or less to their own devices because they could not maintain station with the rest.

Roosevelt described his pleasure at being on the expedition as it steamed "through a sapphire sea, wind-rippled, under an almost cloudless sky." He told his family of the bands playing, of the constant drill and rifle practice, and of the "fear" that they would find Santiago captured before they could get into the fight. It was one of his last letters home before he found himself engaged in all the fighting anyone could want. He thought the hills back of the Cuban coast looked a little like Montana's terrain and was pleased to see the Southern Cross again.

"We are well within the tropics," he wrote, "and at night the Southern Cross shows low above the horizon; it seems strange to see it in the same sky with the friendly Dipper."

On June 20 the convoy reached Guantánamo and the time of writing letters and dreaming came to an end. Most of the ships slowed down or anchored, but the *Segurança* went on to Santiago, where Admiral Sampson joined Shafter, and the headquarters ship went on westward to Aserraderos for a conference with the Cuban general commanding in the area.

Three small boats took the official party ashore; the Army and Navy brass in the first two and the war correspondents— Richard Harding Davis; Frederic Remington, the artist; Stephen Bonsal; and Caspar Whitney—in the third. The decision to confer with García on land was made, according to Sampson's chief of staff, Captain French Ensor Chadwick, because García became sick at the slightest motion of a water-borne vessel. This friendly gesture on the part of the Americans entailed considerable difficulty as García's field camp was atop a mile-high hill. Sampson and Shafter looked at the narrow trail with some concern, but the Cubans produced two mules and the officers mounted and started up the path. A Cuban guerrilla with a nice sense of humor told Bonsal that the tiny animal almost disappeared from sight when the three-hundred-pound Shafter got into the saddle, and carried the general with his knees bent.

García advised Shafter to land at Daiquirí and Siboney, to the east of Santiago, because few Spanish troops were in the immediate vicinity and because the beaches there offered a better landing place from the open sea. The three commanders drew up detailed plans for moving Cuban troops to points where they could assist the Americans and for shore bombardment in advance of the landing. Daiquirí is sixteen miles east of the entrance to Santiago, and while it then had no facilities, a small peninsula afforded some protection to the prevailing winds blowing out of the southeast. Siboney, five miles closer to Santiago, it was decided, would be used as soon as troops got ashore to secure it.

As Sampson and Shafter left to prepare their orders, García was almost speechless with joy. The presence of the transports, added to the now familiar battle fleet, gave proof that the naval and military might of the United States was at last ready to lend the insurgents a hand. Shafter, who had noted that the guerrillas had little to eat except wild fruit and palm hearts, washed down with black coffee, sent two thousand rations ashore as soon he reached the *Segurança*. The Cubans had waited for a long time. It seemed to all of them that deliverance from their oppressors was now assured.

The orders of battle were well planned. Shafter had a keen eye for terrain and was, with General Miles, the most experienced general in the American Army. He left little to chance. Sampson was equally precise in making sure that every man knew his station and duties.

First they asked García to send men to demonstrate at Cabañas and Aguadores in order to make the Spaniards believe the landing would take place there. Other Cubans would join a force of guerrillas behind Daiquirí to capture the three hundred Spanish troops guarding that town. Still others, about three thousand in number, would move west of Santiago to prevent any Spanish units from coming to the relief of General Arsenio Linares, commanding at that city.

Having been told that a strong enemy force was entrenched

at Siboney, Shafter decided to land a regular Army division under Brigadier General Henry L. Lawton and a volunteer division with some regular components under General Wheeler at Daiquirí to envelop the Spaniards at Siboney. Then he would use Siboney as his main landing area. To confuse the enemy further, Shafter arranged for some of the transports with Brigadier General Jacob F. Kent's and Brigadier General Samuel S. Sumner's divisions to approach Cabañas and take action to simulate a landing.

Admiral Sampson's order of battle was equally involved. To shell the area behind Daiquirí before the troops started ashore, he assigned the *Detroit, Castine, Wasp,* and *New Orleans* as bombardment ships. The *Scorpion, Vixen,* and *Texas* were to shell Cabañas; the *Eagle* and *Gloucester* to do the same at Aguadores; and the *Hornet, Helena,* and *Bancroft* were ordered to demonstrate before Ensenada de los Altares.

The *Suwanee, Osceola,* and *Wompatuck* were instructed to get new Manila hawsers for use in towing boats loaded with soldiers up to the beaches. The steam launches and pulling boats of the big battleships and armored cruisers were also designated for the same purpose. The Army had little experience with amphibious operations and had provided only four craft of shallow draft for the entire convoy. Two of these had gone adrift on the long voyage from Tampa, and there was nothing to be done but rely on the Navy's small boats.

Not for an instant did Sampson forget that his major task was the continued immobilization of Cervera's squadron or its destruction if it tried to escape. So he replaced the merchant cruiser *New Orleans* with the *Indiana* and left the latter with the *New York, Brooklyn, Massachusetts, Iowa,* and *Oregon* on guard at the entrance to Santiago harbor. He would send everything else to help Shafter—gunboats, torpedo boats, armed merchantmen, tugs, launches, and the like—but the battle line would remain where it belonged. The last paragraph of his Order of Battle, dated June 21, 1898, reveals how his mind worked:

The attention of Commanding Officers of all vessels engaged in blockading Santiago de Cuba is earnestly called to the necessity of the utmost vigilance from this time forward—both as to maintaining stations and readiness for action, and as to keeping a close watch upon the harbor mouth. If the Spanish Admiral ever intends to attempt to escape, that attempt will be made soon.

General Shafter, prowling about the deck of the *Segurança,* perspiring in his woolen uniform, his face aflame under a giant white pith helmet, was eager for the invasion to begin. He worried most of all about illness and disease, both induced by the humid, subtropical climate and the mosquitoes rampant in all the Caribbean islands. He had done a little research while waiting for troops to gather at Tampa and knew that an English expedition to take Havana in 1761 had failed because of weakness and disease and that an army Napoleon sent to Santo Domingo in 1801 had lost two-thirds of its men to yellow fever. Moreover, the transports were almost out of water and the best way to cope with that situation was to put the men ashore.

The men Shafter had available in the Fifth Corps were organized into two divisions and an independent brigade of infantry and one cavalry division, dismounted, four batteries of light field artillery, a detached observation balloon unit, and a Gatling gun unit, with supporting forces.

With few exceptions, all these units were regulars. The First Division, commanded by General Kent, consisted of three brigades of three regiments each. The Seventy-First New York Volunteer Infantry was the only nonregular unit in the division. The Second Division, commanded by General Lawton, also had three brigades of three regiments each. The Second Massachusetts Volunteer Infantry was the only volunteer regiment in that division.

Brigadier General John C. Bates commanded the Third (provisional) Division, in which there were two regular infantry regiments and six volunteer regiments of foot soldiers.

Major General Wheeler led the Cavalry Division with two brigades of dismounted men. Five regiments were regulars and the sixth regiment was the First U.S. Volunteer Cavalry—the Rough Riders. There was one small detachment of mounted cavalry attached to the corps. This unit of regulars was commanded by Lieutenant Colonel William A. Rafferty.

Shafter had at his disposal only four batteries of light guns, four guns to a battery. These sixteen guns were antiquated in design, used black powder, and were difficult to aim. It is significant that these guns were built but a short time before the French perfected their famous seventy-fives, weapons so superior to ours that comparison is foolish.

Opposed to the Americans were about 36,000 Spanish troops in Santiago province, 19,000 of them at Santiago, and the balance scattered in five or six different encampments. All were organized into a single corps under General Linares. The rest of the 160,000 Spanish troops in Cuba were garrisoned at the western end of the island, in and near Havana.

This was the general disposition of troops on the morning of June 20, the day chosen for the landing. It looked very orderly on paper but was quite the opposite in fact. Although ordered to stay bunched off Siboney and Daiquirí, the transports had scattered to the four winds during the night. The steam launches, towing strings of boats, went looking for their assigned ships and lost hours finding them. One transport, in fact, loaded with men in a unit designated to be one of the very first to hit the beach, wandered so far away that it was late in the afternoon before it was discovered and unloaded.

Fortunately for everyone, the actual landing was unopposed.

As soon as the morning sun provided enough light to aim the big guns, the four Navy ships started bombarding the countryside behind Daiquirí. For most of the troops looking on from the transports' decks, it was the first time they had heard the sound of guns fired in anger. Shells were lobbed into the valleys between the hills and over the hills themselves, although there were no specific targets. The beaches looked deserted, and only the fact that an old pier and several gondola cars used for hauling iron ore to the pier were blazing fiercely revealed that the enemy must have been nearby just before the ships started their cannonading. The soldiers could hear the echoes of the shells as they exploded, kicking up great dust clouds, or tore the tin roofs off stone blockhouses the Spaniards had erected many years before.

Not all the men could enjoy the luxury of being spectators. Hundreds were scrambling over the sides of the transports and jumping into the boats towed in strings behind steam launches. Navy men laughed gleefully at the awkward behavior of the soldiers, who found it exceedingly difficult to judge when to jump. Some jumped too early and crashed when the boats moved upward on a wave. Others waited too long and fell many feet as the boats dropped away in a trough.

When a string of smallboats was filled the launch sputtered off toward shore, dragging its tow like a writhing snake behind it. Most of the boats were filled with too many man and few had any freeboard. Waves broke over the gunwales, soaking the men, and the erratic movement of the little craft made some of the soldiers seasick. Soon the water between the transports and the shore was dotted with the bobbing convoys. If the enemy had dug in, waiting out the naval bombardment, as the Japanese did later in the Pacific islands and the Germans on the Normandy beaches, it would have been slaughter. But the Spanish troops had cut out for the hills before dawn, setting fire to some buildings as they left, and the first Americans went ashore standing up. Not one enemy gun barked defiance. One boatload of Americans drew up to the ore plant's pier and the men scrambled onto the stringpieces. At almost the same instant another string of boats disgorged its men on the beach beyond, and no one could claim to be the first man ashore. It was about 10:25 when these men touched firm ground and a great shout went up, both on the beach and on the transports and men-of-war. The commanders of the latter, realizing that there was no answering fire, ceased bombarding the town and its outskirts.

During the first few minutes of the debarkation Colonel Roosevelt, whose regiment had been given low priority for going ashore, fumed and fretted on the *Yucatan*, eager to get into the fray. When the launches came back to reload their boats, Roosevelt saw his chance in the mounting confusion. He "threw his rank" with a young naval officer who had been an assistant to Roosevelt when the latter was Assistant Secretary, and the poor devil could do nothing but agree to ferry some of the cavalry to

the beach. The colonel was one of the first to scramble into the
boats and so, with a goodly number of his men, reached the
shore within an hour or so of the start of debarkation.

These first arrivals found no Spaniards and only a few Cubans
who had dared to enter town during the bombardment. Many
of the workers' huts were blazing, and the buildings of the
Juragua Ore Mining Company were all on fire. Large land crabs
scuttled into the underbrush, but many that had infested the
flimsy thatched-roof houses were roasted alive in the flames,
creating a horrible odor that nauseated many of the soldiers.

Although Shafter's battle order assigned the first troops ashore
to Lawton, that old fighting cock Joe Wheeler was not far behind and outranked Lawton, anyway. Fighting Joe saw a Spanish flag still waving above a stone blockhouse on a hill back of
town and ordered some of the Rough Riders to pull it down.
The volunteers raced up the hill, tore down the enemy banner,
and ran up the Stars and Stripes. As soon as the ensign fluttered
in the sunshine, men on the beaches, in town, and on the ships
off shore saw it and sent up another cheer. Captains pulled the
lanyards of their steam whistles, and a few exuberant men
wasted ammunition by firing into the air. It should be noted
that the correspondents also observed the action and were quick
to mention that it was Roosevelt's men who had done the deed
when they filed their first dispatches.

Already a favorable tide of publicity was running for the
ebullient politician-turned-soldier. Other officials seemed to
make mistakes when it came to dealing with the press. Roosevelt
never did.

Just the day before, Shafter had issued a firm directive that
no correspondents were to go ashore with the first assault waves.
Davis, impeccably turned out in his tailored riding breeches and
boots, thin shirt, and sun helmet, expostulated with the commanding general in behalf of his professional associates and
finally for himself alone, arguing that he was no run-of-the-mine
reporter but "a descriptive writer." This was too much for
Shafter.

"I do not care a damn what you are," said the General. "I'll
treat you all alike."

The lack of docking facilities at Daiquirí made it necessary for the horses to swim ashore. Some swam for Florida.

Davis sulked in his cabin and almost did not go ashore at all, and from that time forward Shafter fared badly in most of the stories sent to American newspapers.

One reporter disobeyed the orders, gave his clothing and gun to a soldier to carry ashore, and jumped out of a porthole. It was a longer swim than he had anticipated but as he was tiring, a string of boats went by and he grabbed a painter and thus made it the rest of the way. The balance of the press went ashore in better style that evening, when even the rawest recruit in the corps realized that the Spaniards had missed their best opportunity and would not oppose the landings at the critical moment.

The debarkation went on all day and into the evening, with very few tragic incidents. Two Negro infantrymen were drowned when trying to land on the ore pier and several men were injured, but it must have been one of the least costly amphibious landings in military history.

There was considerable trouble unloading the horses and mules for the artillery and supply wagons. There was nothing to do but drop them into the sea from the lowest possible deck or opening in the hull and let them swim to shore. Many of the animals, exhausted from their long stay in the dark holds, panicked when suddenly dumped into the ocean. Most headed for shore but many swam out to sea. Just when it seemed that many of the mounts would be lost, a bugler on the beach blew "right wheel" and the horses, remembering their training, turned and swam to land. It was several days before the animals regained their strength, and this later contributed in part to a shortage of rations at advanced positions.

While Lawton and Wheeler were getting most of their men on shore, Kent's troops, still on ten of the transports, went off to Cabañas to make it look as if they were going to land there. The feint may have worked, for no Spanish forces—it was found out later—left Santiago or other points in the vicinity to reinforce those troops supposedly guarding Daiquirí, Siboney, and the hinterland behind them.

A more determined army could have easily mustered between three and four thousand men who were within a half day's marching time of Daiquirí and sent them to turn the landing into a catastrophe for the Americans. The Spanish soldiery's morale was already at low ebb after years of inconclusive fighting with the Cuban insurgents. Otherwise they could have struck a decisive blow for the Spanish Empire in the West Indies. But the chance was thrown away and an invading army came ashore with only two men lost in the process.

11

★   ★   ★   ★   ★   ★

First Blood at Las Guásimas

WHILE MOST OF THE MEN at Daiquirí tried to dry out their clothing, cook meals over open fires, and generally make themselves into a more warlike body, that old Confederate cavalryman Joe Wheeler reverted to his earlier battlefield experience and began questioning the natives for military information. It was an obvious thing to do, but in the excitement the men who had learned of war only from textbooks forgot their lessons. Fighting Joe was cut from a different bolt of cloth.

Cuban irregulars told him that a Spanish force was entrenched in the hills back of Siboney, the town five miles to the west which would be the main port of debarkation once it was secured. This information served his purpose well. He wanted to get on with the business of fighting Spaniards, and here was an opportunity. Calling in the brigade commander, Brigadier General S. B. M. Young, and Colonel Wood of the volunteers, he sketched out a plan to strike the first blow even while the troops were marching down the coast toward Siboney. The second night after the landing, Lawton's main force was in control of Siboney, and the Second Brigade of dismounted cavalry, with Wheeler leading the way, was even farther in the van. They went into bivouac knowing that the morning would bring fighting, and some of the men, tired as they were, found it difficult to fall asleep.

Wheeler's information was to the effect that the enemy was posted at the junction of the only two routes leading from Siboney to Santiago. One of these was a rough wagon road that climbed the hills from town, turned east for a while, as if away from Santiago, but then swung north and finally west about four miles in from the coast. The other route was only a path, which, as it was suitable for men and mules only, climbed almost straight up the ridge behind Siboney and made a beeline toward Santiago. The two routes met in the jungle at a crossroads called Las Guásimas after the guasima trees that grew there in lush abundance.

It rained that night, quenching the cooking fires and turning the ground into mud one soldier said was exactly like the mud in his father's pigsty back home in Virginia. When the bugler blew reveille at 3:15 A.M., it was a sodden mass of soldiery that arose to do battle.

Young started off with more than four hundred regulars from the First and Tenth Cavalry Regiments on the wagon road while Colonel Wood, who must have wondered why he had left the pleasant duties of caring for Mr. McKinley's health, led five hundred Rough Riders up the more precipitous goat track. General Wheeler elected to go with the regulars, but the newspaper men stayed with the Rough Riders, sold on their own judgments that the First Cavalry Volunteers would be where history was made or would make it themselves. Richard Harding Davis must have been the dressiest man in Cuba. He had changed into a white sack suit because of the heat and draped a puggaree over his pith helmet to keep the sun off his neck. He was having a bout with sciatica, so on this expedition he rode an Army mule.

The scene they left behind them was something that belonged in a comic strip rather than in the annals of an armed invasion. Troops were pouring ashore at Siboney under the searchlights of the naval ships to find that those who had marched to the port from Daiquirí were dancing naked around the campfires in the rain, shouting and rough-housing like schoolboys on vacation.

The sun came up that twenty-fourth day of June as the dismounted cavalrymen neared the top of the ridge. Birds called

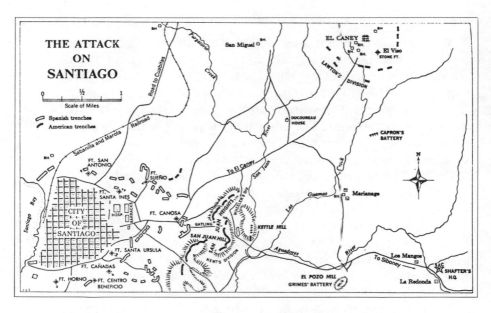

THE ATTACK
ON
SANTIAGO

Scale of Miles

Spanish trenches
American trenches

Sabanilla and Marota Railroad
Road to Cuabitas
Parajanito Creek
San Miguel
EL CANEY
STONE FT.
El Viso
LAWTON'S DIVISION
DUCOUREAU HOUSE
CAPRON'S BATTERY
FT. SAN ANTONIO
FT. SUEÑO
To El Caney
Marianage
Guamas
FT. SANTA INES
San Juan River
Las Guamas River
CITY OF SANTIAGO
HOSP.
FT. CANOSA
GATLING
SAN JUAN HEIGHTS DIV.
KETTLE HILL
SAN JUAN HILL
SAN JUAN
KENT'S DIVISION
Aguadores
Los Mangos
To Siboney
SHAFTER'S H.Q.
FT. SANTA URSULA
FT. CAÑADAS
FT. HORNO
FT. CENTRO BENEFICIO
EL POZO HILL
GRIMES' BATTERY
La Redonda
Santiago Bay
N

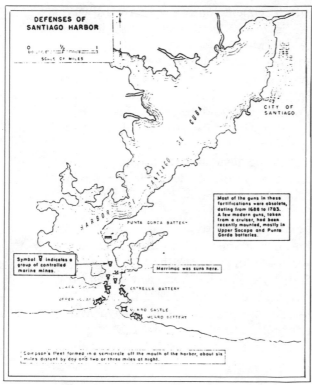

DEFENSES OF
SANTIAGO HARBOR

SCALE OF MILES

BAHIA DE SANTIAGO DE CUBA

CITY OF SANTIAGO

Most of the guns in these
fortifications were obsolete,
dating from 1688 to 1783.
A few modern guns, taken
from a cruiser, had been
recently mounted, mostly in
Upper Socapa and Punta
Gorda batteries.

PUNTA GORDA BATTERY

Symbol ⊽ indicates a
group of controlled
marine mines.

Merrimac was sunk here.

ESTRELLA BATTERY

MORRO CASTLE
MORRO BATTERY

Sampson's fleet formed in a semicircle off the mouth of the harbor, about six
miles distant by day and two or three miles at night.

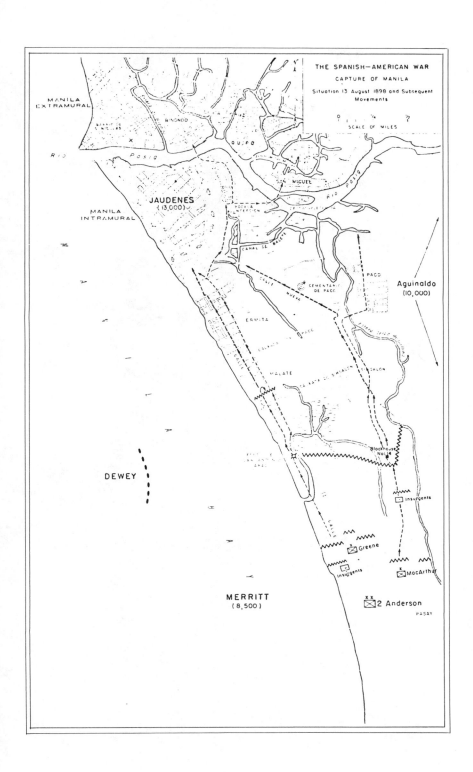

THE SPANISH—AMERICAN WAR

CAPTURE OF MANILA

Situation 13 August 1898 and Subsequent
Movements

SCALE OF MILES

MANILA
EXTRAMURAL

BINONDO

QUIPO

SAN MIGUEL

RIO POSIG

PASIG

JAUDENES
(13,000)

MANILA
INTRAMURAL

CANAL DE BELEY

PACO

CEMENTERIO
DE PACO

Aguinaldo
(10,000)

ERMITA

PACO

MALATE

SALON

Blockhouse
No 14

DEWEY

Insurgents

Greene

Insurgents

MacArthur

MERRITT
(8,500)

2 Anderson

PASAY

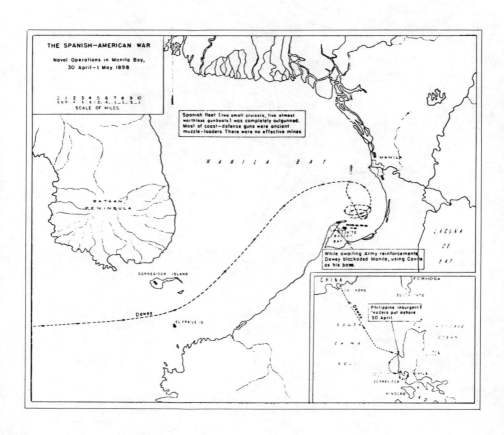

THE SPANISH—AMERICAN WAR

Naval Operations in Manila Bay,
30 April–1 May 1898

0 1 2 3 4 5 6 7 8 9 10
SCALE OF MILES

Spanish fleet (two small cruisers, five almost
worthless gunboats) was completely outgunned.
Most of coast–defense guns were ancient
muzzle–loaders. There were no effective mines.

M A N I L A   B A Y

MANILA

BATAAN
PENINSULA

LAGUNA
DE
BAY

CAVITE
BAKOOR
BAY

CORREGIDOR ISLAND

While awaiting Army reinforcements,
Dewey blockaded Manila, using Cavite
as his base.

Dewey

EL FRAILE IS.

CHINA

FORMOSA

HONG KONG

SOUTH CAPE

Dewey

Philippine insurgent
leaders put ashore
30 April.

S O U T H

C H I N A

S E A

PACIFIC
OCEAN

MANILA

CORREGIDOR

MINDORO

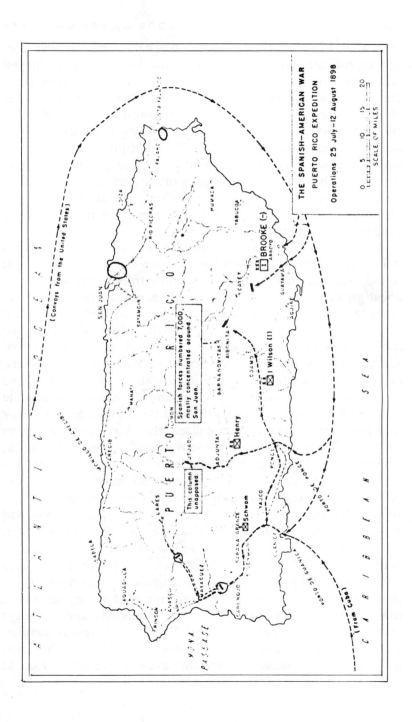

THE SPANISH-AMERICAN WAR
PUERTO RICO EXPEDITION

Operations 25 July–12 August 1898

0 5 10 15 20
SCALE OF MILES

from the jungle on either side of the path, and the war correspondent and future President of the United States enjoyed
that esoteric conversation common to bird watchers when there
are many new species to observe. Both of them, as well as other
observant men, noticed that the rain forest was full of wood
cuckoos, whose calls could be heard echoing back and forth in
the woods ahead of them. If the Cuban scouts whom Wheeler
had sent ahead had thought about it, they might have told the
Americans that the Spanish soldiers often simulated the notes of
the wood cuckoo to signal one another, just as American Indians did in the days of the early pioneers. but they forgot, or
were too busy doing something else.

A little before 7:30 A.M., an advance unit under Captain
Allyn K. Capron went ahead with some Cuban irregulars and
found evidence that a body of Spanish troops was somewhere
ahead of them. They halted for a while, and in the interim the
men on the wagon road found a stone breastworks thrown up
several thousand feet ahead, barring the road. Wheeler tested
the defenses by ordering several shots fired at the obstruction.
Instantaneously there was the sound of hundreds of Mausers,
and bullets zipped through the branches above their heads. Some
struck men on the narrow road, making sickening sounds quite
different from those that went through the leaves and vines. For
a moment the surprise immobilized the Americans, but then
they dived into the jungle for cover and started firing back.
Colonel Wood, hearing the fusillade to his right, knew that the
junction of the path and the wagon road must be very close
ahead. Calmly he extended his men as skirmishers, and they too
soon came under heavy fire. A reporter noted that Wood was
slow in his movements and very calm under the rain of bullets
but that Roosevelt "jumped up and down" in his eagerness to
get men moving forward. Both the road and the foot path were
narrow defiles through thick jungle. It was almost impossible to
see more than ten feet in any direction except on the wagon
road. Capron went down, mortally wounded, and Sergeant
Hamilton Fish, scion of one of New York's most famous families,
slumped to the ground, a bullet through his brain. Other men
fell, dead or wounded, and stretcher bearers had all they could

do to carry them back to where one surgeon and a hospital corpsman were operating at a clearing beside the road.

Wheeler, who realized he had blundered into a force that outnumbered his own 3 to 2, wished he had a field piece or two to blast the stone breastworks. Lacking anything heavier than Hotchkiss guns, he ordered several forward and then urged his men to move to the right and left to envelop the enemy. The fighting was taking place in a saucer-like depression under a slight rise that gave the Spaniards a distinct advantage. Davis jotted down in his notebook that the Spanish fire was mercilessly accurate, and every reporter commented upon the peculiar z-z-z-z-z-eu whine of the Mauser bullets as they flew by. The hand-cranked Hotchkiss guns seemed to draw enemy fire, and soldiers moved away from them as if superstitious.

The mounting sun turned the jungle into a torture chamber where men died, were wounded, or fell in their tracks from overexhaustion. At the field hospital in the rear the medical men were doing their best, blood dripping from their arms and uniforms. Stephen Crane, the author-reporter, and others brought in Edward Marshall of the New York *Journal,* whose spine had been shattered. Although he was given up for dead, he survived and wrote later of how a wounded soldier, who himself was in horrible agony, started singing "America" and how the others joined in.

Miles away at Siboney the main force heard the firing in the hills and knew that their comrades were at last engaged in the struggle that all had looked forward to with such enthusiasm. They could not hear the pathetic singing of the wounded men, but they sensed nonetheless that war was not all gay parades and exciting camp life.

General Young threw in all his men, leaving no reserves, and they advanced cautiously through the dense undergrowth, firing as they went. The regulars could hear the Rough Riders firing too, and both groups felt better when a volunteer cavalryman appeared to the left of the regulars' extended line, waving a guidon to prevent Young's men from shooting at the others. It was now about 9 A.M.; every man who could carry a rifle was edging ahead toward the Spanish position, and the flanks of the joined skirmish line were bending in like the jaws of a giant calipers.

Fighting Joe Wheeler, surveying the battlefield as well as he could, realized he had bitten off about as much as he could chew and finally agreed to send for reinforcements, much against his will. Before the courier could make it back to Siboney, however, Lawton had decided that the cavalry brigade was in serious trouble and sent another regiment of regulars to its aid.

As it turned out, reinforcements were not needed. No sooner had Wheeler sent the courier off than the tide of battle changed. The Rough Riders and the regulars both worked their way out of the densest portion of the jungle and found patches of open ground before them, all in plain sight of the enemy behind the stone walls. Running and firing, covering one another, and running again, the Americans went forward in the face of murderous fire. It was too much for the Spaniards. Evidently convinced that a much larger body of troops must be just behind the advancing Americans, they melted away on the road leading to Santiago. The invaders had won their first real battle on Cuban soil.

A final count showed that 964 Americans took part in the battle of Las Guásimas against 1,500 Spaniards. General Linares could have thrown 12,000 troops into the conflict if he had wanted to, as there were that many within a few hours' marching distance, but it was the old story of misjudging the enemy's strength. The Spanish had convinced themselves that they were badly outnumbered. Why else would such a small body of men blunder into their outer works?

Newspaper reports of the battle, besides revealing that sixteen men had been killed and fifty-two wounded, made it clear that the Americans had run into an ambush. But most of them agreed that the troops had fought bravely under wretched conditions, and most of them tended to make the Rough Riders, and Roosevelt in particular, the heroes of the engagement.

There was obviously some back-scratching on both sides. Davis wrote many purple passages lauding Colonel Roosevelt, and the latter wrote in a report that on one occasion Davis had spotted a detachment of Spanish soldiery on a hill across a

"The Heroic Stand of the Rough Riders at Las Guásimas" by W. A. Rogers

ravine and that Roosevelt had been able to order heavy fire on the enemy and drive them away as a result.

Poor Colonel Wood was bypassed in many of the newspaper articles which repeatedly referred to "Roosevelt's Rough Riders," but he seemed to take no umbrage. The regulars, too, always seemed to get second billing in the accounts from the battlefield.

General Lawton, who had been given command of the advance, considered Wheeler's action more than reprehensible and said so, but the old Confederate leader gloried in the situation. It had given him the first victory by land forces in the war, and it had given him a chance to be enshrined for one of the most colorful remarks of the whole war. He had watched his men race across the meadows toward the Spanish breastworks and had seen the enemy legging it for the outskirts of Santiago. In his excitement he had forgotten himself sufficiently to turn to his aides and shout: "We've got the damn Yankees on the run!"

Lawton and Wheeler patched up their differences enough to walk together beyond the spot where the Spaniards had thrown up their breastworks. There before them, beyond the tops of the trees in the valley that extended down from the scene of the engagement, they could both see the red-tiled roofs of the city of Santiago. After the bitter fighting of the morning it was a most entrancing view.

General Shafter, back in his cabin on the *Segurança,* wrote a stiff dispatch to General Wheeler telling him bluntly that while he was happy over the victory, he wanted the old rebel cavalryman to have his men entrench themselves where they were and to start no new battles until he (Shafter) gave the signal. The commander of the Fifth Corps wanted that entire corps off the boats and in position before any more fighting took place. It was a perfectly reasonable thing to want, in the circumstances. Fighting Joe's men had a bellyful of glory, true, but they had gone so far from their still-to-be established base of supplies that most of them went to sleep that night with those same bellies empty.

Weeks later, when various facts were being sorted out and Spanish officers were revealing what their thinking had been at the time, it was believed that the battle of Las Guásimas actually had never been necessary at all. The Spanish had decided, some of the officers said, to evacuate the breastworks on the ridge before any real fighting began. This version does not denigrate the success of the Americans. No one who has experienced the dirty business of war will fail to recognize the psychological effect of such a victory and defeat. The winners are supported in their feeling of invincibility. The losers can remember only that they lost, and it siphons off some of their courage. In that way, Las Guásimas was a most important victory for the United States troops.

When it was all over, and for months afterward, military experts wrote dozens of articles accusing the Spaniards of bad judgment in not making their main stand at Las Guásimas, where the Americans would have been "pinched" in a small sector between Siboney and the battle lines. What the experts did not take into consideration was Sampson's fleet. General Linares did not make that same mistake. He knew that the big guns on the enemy warships could have been brought into play and easily could have fired into the Spanish lines.

As a matter of fact, there was actually no place in the immediate vicinity of Santiago where Linares' troops could be free from naval gunfire, as was proved later. As the crow flies, the Spanish lines at Las Guásimas were only two and a half miles from deep water. Sampson had sixty-four guns in his fleet that could fire from four and a half to six miles. With naval spotters ashore or with Army officers doing the spotting for the Navy, the big guns could have zeroed in on any target from Siboney to Santiago. It was another sign of the Americans' inexperience with amphibious warfare that the fleet did not take any part in shelling enemy lines during the battles that followed the initial action at Las Guásimas. Linares, having missed his golden opportunity to turn the landing into a catastrophe for the Americans, was picking the lesser of two evils in withdrawing to the ridges nearer Santiago. These were four and a half miles away from Sampson's guns, two miles farther than the stone breastworks at the fork in the roads where the first engagement took place.

Aside from one or two conferences between Sampson and

Shafter, and occasional messages sent back and forth between them, there was no effort to establish a combined staff operation. It seemed as if the Army was still thinking in terms of Indian warfare on the western plains, where battles occurred on the spur of the moment, rather than of large-scale fighting where the enemy lines could be observed through field glasses and where guns could be aimed with considerable accuracy, even from as far away as the sea.

There was, however, considerable cooperation between the forces. As Shafter moved inland and to the northwest toward Santiago, his left flank became endangered because of the existence of enemy forces at Morro Castle. To interdict the movement of these men toward the American lines Sampson assigned the small armed yacht *Gloucester* and the armed lighthouse tender *Mangrove* to a point just off Aguadores, between Siboney and the Morro. There was a railway bridge near the former town, and American Navy gunners spent many daylight hours firing at labor parties working on the bridge approaches. They did not damage the bridge, knowing that Shafter might need it later.

This cannonading, and other bombardments by the fleet, were of great interest to Mr. Hearst, who had come to cover the war in his steam yacht *Silvia,* and who moved in and out of the naval formations as if he were directing a motion picture with a hired fleet. On one occasion he sailed between the warships and the shore installations they were firing at, and a return shell missed the *Silvia* only because it ricocheted and bounced over the yacht.

Hearst had interviewed the three leaders of the allied forces—Sampson, Shafter, and García—finding them all courteous, even in the midst of war, and he sent dispatches home informing the public that affairs in Cuba were in the hands of men so able and gifted that there was no need for any concern.

When not entertaining such VIPs as the publisher of the New York *Journal,* Shafter busied himself getting all his troops ashore after Wheeler and Lawton consolidated their position beyond Las Guásimas. He took heart in reports sent in from the first battle. The volunteers had conducted themselves with great initiative and bravery, behaving much the same as the regulars under enemy fire. This was immensely important to the Army commander-in-chief because he knew that he had virtually every regular soldier in the United States Army either ashore or about to be landed there. Any reinforcements that might come from the States would be volunteers, and it was good to know that they had done so well in their first baptism by fire.

There were two problems facing Shafter. One was to whip the Spanish and capture Santiago. But the other problem was one posed by the first—how to get into position with enough men to turn the trick. The terrain seemed against the Americans. For the sixteen miles between the port of debarkation at Siboney to the very outskirts of Santiago there was nothing but jungle, through which ran very few roads—all in wretched condition. The main route from Guantánamo Bay on the east to the provincial capital on the west was a dirt road that wound through the rain forest, up hill and down dale, fording streams without bridges and ankle deep in mud or worse in low places in the valleys. This road bore the awesome name of El Camino Real, or the Royal Road, and it had to serve for most of Shafter's troop movements and the shuttling of supplies. It was on this road that Young and his regulars had marched before the ambuscade at Las Guásimas. Beyond that point it went two miles to a village called Sevilla, and it was here that Shafter eventually established his field headquarters. The road was paralleled for a considerable distance by the meandering Aguadores River, which joined the San Juan River at right angles several miles to the west of Sevilla.

Whenever the road and river met, as they did several times, the road became a quagmire for hundreds of feet on each side of the fords. El Camino Real was seldom wide enough for two wagons or mule trains to pass, and alternate routes toward Santiago were not much more useful than the footpath the Rough Riders had used on the way to Las Guásimas. Davis called the main road "a huge gutter" when the tropical rain storms swept over the eastern end of Cuba, but during the six days following the engagement at Las Guásimas Shafter succeeded in moving most of his troops up to Sevilla and even a bit beyond. Each man took three days' rations with him, and the mules and horses browsed on the grass found in small clearings in the jungle.

Fighting Joe Wheeler sent word to Shafter that there was not enough room for the troops coming up from the port to bivouac at Sevilla, so the commanding general instructed the cavalryman to advance, but not to bring on any further engagements with the enemy. Wheeler therefore moved two miles west to a hill called El Pozo (the well). El Pozo was important because there a road struck off from the Royal Road to the fortified village of El Caney, four miles to the north. Scouts had determined that half a thousand Spanish troops under General Vara del Rey held this village, which was on another, better highway leading into Santiago from the northeast.

Any observer who thought the confusion at Port Tampa was bad would have realized that conditions between Siboney and the front were a hundred times worse. The heat was overpowering. The mercury reached 100 degrees in the middle of the day, and heavy, sudden rains soaked men, beasts of burden, and supplies. Animals that had been too long in the dank holds of the transports sickened and died. Pack trains were used at first because the wagons had been shipped knocked down and had to be assembled on the beach. Hired laborers collapsed in the heat, and when the Quartermaster Corps officers could not get Cubans to take their place, soldiers were impressed. Medical officers were put ashore without their kits and medicines. The field pieces were sent forward without enough reserve ammunition, and some troops had too many rations while others, less provident, did not have enough.

The food was all wrong for fighting in the Tropics. There was plenty of salt pork and hardtack, and sugar and coffee were available in abundance. For some reason there was a real shortage of onions and potatoes which all soldiers like, and an even greater shortage of tobacco. Red meat, which all fighting men thrive on, just did not exist. Because of the wretched food, the heavy woolen uniforms, and the heat, scores of men started coming down with "Cuban fever," an all-encompassing ailment that covered dysentery, malaria, and the dreaded yellow fever.

Wheeler and Lawton could see Spanish soldiers erecting breastworks and digging trenches on two ridges a mile or more beyond El Pozo. The northern hill was called Kettle and the other, slightly to the southwest, San Juan Hill. The San Juan River lay between the most advanced positions of the Americans and the fortified ridges guarding the approach to Santiago. The Royal Road passed between Kettle Hill and San Juan Hill.

Shafter studied the reports that dribbled in from Cuban scouts, staff officers under Wheeler and Lawton whose reconnaissance took them to within talking distance of the Spanish pickets, and Army engineers, and decided on a master plan for breaking through the enemy lines to the city.

Certain underlying conditions controlled much of Shafter's thinking. He wanted the village of El Caney seized to protect his right flank, to keep enemy troops that might be near Guantá-namo Bay from joining in the defense of Santiago, and to allow his troops to move out far enough to cut the pipeline carrying water from the hills at Cuabitas into the city. One other thought kept recurring. Information gained by General García of the Cuban forces indicated that General Escario was leading a relief column of Spanish troops toward Santiago from Manzanillo. According to whose version was accepted, it numbered from 3,700 to 8,000 men. Cuban insurgents were reportedly attempt-ing to delay the force, but as it had left Manzanillo on June 22, Shafter was afraid it might arrive any day and thus give Linares even greater superiority in numbers.

He decided to open his attack with Lawton's Second Division against El Caney and then to attack the fortifications at San Juan Hill and Kettle Hill with Kent's First Division and Wheeler's Cavalry Division. Bates and his independent brigade were to move ahead between these two main areas of attack and cut through to the Santiago-El Caney road, later to be joined by Lawton after he had reduced El Caney. García and his Cubans were to knife through in the same general area, pass around the northern outskirts of Santiago, and interpose them-selves between it and Escario's column, somewhere near El Camino Real—the main road leading to faraway Havana.

An early difficulty presented itself when the staff considered

how to get Lawton's division into position to attack El Caney.
The road leading there left the main route at El Pozo, passed
through the little town of Marianage, and then cut northwest to
the El Caney-Santiago road at a point that came to be marked
on the Army maps as the Ducoureau House. At Marianage a
road that was hardly a mule track cut off to the north to El
Caney, and it was up this trail, and by another rough path
farther east, that Lawton was to move toward El Caney.

Shafter set July 1 as the date for the battle. On the day before,
engineers and soldiers tried to patch up the road from Marianage
to El Caney so that ammunition wagons and a battery of field
guns could get through. Brush was cut in some places, made into
mats, and used to make a corduroy road. Late on June 30
Lawton took his men down the Santiago road to El Pozo, turned
north to Marianage, and went into camp a mile or so up the
trail toward El Caney. Bates was to take his independent brigade
up the jungle path to the east and spend the night in a position
where he could support Lawton in the morning or move south-
westward to link up with the Cavalry Division.

At the final staff meeting at Shafter's headquarters—the commanding general had come ashore finally on June 29 from the
Segurança—command changes had to be made because of illness. Fighting Joe was bedded by a fever that had the medical
officers worried. Sumner, commanding the First Brigade, was
moved up to division command. General Young, of the Second
Brigade, was so seriously ill from fever that he was being sent
back to the United States, so Colonel Wood took over his
brigade. That shift led to Colonel Roosevelt being given command of the Rough Riders on the eve of battle. At the last
minute Shafter asked Kent to move one of his regiments to the
far left to prevent any of the forces at Morro Castle or Aguadores from striking his left flank.

During these last days and hours the Spanish had not been
resting. With surprising industry they had been improving the
fortifications on the ridges in front of the invading force and,
unknown to the Americans, had done an excellent job of making
the little village of El Caney into a forbidding fortress. Holes
had been cut in the walls of a solidly built stone church, and a

small stone and adobe fort called El Viso made into another strong point a few hundred yards away. Most of the houses in the crossroad village were also prepared for defense, and trenches had been dug to connect all the buildings.

At San Juan and Kettle hills the Spaniards had been just as eager to build up their defenses. In addition to the trenches which had been dug days before—and which should have been shelled heavily by the fleet before the battle began—they had strung barbed wire entanglements up the sides of the ridges and another strand at the bottom of the hills near the shore of a small pond.

General Linares planned to defend Santiago with his more than ten thousand men in a most peculiar fashion. He knew the American force lay to the east of town, but this did not prevent him from guarding every approach, even from the west and southwest. He scattered his men in groups all around Santiago Bay, some of them so far away from the approaching scene of battle that they could not have marched to the front in a full day. He was more afraid of the Cuban guerrillas than he needed to be and also feared that troops might come ashore from the sea near the entrance to the harbor. About a thousand men from the Spanish fleet were put on shore under Cervera's chief of staff, Captain Bustamente, and ordered into position at Dos Caminos northwest of the city. Other forces were sent out the Cobre road to make contact with Escario's column, and at least a thousand men were kept immobile on the far side of the bay from Santiago, seeing no action during the critical battles.

Linares set up his headquarters at Fort Canosa, a fortified point about halfway between the city and San Juan Hill. For a reason only he knew, he put less than 150 men of the Talavera Regiment on Kettle and San Juan hills. The defenders of El Caney consisted of three companies of the Constitution Regiment and one company of dismounted guerrillas, in all 520 men.

It was a ridiculous misuse of available troops. If the great generals like Hannibal, Caesar, Frederick the Great, or Napoleon were watching, they must have shuddered at the violation of war's oldest rule—concentrate at the point of danger and have a reserve close at hand for counterattack.

Late on the evening of June 30 Linares must have recon-
sidered and realized that he was weakest at the most dangerous
point. So he made partial restitution by sending two companies
and his two Krupp guns under Colonel José Vaquero, and sixty
volunteers from the city's home guard, forward to reinforce the
men on San Juan and Kettle hills. This added enough men to
make the total holding that position come to 521.

The Americans were busy at the tasks an army performs in
the last hours before a major battle. Lawton, with Capron's
battery of four pieces, had gone as far as he could without fear
of ambush, and had told his men to get some much-needed
sleep. The main attack force under Kent and Sumner rested
near El Pozo, and watched the Gatling gun detachment under
Lieutenant John H. Parker and the Army's one observation
balloon, still deflated, being moved closer to the front.

The soldiers cooked up an evening meal of fat pork and beans
to eat with their hardtack, and sat around grousing about the
lack of smoking tobacco. Chewing and pipe tobacco had sky-
rocketed in price because of the shortage, until some men were
paying two dollars for a package that should have cost eight
cents. Others were reverting to boyhood tricks and smoking
dried grass and leaves. Some even smoked dried manure, so eager
were they for the solace that comes from a pipe.

As in all armies where allies fight together there was a lot of
complaining about the other fighters. The Americans tended to
have a low regard for their "little brown brothers" and accused
them of being on hand when rations were being doled out but
strangely absent when the bullets were flying. The Cubans would
not help with menial tasks, and this galled the Americans, but
the latter overlooked the fact that the insurgents' patrols were
invaluable in keeping Spanish scouting parties tied down close
to their own lines. Even as the Americans sat around their fires
on this last night in June, they were in fact being protected from
sudden sorties or limited attacks by hundreds of Cuban irregulars prowling through the jungle between the two armies.

In his tent near Sevilla General Shafter penned a short note
to Sampson and sent it off by courier before midnight. It read
as follows:

Camp near San Juan River
June 30, 1898

Sir:

I expect to attack Santiago tomorrow morning. I wish you would bombard the works at Aguadores in support of a regiment of infantry which I shall send there early tomorrow, and also make such demonstration as you think proper at the mouth of the harbor, so as to keep as many of the enemy there as possible.

In the light of later information it seems incredible that Shafter did not ask Sampson for heavy bombardment of the city of Santiago and the area between there and the ridges where he planned a frontal attack the next morning. It might appear, in restrospect, that Shafter wanted to win his battle without having to share any of the glory. Sampson had blockaded Cervera early that month and sent word that ten thousand soldiers should be transported to Cuba to seize the city. Perhaps Shafter figured that was his assignment and he would carry it out without naval support. Whatever the thinking, the result was evident. Infantry, with almost no artillery support, would have to assault the heights before Santiago while the big guns of the Atlantic fleet remained tragically silent.

An air of expectancy hung over the American positions as the moon rose on the night of June 30. The orders had seeped down through the ranks by now, and regulars and volunteers alike knew better what was expected of them. They knew that Lawton would lead off with the assault on El Caney—which Lawton and Brigadier General Adna R. Chaffee, commander of the First Brigade in the Second Division, had said would take two hours. Then Sumner, leading Wheeler's Cavalry Division, was to cross the streams that joined to form the San Juan River in front of the ridges, deploy to the right, and assault the Spanish lines. Kent's First Division was to move out behind Sumner, deploy to the left, and coordinate its attack with the cavalry.

The trouble with the second half of the battle plan was that virtually every one of Sumner's and Kent's men had to go forward by marching down the road to El Pozo before striking out north and south. All through the night, until the small hours of

the morning of July 1, men, mules, guns, ambulances, and supplies crawled through the quagmire known as El Camino Real.
One war correspondent wrote that it seemed to him that every
able-bodied man in the United States had been given a gun, sent
to Cuba, and was now trying to go forward on one narrow route
unworthy of the name "road." But he did not explain the significance of the situation. American fighting men have a way of
overcoming obstacles when they are eager to fight the enemy.
Singing, cussing, joking, falling, and rising to march onward
again, the thousands of men made their way through the junction at El Pozo and tried to find their assigned jump-off positions. Some did not make it in time to get more than a couple
of hours of sleep, but they were where Shafter wanted them.

Richard Harding Davis observed the scene and sat down to
send off a dispatch to the New York *Herald* before the guns
started firing. His prose style was much like that of a later correspondent, Ernest Hemingway, who turned to fiction between
wars and achieved a sense of reality few writers have approached.

The hours passed and still the men moved forward in unbroken lines.
The moon rose, and still they passed, great stalwart giants in brown,
and young volunteers in brown, and cavalry mounted and unmounted,
white and colored, and pack trains of mules followed the leader's
bell. . . . In the bushes of the basin beneath us twenty-two thousand
men are sleeping, buried in a sea of mist, waiting for the day.

They could not all have been sleeping, if they were marching
past in an unbroken line, but that was poetic license. By the
time the dispatch had reached Siboney and the end of the telegraph wire, Davis knew most of them would be snatching that
precious hour or two of sleep that would refresh them for the
morrow's battle.

Those few men who could not sleep gazed westward at the
sugar-refining plant atop Kettle Hill and saw how it derived its
name—the equipment looking like a giant tea kettle in the moonlight. Beyond that rise of land and its neighbor, San Juan Hill,
they could see the lights going out in the city of Santiago.

12

★　　**12**　　★　★´　★　★　★

"Don't Bother with the Little Blockhouses"

AS SOON AS THE SUN provided enough light on the first morning in July, the gunners of Captain Allyn Capron's battery went to work. Using their range finders and the magic of triangulation, they studied the distances from their position to the church of San Luis del Caney, the stone blockhouses, and the trenches linking them. The four old guns had been dragged, pushed, lifted, and cussed into place on a hill about a mile and a quarter south of town. Lawton's instructions were to begin firing as soon after 6:30 A.M. as possible.

The commander at El Caney had spent much of the night writing his battle orders. These called for Chaffee to take the right of the division's line with the Seventh, Twelfth, and Seventeenth Infantry Regiments of the First Brigade; Colonel Evan Miles was to advance in the center with the First, Fourth and Twenty-Fifth Infantry Regiments of the Third Brigade; and Brigadier General William Ludlow was to move to the left flank with the Eighth, Twenty-Second, and Second Massachusetts Infantry Regiments of the Second Brigade. All of these were regular Army units except the last, which was made up of volunteers.

These assignments put Chaffee on the eastern approaches of the little cluster of houses making up the village, with the stone fort of El Viso as his first objective. Miles faced almost due north in the center and Ludlow, near the El Caney-Santiago road, faced northeast toward the fortified church where Cortez was reputed to have prayed before leaving to conquer Mexico. Sixty-eight men of Troop D, Second U.S. Cavalry, were assigned to protect Capron's battery.

It was with a real consciousness of relief that Capron, whose son had died a week before in the engagement at Las Guásimas, ordered his gun commanders to start firing. At last he could do something to even that tragic score. The shells overshot the targets on the first rounds, but the aim was corrected and the projectiles started falling on the homes and blockhouses. A column of Spanish soldiers that had been visible a few minutes before scattered like frightened chickens.

Black powder smoke went up from the guns, building into a pall that hung over the hilltop so heavily that the gunners had to cease firing every so often to permit it to drift away. Another cloud of smoke and dust arose over El Caney from the shattered adobe walls and the hits in the village streets.

Simultaneously with the beginning of the bombardment, Lawton's men moved ahead in a wide arc, men dodging and running as the Mausers crackled in the trenches ahead of them. Chaffee pushed his forces to within a hundred feet of the El Viso blockhouse, but they were forced to take shelter behind a ridge facing the fort. Ludlow found his men coming under heavy fire from a number of outlying blockhouses scattered in a chain around the church. Firing grew heavy and continuous. Here and there men fell to lie still or to crawl painfully toward safer positions. Reporters accompanying the first assault said the sound of bullets in the brush on the hillsides and in the leaves of the trees overhead resembled hail, a simile many a soldier knows too well.

After a while stretcher bearers came on the scene, taking the wounded back to a field hospital near Capron's battery. The growing number of wounded underscored what Lawton and his brigade commanders now knew for sure—it would take a lot longer than two hours to capture El Caney.

About nine o'clock one of the field pieces found the exact range for the El Viso blockhouse, and shells knocked a wide hole in the masonry walls. Instead of following up these hits, the battery shifted to other targets, shelling trenches to diminish the fusillades spewing into the Americans' faces. Enemy riflemen used the opening in the fort wall as another loophole, and the chance to pulverize El Viso was overlooked until hours later.

It was bad enough that the artillery had to use old-fashioned black powder, but as there were no enemy field pieces in the village it did not lead to the tragedy encountered at Las Guásimas. It was another story for the unfortunate soldiers in the Second Massachusetts Infantry. The volunteers were using black powder cartridges, and every time a man pulled the trigger he provided the foe with an excellent target.

The 520 Spaniards, safe behind their walls and trench embankments, were armed with modern Mausers using smokeless powder. The bullets whistled through the tall grass and into the mango trees in a grove where Ludlow's brigade was inching forward. Too many of them struck the volunteers from Massachusetts.

Seeing what was happening, Ludlow ordered the regiment to fall back, out of range. It was the only sensible, indeed the only merciful, thing to do. The two regiments of regulars filled in the gap, and the Bay State men went back to form what was, at the moment, the only reserve force available to Lawton before El Caney.

Capron edged his battery forward when he could, constantly plagued by troubles born of using the old powder. In the years when everyone in the States seemed to be urging war with Spain on Cleveland and McKinley, Congress had never got around to appropriating enough money to supply smokeless powder for all the regular forces and had approved almost none for the militia. Many a man died in the assault on Santiago because of this parsimony. And the field artillery was always hampered in its usefulness for the same reason.

One of the correspondents with Lawton's division sent his

paper a description of the furious battle between thousands of riflemen in the open and five hundred of the enemy in their strongly fortified positions. He told how he watched as some of Chaffee's men in the Twelfth Regiment rushed forward, bent over almost double to stay out of sight of a group of Spaniards beyond a slight rise of ground. The purpose, the writer said, was to avoid flushing the enemy and having them run off. "Later in the day," he added, "we began to wonder if they were ever going to run."

Vara del Rey's stubborn defense of El Caney kept Lawton from wheeling to the southwest and joining in the attack on San Juan and Kettle hills, which had been Shafter's plan. The commander-in-chief had hoped that Lawton's division, coming in on the Spanish left, could flank the defenses so painstakingly set up by the enemy on the ridges directly in his front.

Shafter went forward to a high hill where he could see what was going on in his front quite clearly but could only guess what was happening at El Caney from the smoke rising from Capron's battery. He saw the men of Kent's and Sumner's divisions pushing ahead on the Santiago road in an effort to get into position for the assault on the ridges, and could do little but pray that somehow the worst traffic jam of the whole campaign might be cleared out sufficiently for the troops to attack together.

The congestion on the beaches at Daiquirí and Siboney had been troublesome. That on the road leading to the engagement at Las Guásimas was worse, and the continuing tie-ups in the days when men were moving from the shore to El Pozo had become a nightmare. But now pandemonium existed everywhere.

Before Adna Chaffee marched off to help capture El Caney, he had surveyed the terrain in front of the hills and had reported to Shafter that the movement of all the troops down the one road when the assault began would be disastrous. Chaffee proposed that small openings be cut out of the jungle at right angles to the road and that sortie points be hacked out from those openings. Then, he suggested, the troops could move forward before the battle, take positions in these man-made "trails," and debouch together on the order to attack.

It was a most intelligent proposal, but it was not acted upon.

Two divisions tried to jump off for an assault against entrenched positions, using a single road at right angles to the enemy.

Battle orders called for Cuban irregulars to lead the way down the road toward the pond at the base of the ridges, cut right, and move around the enemy left. The dismounted cavalry was to follow, and Kent's division was to march on its heels, swinging to the left when it reached open ground.

Lawton had been fighting at El Caney at least an hour when Captain George S. Grimes's battery, posted on El Pozo Hill, opened the battle for San Juan and Kettle hills. The first shells fell in front of the enemy lines, doing no harm, but the telltale smoke from the guns' black powder allowed the Spanish gunners to aim their counterbattery fire with deadly accuracy. Because of the glutted road, and surely because of stupidity on the part of some general officer, the Cuban detachment and most of the dismounted cavalry were within a few score feet of Grimes's field pieces awaiting an order to advance. The third shell from the Krupp guns in the Spanish lines exploded in the midst of these men, killing several, wounding more and, as Colonel Roosevelt expressed it, turning the demoralized Cubans into "frightened Guinea hens."

Roosevelt ordered his Rough Riders to disperse in the jungle and Grimes stopped firing. Spanish gunners continued, however, for fifteen or twenty minutes. After a while the Americans moved forward again and almost at once found themselves forced to ford the stream. Another traffic jam developed, and sporadic firing from the Spanish lines took a steady toll of the men laboring to cross the small creek.

John Black Atkins, a British war correspondent, said the leading units finally got across and the Cuban irregulars swung away to the north, as ordered. "A little further down the lane they branched off to the right," said Atkins, "and disappeared for the day."

Regiments of dismounted cavalry, regular and volunteer, hurried forward only to find themselves tangled up with some of Kent's people, who should not have moved until Sumner's division had spread out from the road.

Shafter could see none of the details of the confusion from

"Grimes's Battery Going Up El Pozo Hill" by Frederic Remington

his observation point on the hill. But his adjutant general, Colonel E. J. McClernand, who had been sent beyond El Pozo to represent him, tried to straighten things out. He ordered Kent's men to let the cavalry through, as had been intended in the first place, and Sumner's men squeezed their way forward, taking forty precious moments to do it. It was no wonder Stephen Crane compared the route at the bloody angle to the sunken road at Waterloo.

Then occurred one of the worst fiascoes of the day—the advance of the Army's one and only observation balloon, which provided enemy gunners with a made-to-order target.

The idea of using balloons, first found useful in the Civil War, was a natural aftermath of the Navy's success in bottling Cervera in Santiago harbor. During the period when cities on the Atlantic seaboard panicked at the thought that Spanish warships might attack them, several Signal Corps balloons had been sent to help them defend themselves. When the need—which was never proved—ended, the balloon that had been assigned to New York was deflated and sent to Fifth Corps headquarters at Tampa. With it went Lieutenant Joseph E. Maxfield of the Signal Corps—alone. In the mix-up at Tampa the balloon was lost for days. Maxfield finally pleaded for some enlisted men and got twenty-four, using them to track down the waylaid balloon. His energy paid off. The missing item was found, repaired, and put on a transport. From Siboney his group moved it to El Pozo and finished patching up the many rents caused by the varnish melting in the ship's hold. It was a marvel that he made it tight and that he had brought along enough hydrogen gas to inflate it. Finally, on the last day of June, the eve of the battle for Santiago, Maxfield and Lieutenant Colonel George M. Derby, chief engineer on Shafter's corps staff, made three ascents to study the ground before the Spanish trenches.

They reported to Shafter that they could see over the hills to where Cervera's fleet lay at anchor and that a lot of barbed wire had been strung on the slopes of the hills in front of them. The next morning, again under instructions from Shafter, the two men went up again, the mooring-rope handlers clustered in a stream bed near the El Pozo sugar house. It was about 8:30

A.M. when the big, gaudy, cumbersome balloon rose hundreds of feet in the air almost directly above where Roosevelt and Kent were trying to disentangle their men at the first ford.

Derby could see the enemy trenches with the help of his binoculars, but they looked empty. He saw something else much more important: another road to the south roughly paralleling the one packed with humanity directly below the balloon. The engineer officer wrote out a message to that effect, weighted it with a pebble, and tossed it down to an officer in Kent's division. It might have been a signal, for almost immediately the troops that he had not been able to see in the distant trenches suddenly rose up and started firing at the balloon. Some of the bullets punctured the big envelope, but most of them hit soldiers in the column below. The Spanish were smart enough to know that the balloon marked the presence of troops, and the Krupp guns joined in the firing. The van of the American column ground to a halt under the attack, but those behind could not stop, and masses of men milled about in the deadly rain of bullets. Some shook their fists at the balloonists, holding them responsible for their plight—and rightly so.

Maxfield's ground crew tried to "walk" the big silken globe away from the road, but the ropes became enmeshed in tree branches. As it was the only target the Spanish could see clearly, they peppered it until it looked like a sieve. Derby and Maxfield, unable to ascend or descend while the ropes were tangled, were in a most uncomfortable position, but they had charmed lives that day. Finally enough hydrogen escaped so the big envelope sank slowly and gently to the ground. Neither balloonist was hurt beyond a few scratches but the Americans who were suffering under a galling fire cheered when the envelope touched earth. "It was a relief to know that it was crushed to earth, never to rise again," one officer testified long afterwards at a Congressional inquiry.

Another fighting man who would be heard from years later agreed that the whole incident had been a fiasco. He was Lieutenant John J. Pershing, and what he said was this:

When the Tenth Cavalry arrived at the crossing of the San Juan

River, the balloon had become lodged in the treetops above, and the enemy had just begun to make a target of it—no doubt correctly supposing that our troops were moving along this road and were near at hand. A converging fire from all the works within range opened upon us that was terrible in its effect; the 71st New York, which lay in a sunken road near the ford, became demoralized and well-nigh stampeded.

Many of Kent's men did use the alternate trail that Derby had spotted from the air, and to this extent the balloon served a useful purpose. But it should never have been put up so close to a large body of men so tightly packed together.

While men were dying under the combined artillery barrage and the steady fire of the Mausers, there was a singular absence of directives from higher up. Each division and brigade had been told in general terms to move forward to the edge of the woods just beyond the San Juan River, and there get ready for the assault. Between the edge of the jungle and the Spanish lines there was considerable open ground, as if an orchard had once been set out on the slopes. Stephen Crane thought it looked a little like the hills of Orange County, New York, where he had spent several years of his young life.

A few farm buildings were scattered on the sides of the ridge and had been turned into blockhouses with sandbags and holes poked through the walls. Bullets flew from trench and block-house in a steady, savage, insistent fusillade. Other bullets came from snipers who had climbed into trees on the fringe of the woods and who shot straight down on the unwary Americans until they were themselves spotted and knocked from their perches by angry men in the melee below.

No one at the rear seemed to know how to stop troops from marching forward into the glutted road. It was as if gallons of water were pouring into a quart can, and the only possible result was chaos confounded by the steady fire from enemy entrenchments.

Sumner got most of his first regiments through the bottleneck the men had already christened "the Bloody Angle" and tried to move out to his right. Then he was ordered to link up with Lawton—an order that revealed how ignorant of true conditions the corps staff was at the moment. Lawton was pinned down with his seven thousand men at El Caney, four miles away, and a link-up was out of the question. Sumner got his men back into the cover of the woods and waited—and waited, and waited. Men were dropping all about and the stretcher bearers had to buck the oncoming regiments as they piled into the clotted road beyond El Pozo.

General Kent had no orders beyond his early one to strike out to the left when he could debouch from the road. The delay in front of him made him furious. As he was mounted, he could hurry faster than most of the soldiery, and he threaded his way up to the angle where men of his First Brigade, led by the Sixth Infantry, were manfully trying to carry out their instructions. The Sixth squeezed through and the Sixteenth Infantry followed before Kent learned of the alternate route spotted by the balloon observers. Swiftly, he altered the marching orders, and sent the last regiment of Brigadier General H. S. Hawkin's brigade—the Seventy-First New York Volunteers—up the other trail.

This led to one of the most hotly discussed incidents of the whole campaign and to charges ranging all the way from stupidity to rank cowardice. General Kent put it this way:

This would have speedily delivered them in their proper place on the left of their brigade, but under the galling fire of the enemy the leading battalion of this regiment was thrown into confusion and recoiled in disorder on the troops in the rear. At this critical moment the officers of my staff practically formed a cordon behind the panic-stricken men and urged them to again go forward. I finally ordered them to lie down in the thicket and clear the way for others of their own regiment who were coming up behind. This many of them did, and the second and third battalions came forward in better order and moved along the road toward the ford.

Arguments have persisted even to this day about the behavior of the Seventy-First New York Volunteers. Pershing's comment supported Kent's words. Others said that the volunteers suffered more than any other regiment in the area because they—like the Second Massachusetts at El Caney—were using black powder and thus giving their position away to the enemy. Most

of the New Yorkers, once they saw their brothers-in-arms pressing ahead, recovered from their confusion and moved on to
where they belonged, on the left flank of their brigade.

Some of the newspaper reporters' dispatches were delayed.
Some correspondents wrote long after the events they witnessed,
and a few wrote of things they had not seen. Sylvester Scovel
had gone off to Jamaica in the *World*'s boat and didn't get back
to Santiago until after the battle was over. Then he wrote of
the panic that overwhelmed some of the men of the Seventy-
First New York, and the story appeared on July 16 in Pulitzer's
paper long after the battle was over. It was unsigned, and many
incorrectly ascribed it to Stephen Crane.

Hearst, by then back in New York, jumped at the chance
to make hay with the incident. The *Journal* called its rival's
article a slur and a slander upon the heroism of the men from
the metropolis. Poor Crane never completely got out from under
the cloud. As late as 1924 Don Seitz, business manager of the
World, repeated the calumny in his biography of Pulitzer, and
other writers did the same.

All of them failed to take into account the official reports
by Pershing, later American General of the Armies in World
War I; General Kent; Captain (later Rear Admiral) French E.
Chadwick, Sampson's chief of staff; Colonel Roosevelt; and
others.

The advance to the jump-off line was more than men should
have been asked to make under the intolerable conditions.
There should have been more than one way to move to the
front. If no other routes could have been found, they should
have been cut through the woods. If this were out of the question, the troops should have been put in position in the night,
silently, rather than as if they were marching in a Fourth of
July parade back home.

But Shafter was ill, nearly prostrated by the heat, and without correct information about the movement of many of his
units. While the Spaniards were having a holiday firing at the
Signal Corps balloon, the commanding general concluded that
Lawton at El Caney was in serious circumstances. He sent a
courier to the Second Division commander about 10 A.M. with

this message: "Lawton: I would not bother with the little block-houses. They can't harm us. Bates's brigade and your division and García should move on the city and from the right of the line, going on the Sevilla road. Line is now hotly engaged."

The message revealed just how deep the confusion was. Law-ton was not concerned about the little blockhouses alone. He had not captured a single building or foot of enemy trench. Bates's brigade was not close enough to join Lawton in any march, and the route they were supposed to use to advance to Santiago after the reduction of El Caney was not the Sevilla road but the El Caney road. Finally, the "line," as Shafter called the main force in front of San Juan Ridge, was not hotly en-gaged. It was jammed into a small area of jungle, overcrowded highway, and stream beds, forced by a lack of specific orders to wait there under a murderous rain of bullets and shrapnel.

Bates's brigade had been told to move up to the front from Siboney on the day before the battle. It had marched most of the evening, arriving at a point between Las Guásimas and La Redonda around midnight. Early the next morning the brigade reached Shafter's headquarters and was ordered to go to El Caney. Without stopping to rest or eat, the men marched to Marianage and then along the wretched woods path toward El Caney. Nearly exhausted by the long trek, they were put into Lawton's lines to the right of Miles, but it was then well after noon.

13 ★ ★ ★ ★ ★ ★

San Juan Hill

CONDITIONS IN FRONT of the Spanish works on San Juan Ridge had worsened steadily. At about the moment that Bates reached El Caney, Kent was maneuvering to get his brigades lined up for an assault on the enemy position. He had handled the unfortunate incident involving the Seventy-First New York Volunteers and had managed to get most of General H. S. Hawkins' brigade past the Bloody Angle, but the entire area had become a vast slaughter pen where men were dying who could not even see the enemy, to say nothing of firing in their own defense.

Kent urged Colonel Wikoff and the Third Brigade to move down the alternate trail. The infantrymen of the leading regiment, the Ninth U.S., were obeying, often stepping over and around the prostrate figures of some of the New York volunteers, when a bullet struck Wikoff. He fell, mortally wounded. Lieutenant Colonel Worth of the Thirteenth took over and almost immediately fell, seriously wounded. Command of the brigade devolved upon Lieutenant Colonel Liscum of the Twenty-Fourth Infantry, but five minutes later he too was struck. Command finally fell into the hands of Lieutenant Colonel E. P. Ewers of the Ninth Infantry.

There have been battles where enlisted men suffered almost alone, but this was not one of them. The infuriating fire from the Spanish position made no distinction between officer and soldier.

The Cavalry Division, which had moved out from the road first, crossed the San Juan River to find itself suddenly in the open. Sumner urged his troops to fall back to the creek bed and to move to their right up the stream. The riverbank gave them some protection as did a few trees growing along the river. Having succeeded in getting his foremost regiments into a somewhat safer position, the general waited for signs that Kent's division was where it could join in the assault. But the men at the base of Kettle Hill could see little that was going on in the woods near the Bloody Angle. Sumner asked an officer to carry a message back that he was ready to launch his attack, but the officer was killed. Another and then another officer fell trying to carry out the same mission.

Through the smoke from Grimes's battery—which had resumed firing in an attempt to cover the foot soldiers pinned down near the river—appeared the figure of General Wheeler, wan and shaky, who had risen from his sick bed against the doctor's orders. He did not supersede Sumner—that would have been catastrophic under the conditions—but he did look over the situation with the eye of a field general who had known intimately the confusion of battle. He sensed that retreat would be madness, even if it could be carried out. Leaving the troops immobilized where they were would have been inhumane.

An attack was the answer. At about this moment one of Sumner's couriers got through with the word that the Cavalry Division wanted to go ahead, and Fighting Joe read the message. Addressing no one in particular, although Lieutenant John D. Miley of Shafter's staff was standing nearby, Wheeler announced that Sumner was asking if Shafter's orders "contemplated" an assault on the Spanish trenches. It may have been that this was all that was needed—the phrasing of the question, the pinpointing of light on the problem—but it worked. Miley assumed the responsibility of speaking for Shafter, who was lying on a cot two miles away, and said everyone should advance. It was not a crisp order—nothing that history could immortalize, not a heroic call to arms that could be graven on bronze—but it moved two bloodied, battered, and extremely unhappy divisions off dead center. They wanted to fight and now at 2 P.M., six hours after Grimes's battery had opened the battle, they were going to have their chance.

By a process more like osmosis than military command, the various regiments began to move forward. Word spread along the packed road from El Pozo and the Bloody Angle and the muddy ford, out to the border of the woods and along the riverbed, off to where Kent's men were forming lines at a barbed wire strand that bayonets could not cut, and off to the meadow's edge where the socially elite from the Atlantic seaboard were lying in the mud with the marshal of Dodge City and the cowboys of Arizona a few rods from the colored men of the Ninth U.S. Regular Cavalry. It seeped back to a point on El Camino Real, where Lieutenant John H. Parker had been waiting impatiently to move his four Gatling guns forward so they could do some good.

Suddenly the thousands of men started forward, some in tight ranks, some at the double, and some jogging forward, firing, stopping, firing, stopping, but always moving ahead. It was like the swarming of bees, an angry mass movement, all in one direction.

Units fought more or less in the position they found themselves in when they emerged from the congested areas in the woods. This had the effect of putting the Sixth and Sixteenth Regular Infantry Regiments in the van on the left. General Hawkins, paying no attention to heavy fire from the hilltop, led these men personally. On his right, and nearest to the enemy, were the First and Ninth U.S. Cavalry Regiments and Roosevelt's Rough Riders, all dismounted. They were nearest to the enemy because Kettle Hill extended out from the main ridge several score feet or more.

Richard Harding Davis—who had covered many a battle—found this one more exciting than some he had witnessed where cavalry charged with lowered guidons and massed infantry went forward at a flawless quickstep. The Americans before San Juan Ridge, he said, strode through the tall grass, in broken lines, falling and picking themselves up, tearing down barbed wire strands when they were in their way as if bullets from the ridge were not whizzing all around them. "They walked," he said, "to greet death at every step . . . a thin blue line that kept creeping higher and higher up the hill."

Behind the leading regiments came other troops including many of the Seventy-First New York, eager to redeem themselves in the climactic assault. And just behind the van came Lieutenant Parker with three of his four Gatlings, racing to get them into position in support of the riflemen.

The Rough Riders were instructed to support the First and Ninth Cavalry, the latter a Negro regiment under command of Colonel John M. Hamilton, in their battle for Kettle Hill. All moved forward from the creek bottom at the same time, suffering considerable casualties as they progressed. Roosevelt, mounted on a small pony he had brought all the way from the States, rode before his men with absolute unconcern for the firing from the Spanish trenches.

The Ninth charged up the slope and came under cruel fire. Colonel Hamilton fell dead. The regiment stopped to regroup, waiting for orders. This left them directly in the way of the Volunteers. Roosevelt knew his instructions—to get to the top of the hill.

"If you're not going up," he shouted to the men of the Ninth, "get out of my way, for I am."

The Rough Riders followed their colonel. The Negro soldiers did the same. They all arrived at the top together with the soldiers of the First Regiment, finding that most of the enemy had abandoned their trenches and the buildings of the sugar refinery.

While the cavalry was storming Kettle Hill, Hawkins' men were having heavy going. The Spanish on the main ridge poured a continuous fire down upon the advancing blue lines. The regular infantrymen suffered badly. Roosevelt's order to his men to fire across at the positions on San Juan Hill to aid their countrymen had a beneficial effect. Suddenly the Rough Riders and their companions in the other two regiments heard the rattle of machine guns. At first they thought they were caught in a counterattack, but then they saw Parker's Gatlings, firing

"Left Flank of Rough Riders Charging Blockhouse" by Howard Chandler
Christy

from across the brook. The enfilading rifle fire from Kettle Hill
and the hailstorm of bullets from the hand-cranked machine guns
gave Hawkins and his men the help they needed to mount the
rest of the way up San Juan Hill.

General Hawkins said later that "the very audacity of the
assault seemed to demoralize the enemy." Lieutenant Parker had
his own idea about it. His report explained his feelings:

Inspired by the friendly rattle of the machine-guns, our own troops
rose to the charge, while the enemy, amazed at our sudden and tremendous increase in fire, first diverted his fire to my battery and then,
unable to withstand the hail of bullets, augmented by the moral effect
of our battery fire and the charging line, broke madly from his safe
trenches and was mercilessly cut by the fire of these guns during his
flight.

There was no need for rival claims. There had been mistakes
and bad judgments everywhere, but there was also enough
heroism to suit anyone. When, after the unconscionable wait
in the woods near the Bloody Angle, the assault was made,
courage was the commonest possession on the battlefield.

A military man, writing years later of the assault on the
ridge, said that "it was a tangle of organizations which ascended
the hill together." It had to be an accurate appraisal. They had
been all tangled up since dawn; how else could they have
fought?

Davis was more flowery in the book he wrote after the war.
Part of his story said:

The men of the Ninth and the Rough Riders rushed to the blockhouse together. The men of the Sixth, of the Third, of the Tenth
Cavalry, of the Sixth and Sixteenth Infantry, fell on their faces along
the crest of the hills beyond, and opened upon the vanishing enemy.
They drove the yellow silk flags of the cavalry and the Stars and
Stripes of their country into the soft earth of the trenches, and then
sank down and looked back at the road they had climbed and swung
their hats in the air.

There were other regimental commanders near at hand, but

Roosevelt, the only one on a horse, had an advantage he was quick to seize. Gathering the men, he led them in a dash down the far side of Kettle Hill, across a depression with a small pond in the middle, and up the northern flank of San Juan Hill. The movement helped consolidate the American position. From the ridge they could see Spanish soldiers retreating to another outcropping of hills almost a mile to the rear. It was Fort Canosa, the last barrier of any consequence on the road to Santiago.

Sumner and Kent ordered the troops to halt at San Juan Hill, dig in, and prepare for a counterattack if one came. But the enemy had had enough for that day, and the fighting died down to sporadic long-distance firing and then even that came to an end.

When the guns went silent the men could hear clearly the sound of firing at El Caney—the steady rat-a-plan of riflery and the occasional heavy thump of Capron's field pieces. The battle for the little town was still raging four miles away.

Nothing Lawton had done had worked. Massed infantry assaults had led to heavy casualties and little else. Capron's guns had been in action almost continuously, but they too had been unable to shake General Vara del Rey's determination to hold on. Men had eaten in relays, chewing on their hardtack and bacon as they lay behind whatever natural barrier gave them protection. But the battle had never actually stopped. An attack from the left a little after noon caught some of the enemy outside their fortifications, and Vara del Ray fell dead, both his legs shot off. Two of his sons died in the same firefight. Their leader's death made little difference so far as the Americans could judge. The Spanish troops at El Caney fought well that day, winning a place with the most heroic defenders in history.

Joseph Chamberlain of the New York *Post* put into words the eulogy all observers felt:

I shall never cease to see, when the word Caney is spoken, a line of some fifty or sixty light-blue-clad men standing in a trench, the line bent in the middle at right angles by the square turning of the ditch; at the bending of this line some blue-jacketed young officer standing, always exposed to the belt, and sometimes, as he stood up on the level ground, exposed to the feet; the men rising at the word of this officer's command for hours and hours, delivering volley after volley full in our faces.

Perhaps influenced by the bravery shown on both sides, some of the correspondents behaved in a like manner. James Creelman of the New York *Journal* led a group of soldiers from Miles's and Bates's brigades up the slope toward El Viso exposed to constant fire, waited for a pair of wire cutters to be brought forward, passed through the entanglement, and was first into a trench on the brow of the hill. It was filled with dead and dying Spaniards. Creelman raced ahead to the fort, accepted the surrender of the handful of defenders still living, and picked up the Spanish colors from where one of Capron's shells had knocked them from a flagstaff.

Minutes later a bullet struck Creelman in the shoulder. Soldiers carried him out of the fort, laid him under a mango tree, and covered him with the Spanish ensign. There William Randolph Hearst found him and bent down to listen as Creelman dictated his story.

It was a strange war, this one, where reporters conferred with generals and led troops in heroic assaults.

El Viso fell into U.S. hands about 3 P.M. but it did not end the battle for El Caney. Where before the Spanish had been firing from the fort, they now fired at it from the church, knowing it held Americans. Ludlow, off on the road leading out of the village toward the bay, strode up and down his lines directing fire at different targets and leading his men closer and closer to the enemy lines. Bates's men, still weak from their long march and hours of fighting, kept up the pressure in the center.

The sun, which had cast long shadows toward the west when Allyn Capron first shouted, "Fire!", was now itself low in the west, sending the shadows eastward.

Capron lobbed shells at El Caney in a continuing, relentless, softening process. As he moved his guns forward from one eminence to another, the projectiles battered the walls into rubble but the defenders hung on, suffering hideous casualties.

"The Last Stand of the Spanish at the Western Entrance to El Caney" by Howard Chandler Christy

What brought Lawton's men victory at the end, in addition
to their own incredible bravery, was a shortage of ammunition
in the Spanish positions. Lieutenant Colonel Punet, in command
after the death of the heroic Vara del Rey decided that further
resistance was futile and gave the men permission to attempt
to break out and seek shelter in Santiago.

Heavy barbed-wire entanglements had prevented the Americans from fully encircling the village, so there was an escape
route to the north. Firing with their last ammunition, the Spaniards dashed from the trenches and church. Punet and about a
hundred of his men made it through the gantlet.

Left in the tiny village of El Caney, now little more than
blasted trenches and rubble, were 235 dead and wounded and
120 others captured by the Americans. The balance of the 520
who began the action had been driven into the countryside.

Our losses were equally grave. There were 4 officers and 77
men killed and 25 officers and 335 men wounded. It had been
a bitter battle with honors for heroism on both sides.

Many a soldier, looking over the battlefield as the sun started
to sink beyond the bay, wondered if bravery should have been
called upon to do what brilliance might have avoided. It is the
sort of question young field officers discuss at staff and command
schools.

Was the battle necessary? There were only the 520 Spaniards
in the village, four miles away from the main action. Would
it have been wiser to ask two regiments to pin them down and
keep them from reinforcing their comrades at San Juan Hill?
Would a better general have used Capron's battery to punish
the defenders and kept his infantry out of the battle? What
would have happened if El Caney had been totally ignored?
After the victory at San Juan, this small outpost could have been
reduced at our leisure or ignored.

The British military observer, Captain Lee of the Royal Engineers, passed the final judgment as he watched troops in the
open assaulting the well-defended blockhouses. "Is it customary
with you," he asked an American officer, "to assault blockhouses
and rifle pits before they have been searched by artillery?"

The officer said, "Not always," but the question should have been addressed, in all fairness, not to a major leading his men into the face of deadly musketry, but to Shafter, lying indisposed in his tent four miles away.

Lawton's troops had slept no more than four hours the night before and had been engaged in a bloody firefight from dawn to dusk, but he was a good soldier and obeyed orders. He led his men down the road toward Santiago, as he had been told to do twenty-four hours before. As the light died his van came under sporadic fire and he decided he should not ask his men to face a night battle. At the Ducoureau House he left the main road, cut back on a path to Marianage and so to El Pozo. The next forenoon the Second Division joined the troops in the line on San Juan Hill.

14

★ ★ ★ ★ ★ ★

Colonel Roosevelt, the Critic

WHEN DARKNESS CAME to the battlefield it was an act of kindness for most of the men. It hid a scene of suffering and horror, of fear and sorrow, hatred, even dishonor. The day had granted the Americans a great victory, but the price paid for it was beyond the power of ordinary men to estimate.

Night brought an end to the killing, but it was hideous with the cries of the wounded, lying now in a mist rising from the river in a white blanket, that became a shroud for too many, both American and Spanish. Stretcher bearers carried in the victims in such numbers that the hospital could not handle them. General Shafter paled at the evidence of heavy casualties. They moved him to send off an early report to Washington that he had underestimated the number killed and wounded in the single day's battle. When the message arrived, McKinley and his aides shuddered to think what the public's reaction would be to such news. More than three decades had passed since Americans had read the dreadful casualty lists of Civil War battles.

A final count revealed that 1,475 American soldiers had been killed or wounded in the crowded labyrinth beyond El Pozo, on the slopes of San Juan Hill, and before El Caney. Their comrades-in-arms, weary though they were, had to carry the wounded back to the field hospital, denuding the forward lines of many defenders. All night long the officers on the ridge, knowing how shy of fighting men they were, feared that a counterattack would find the American forces too weak to hold their positions. Rumors of danger multiplied with the darkness, and men found themselves firing at strange noises and shadows. General Wheeler sent word to Shafter that some officers wanted a withdrawal, but he warned against it for reasons of morale. During the late hours of the morning ammunition was rushed up to the lines on San Juan Hill, as were two Colt guns and a dynamite gun sent to reinforce Parkhurst's and Best's batteries. The cannoneers worked most of the night digging pits, but the rocky soil defeated their efforts and when the sun came up they had only about a foot of protection. Two new regiments were brought up from Siboney, the Thirty-Fourth Michigan going into reserve behind Kent's people and the Ninth Massachusetts being placed on the extreme left of Bates's brigade.

The situation at El Caney was even more fearful because there the suffering of the soldiery had a counterpart in the suffering of noncombatants. The men of Lawton's division had no knowledge of the presence of women and children in the fortified village until the bloody business was over. Then mop-up squads found scenes of incredible suffering and horror. The Spanish had known for days that El Caney would be attacked, yet they had done nothing to remove the aged, the young, and the women. All through the holocaust of fire from the musketry of thousands of infantrymen and the bombardment from Capron's field pieces, the noncombatants had cowered in basements and odd corners as walls fell and houses turned to rubble.

When the victors entered the village, children screamed at the sight of the enemy, and women recoiled from the men who had been killing their husbands all through the long day. Some of the scenes were taken straight from Goya's etchings. A beautiful woman ran out of a side street bearing a crucifix and guided the Americans to a room where her husband lay dead on the floor where he had fallen while trying to defend his wife's honor from a drunken officer. In another riddled house a squad of Americans came upon a young woman's body, the haft of a dagger sticking from her breast, the steel buried deep in the flesh. Nearby was a soldier so drunk he could neither remember what had happened nor realize that his comrades had failed in their valiant defense while he was trying to seduce the girl and had killed her when rebuffed.

The church of San Luis del Caney had been turned into a field hospital by the Spanish and a surgeon was operating just inside the doorway—the only place where there was any light. One of the American war correspondents reported that the scene was like a mural by an old master. The almost naked body of a soldier lay on an operating table with a figure of Christ on a crucifix just above him, both illuminated by a strange effulgence from the last rays of the sinking sun.

Shafter had no reserves to put in the line once the two new regiments had taken their stations. Lieutenant Parker placed his four Gatling guns in position to serve as a second line of defense. They were below the brow of the ridge, where the gunners were relatively safe from stray bullets. He thought they had done much too heroic work to expose them to needless risk.

The American soldiers could hear the enemy at Fort Canosa, and fired in that direction out of fear, but most of them were so weary from the grueling wait under fire and the charge up the hill that they fell asleep on the ground. Some suffered only from fatigue but others were feeling the first onslaught of fever. They stayed where they were, knowing that the hospital at Siboney was already full of men, many of them mentally deranged by their high fevers.

As in so many of history's conflicts where victory and defeat are not determined immediately, each side in this one feared the other had come off better. As a matter of fact, however, the Spanish defenders were in far worse shape than their adversaries. General Linares, who had begun the battle as commander of his forces, was seriously wounded. Captain Bustamente, who led a thousand men from the fleet into the lines around the city, was wounded and died soon after. Sixteen officers and hundreds of men were dead. General José Toral took command, fearing that no matter how serious the American situation was, his was worse.

Shafter awoke from a few hours of tormented sleep to learn that the list of casualties was growing hourly. He asked Admiral Sampson to send surgeons ashore to help Army medical men who had been treating the wounded for nearly twenty-four hours without respite. Clara Barton, with a volunteer group of Red Cross nurses, left the *State of Texas*, a passenger ship chartered by the Army as a floating hospital, and rendered wonderful aid. Their tender ministrations were certainly important, but even more valuable were the supplies of medicine and drugs they took ashore with them.

They discovered new evidence of the same confusion that had marked every step of the war. One ship carrying medical supplies was "lost" for a week, and another was stationed with the blockading fleet before the entrance to the harbor and remained there five days and nights before it was ordered to Siboney.

There was a tent hospital for one hundred men only. All other wounded lay in the open. There was a shortage of rubber blankets to keep the ground dampness from the injured. There were no cots, hammocks, or pillows, almost no woolen clothing except what the men had on, and no special food for the feverish and severely wounded men. Stretcher bearers lifted men from the operating table during the first twenty-four or thirty-six hours after the battle, carried them out under the sun or the stars, and laid them down on the wet ground. Some were naked except for the bandages covering their wounds.

It was no better for the troops in the trenches, except that they were not wounded. Rations were delayed or nonexistent. Many men had not eaten since the day before the battle, and even water was in short supply.

When morning came on July 2, a desultory fire broke out between the two armies. Their positions were so close that rifle bullets could kill easily, and the big Spanish guns raked the top of San Juan Hill without any effective counterbattery fire.

Our big siege guns, so carefully loaded at Tampa, were still somewhere in the holds of transports lying at anchor off Siboney. Had they been pushed forward before the battle began, they could have done incalculable good, but Shafter's men fought supported only by sixteen small field guns, four Gatlings, and two or three other guns, all too small for the purpose at hand.

The commanding general wrote to Sampson, urging that the fleet force an entrance to the harbor, but the Admiral, knowing of the mines in the channel, wisely refused. Late in the afternoon of the second, Shafter called in Wheeler, Lawton, Kent, and Bates for a conference at his headquarters. He was in such pain and so weak from the heat that his staff had to unhinge a door from the sugar factory and tilt it at an angle so Shafter could recline on it to conduct the meeting. All day long he had been hearing reports from the front telling of heavy casualties from the almost continuous firing, and he knew his men were extended beyond safe limits. He asked his generals if they thought there should be a withdrawal to a line much nearer Siboney. Some did and some did not. After an inconclusive discussion, Shafter said he would think it over before making up his mind.

But, most important, he assured them that if he ordered a retreat or a simple withdrawal to safer ground, he would assume the full responsibility. This is how he put it, according to McClernand's ungrammatical notes: "Gentlemen, it is possible I have gotten you too far to the front, but I have always thought I had the courage to admit an error if I made one, and if we fall back I will take all blame, if any comes, upon myself; unless, however, you get orders to the contrary you will hold your positions."

Although there was no movement of troops on either side on July 2, the Americans suffered 150 casualties, which amply testified to the fierceness of the firing between the lines. These casualty reports apparently inspired Shafter to send a message to Washington stating that he was seriously considering a withdrawal of five miles. Colonel McClernand did his best to persuade the general not to send it, but got nowhere. Shafter was an obstinate man. However, McClernand did win him over to a proposal that a flag of truce be sent out between the lines with a message demanding a Spanish surrender. Both officers thought Toral might be impressed by the indication the Americans felt sure of their position. Even if he refused, the temporary truce brought on by the appearance of a white flag on the battlefield might give the troops some rest.

Before a decision on a withdrawal could be wrung from the commanding general, he received a telegram from Secretary of War Alger, answering his own about the possibility of retreat. It follows:

Your first dispatch received. Of course, you can judge the situation better than we can at this end of the line. If, however, you could hold your present position, especially San Juan Heights, the effect upon the country would be much better than falling back. However, we leave all that matter to you. This is only a suggestion. We shall send you re-enforcements at once.

The commander in the field, now running a fever from malaria in addition to the prostration brought on by the relentless heat, must have appreciated the Secretary's faith in his judgment. Alger was a patient man, more than willing to rely upon the men he had assigned to tasks far overseas.

Fighting Joe Wheeler wanted nothing to do with a withdrawal and said so bluntly. If there was no surrender of the city of Santiago, he argued, the Army would have to fight again to recapture the ground given up in such a retreat. Even with new troops coming from the States, this could mean more heavy casualties.

As the debate went on, another factor was injected—one that was to bear heavily on everything that happened subsequently during the Cuban campaign. It was the dread specter of disease. General Ireland, the Army's surgeon general, told Shafter, according to McClernand, that "disease had driven its fangs into our men before the day of battle."

Malaria and dysentery were rampant in all units and yellow fever, much more serious, had been reported by several regimental doctors. Both wounded and unwounded soldiers were coming down with fever. The buildings of the Spanish-American Iron Company in Siboney, the largest structures within the American lines, had to be transformed into a general hospital. They were roofed with zinc sheathing and offered the first adequate protection any of the wounded had known.

Some of the worst of the injured were put aboard the hospital ship *Olivette*. The transports *Cherokee* and *Breakwater* were transformed into additional floating hospitals. Sampson sent small boats to transfer the men from shore to ship.

The information hinting that disease would ultimately be a more deadly foe than the Spanish troops affected Shafter deeply. It was also commented upon in the dispatches the correspondents were sending their papers. In the main, however, the reporters were more concerned about the exigencies of the battlefield itself, the lack of fresh troops, and the failure to bring the siege gun train up to the lines.

Caspar Whitney and Frank Norris wrote of the lack of exultation in the ranks on the day after the victories at San Juan and El Caney. Whitney painted a gruesome picture of the battlefield, with "men dying, men wounded, passing back to the division hospital, some being carried, some limping, some sitting by the roadside, all strangely silent, bandaged and bloody."

The man most of the other war correspondents looked upon as the peerless commentator on affairs of war, was even more frank in his dispatches. Davis was tormented by his sciatica, made worse by the dampness and heavy rains, and this may have had an effect on his writing. At one point he said: "The situation here is now critical—alarming—and it would be false to make it out otherwise. The troops should never have been sent here without the full force of artillery at Tampa, and until it arrives they can neither advance nor retreat. They can only lie on their faces or be shot at if they rise."

That was bad enough, naturally, but there was still a lot of venom circulating in Davis' veins. Remembering Shafter's rough outburst on the *Segurança,* the *Herald*'s representative added these words:

Truthfully the expedition was prepared in ignorance and conducted in a series of blunders. Its commanding general has not yet even been within two miles of the scene of operation. That officer rode to a hill two miles from San Juan the day before the battle. He was overcome by the heat and has been lying on his back the greater part of the time ever since. General Wheeler, who refused to remain in bed with his fever, is here beside me on a poncho with bullets passing over him.

It was a merciless hatchet job, unfortunate because of the personalities involved, but it was the simple truth. The war had been run as if by amateurs. Most of the mistakes could have been avoided, but were not. Most of the situations could have been foreseen, and better staff work would have altered everything for the better. The corpulent commander—whom Walter Millis referred to as weighing a seventh of a ton—had had to rely upon the raw courage of foot soldiers who had not let him down. But the price they paid for the victories was shamefully high.

The man whom the headline writers back home were eulogizing—"Teddy" Roosevelt—was probably the most heartless observer of all. After the battle for San Juan had been won and he had organized the men of his brigade into a fighting unit he was sure could hold its sector, he turned to his other love—writing. He penned a letter to Henry Cabot Lodge that must stand as one of the most serious attacks on a military superior in the annals of war. Lodge was smart enough to withhold its publication for a long time. It follows:

Not since the campaign of Crassus against the Parthians has there been so criminally incompetent a General as Shafter; and not since the expedition against Walcheren has there been grosser mismanagement than this. The battle simply fought itself; three of the Brigade Commanders, most of the Colonels, and all the regiments could not be surpassed; but Shafter never came within three miles of the line, and never has come; the confusion is incredible. The siege guns have not yet been landed! The mortars have not yet started from the landing place. Our artillery has been poorly handled. There is no head; the orders follow one another in rapid succession, and are confused and contradictory to a degree. I have held the extreme front of the firing line; I shall do all that can be done, whatever comes; but it is bitter to see the misery and suffering, and think that nothing but incompetency in mustering the nation's enormous resources caused it. The fighting has been very hard. I don't know whether people at home know how well this regiment did. I am as proud of it as I can be; and these men would follow me anywhere now. It was great luck for me to get the command of it before the battle.

Roosevelt need not have worried about whether the public knew how well the regiment did. In most of the papers back home it would have seemed that the Rough Riders were fighting the Spanish single-handed. The colonel's name was in hundreds of headlines and his picture on many a front page. He was well along on his way to the White House.

The man for whom he had so little respect seemed to entertain a similar lack of respect, but his was aimed toward volunteers in general. In the message he sent Alger on the morning of July 3 he described his situation and sketched in some of the details of the battle. "The behavior of the regular troops was magnificent," he said, but never once mentioned the volunteers or state militia.

There must have been a great deal of confusion in Santiago. The French consul led four hundred noncombatants out of town and into the Cuban lines commanded by García. The neutral diplomat indicated that the enemy was not contemplating surrender. On the contrary, troops were busy digging better positions and fortifying outlying buildings.

A strange movement of Santiago residents began soon after the cessation of heavy fighting. They carried some of their personal belongings as they walked along the road leading to the country. One of the routes chosen was the Santiago-El Caney road, where Spanish and American troops faced each other near a masonry bridge south of the little hamlet of San Miguel. The fugitives from the city were women and children and the aged.

Newspaper reporters told of an old woman of seventy carrying a woman of ninety-two on her back, trudging through the dust kicked up by those ahead of her. Some of the young women had put on their best finery for the escape to the rural area. They were corseted, one correspondent said, in such a way as to reveal to the fullest their ripe, feminine contours, but the foundation garments must have tortured them in the 90- and 95-degree heat. A group of prostitutes, apparently in the best of humor, had decided that business could hardly be profitable in the city where every able-bodied man was in the lines or digging trenches. They walked along toward the hills near Cuabitas, evidently looking for a new location to ply their trade. In a way, their decision to leave Santiago was eloquent proof that conditions in the town were chaotic, if not utterly hopeless.

Shafter and his staff decided that the suggestion McClernand had made late the night before about a surrender demand should be carried through. The general had a short message drawn up and asked General Wheeler to assign an officer to carry it to the Spanish lines under a flag of truce. It read:

> Headquarters United States Forces
> Near San Juan River, Cuba
> July 3, 1898—8:30 A.M.
>
> *To the Commanding General of the Spanish Forces,*
> *Santiago de Cuba.*
> Sir: I shall be obliged, unless you surrender, to shell Santiago de Cuba. Please inform the citizens of foreign countries and all women and children that they should leave the city before 10 o'clock tomorrow morning.
>
> Very respectfully, your obedient servant,
> W. R. Shafter, *Major-General, U.S.A.*

Colonel J. H. Dorst, with a few men to carry a large white flag, climbed out of the American trenches atop San Juan Hill a short time later and walked into the Spanish lines at Fort Canosa. Firing ceased on both sides at the first appearance of the truce flag. Dorst handed Shafter's surrender demand to a senior officer of the Talavera Regiment and returned to his own lines, not waiting for an answer. There was some sporadic firing after the incident, but both sides seemed to prefer a wait-and-see attitude and the musketry almost died out for the balance of the day.

If the men could have used this period of relative peace for washing and eating, they would have been much happier. Some of them, Colonel Roosevelt wrote Senator Lodge, had been in the same clothing for a month; others, he said, were in tatters. He complained that despite all he had done, he still could not get good dried meat, cornmeal, rice or canned fruit for the Rough Riders. The colonel was in a sour mood and excoriated

Shafter anew for lack of administrative ability. He was proud
of his men, though, and told Lodge, "I feel terribly to see them
suffering for lack of good food, to see my sick men in high
fever lying in mud on their only blankets without even so cheap
a comfort as a little rice or even sugar for their tea and coffee."

Later, however, his natural ebullience overcame the feeling
of anger at his superior.

"Did I tell you I killed a Spaniard with my own hand when
I led the storm of the first redoubt?" he asked Lodge.

He had not told him. This was the first time Roosevelt had
written about it to anyone, and it had the same element of
juvenile pride in it that one notes when a boy announces he
has just passed the merit badge test for canoeing.

If the flamboyant leader of the Rough Riders was contented
with his own place in the Valhalla of battle heroes, few other
commanders in Cuba could say the same. Shafter wired Alger
on several occasions that he was almost prostrate from exhaus-
tion and had eaten virtually nothing for four days. He even went
so far as to suggest that he had considered handing field command to his next in rank, General Wheeler, but the latter's own
illness had made such a move unwise. Shafter made a speech
the year after the war in which he recalled that all of his general
officers "were ailing more or less."

The enemy high command was plagued by another variety
of misfortune. Although acclimated to the heat and not suffering from illness, they were involved in a tug of war over the
relative importance of the city of Santiago, and the fleet led
by Admiral Cervera. Linares did not want to see the sailors leave
his lines, but Cervera needed them if he was to engage in a
fleet action.

Dissension had been evident among the Spanish leaders ever
since Cervera arrived. Truthfully it had existed before, in a
way, because the admiral had claimed all along that his antiquated, run-down fleet should never have left the Cape Verdes.
Almost out of coal, he had had to choose between Santiago and
San Juan, knowing that he would be trapped in either port.

While Shafter and the Fifth Corps were steaming toward
Siboney and Daiquirí, and while they were landing and advanc-

ing toward Santiago, conditions in the city had become desperate. Most of the population was down to a diet of rice and coffee. Cervera had found precious little coal in the harbor and was trying to economize by shutting off the boilers in some of the ships each day. This was no way to prepare for a sortie in the event of fortuitous circumstances and he told Captain General Blanco so.

Blanco, sitting in Havana, thought Cervera could break out and said so on many occasions during the American buildup. He cited several minor instances where Spanish ships had evaded the blockade at other ports, not realizing, or not choosing to realize, the difference between a fleet like the one Sampson commanded and the grab-bag squadrons of armed merchantmen and similar inferior vessels guarding other Cuban ports.

Eventually Blanco asked for supreme command in Cuba, and the government in Madrid granted his wish on June 23. From that moment pressure on Cervera to break out was increased. But the Admiral laid his cards on the table in a telegram to his new commander. It said in part:

I believe it my duty to set forth condition of squadron. Out of 3,000 rounds for 5.5-inch Hontoria guns, only 620 reliable, rest have been pronounced useless, and were not replaced by others for lack of stores when we left. Two 5.5-inch Hontoria guns of *Vizcaya* and one of *Oquendo* defective, and had been ordered to be changed for others. Majority of fuses not serviceable. We lack Bustamente torpedoes. *Colón* is without heavy armament. *Vizcaya* is badly fouled and has lost her speed. *Teresa* does not have landing guns, and those of *Vizcaya* and *Oquendo* are unserviceable. . . . Blockading fleet is four times superior; hence our sortie would be positively certain destruction.

Writing to General Linares, the Admiral went even further in outlining the inevitable results of a sortie. He was a brave man and was willing to accept orders, but he did not want disaster on his conscience when he knew the result beforehand. He wrote in part:

I, who am a man without ambitions, without mad passions, believe that whatever is most expedient should be done, and I state most emphatically that I shall *never* be the one to decree the horrible and useless hecatomb which will be the only possible result of the sortie from here by main force, for I should consider myself responsible before God and history for the lives sacrificed on the altar of vanity, and not in the true defense of the country. . . . It is therefore for him [Blanco] to decide whether I am to go to suicide, dragging along with me those two thousand sons of Spain.

While the American forces fought their way past Las Guásimas and waited to mount the assault on San Juan and El Caney, the feuding among the Spanish leaders grew more bitter. The Spanish minister of marine in Madrid told Cervera that loss of the fleet in battle would be more honorable than its capture or its destruction by its own men. Blanco kept belittling the danger of battle, urging the fleet to leave in the darkness of night. It was as if he had not been told of the relentless searchlight watch Sampson had initiated almost immediately upon converging his forces outside the harbor.

Two days before the Americans launched their frontal attack on the city's eastern defenses, Blanco wired the admiral the order Cervera knew was coming. "In case the situation should become aggravated, so that the fall of Santiago is believed near," instructed Blanco, "the squadron will go out immediately as best it can, entrusting its fate to the valor and ability of your excellency and the distinguished captains commanding it, who no doubt will confirm by their actions the reputation they enjoy."

On the night after the battles at El Caney and San Juan Heights, General Toral cabled Blanco of the defeat and told him that if the sailors were withdrawn from the lines the city would fall immediately.

An urgent telegram was sent from Havana at 10:30 P.M. on July 1, reflecting Toral's pessimism and Blanco's conviction that Santiago's fall was only hours away. It contained these sentences: "In view of hostile progress in spite of heroic defense garrison, and in conformity with opinion government, you will re-embark crews, take advantage of first opportunity, and go out with the ships of your squadron, following route you deem best."

Exactly fifteen minutes later, Blanco, now sure the Americans were about to enter Santiago, sent off another wire to Cervera, urging him to hasten his departure.

All through the next day, while firing between the lines was going on with little interruption, the sailors were ferried back to their ships. Those of the *Vizcaya,* who had been deployed far out on the Camino Real del Cobre, arrived on the warship "completely exhausted."

The orders to break out had been given by Captain General Blanco and the government in Madrid. They were explicit. Admiral Cervera, a man without "mad passions," would obey them to the letter.

15

★ ★ ★ ★ ★ ★

Courage Is Not Enough

O N THE BEACH at Siboney the morning sun shone down upon a scene of most unwarlike nature. Several soldiers were saddling a horse, having curried it with loving care. Other soldiers, taking advantage of the warmth that came with the tropical sunlight, were bathing in the surf. Every now and again they peered down the coast toward the entrance to Santiago harbor. An hour or so later they saw the armored cruiser *New York* steaming along in their direction and knew that Admiral Sampson was on his way to an important battlefield parley with their commanding general. He would ride to the camp near the San Juan River on the horse they were grooming.

The man-of-war was still a considerable distance off when they saw her turn back, a heavy plume of black smoke emerging from the stacks as engine room crews built up steam. From far to the west they heard the crump, crump of heavy guns and realized that Sampson would not be needing the saddled horse that day.

The *New York* had not been long on her way from her station guarding the harbor when Captain "Fighting Bob" Evans on the *Iowa* heard his lookouts cry out, followed by the ringing of "general quarters." He looked up the channel and saw the

Spanish warship *María Teresa*, a bone in her teeth, charging straight toward the open sea.

Guns in the *Teresa*'s bow turret barked as she came under the shadow of Morro Castle. Five miles away Sampson heard them too and ordered the helm put over hard. The Spanish fleet was making its bid for freedom, and he wanted to be in at the kill.

Commodore Schley, who had been a reluctant commander at Cienfuegos, moved swiftly. Command had fallen on his shoulders when Sampson steamed off to confer with Shafter, and he was quick to sense that the glory that had escaped him up to the present was now within his grasp. Flags were sent up on the *Brooklyn* ordering, "Clear ship for action." The other American vessels in the arc outside the channel mouth acknowledged, and all moved in toward where the *Teresa,* with others of Cervera's fleet now coming into view behind her, was turning slightly to starboard to round a rocky shoal called Diamond Bank.

Captain Evans called it a beautiful sight and noted that the men of the *Iowa* cheered the Spanish fleet in sheer admiration for the enemy's bravery. That it was. Captain Victor Concas, Cervera's chief of staff, described it best in his memoirs, pointing out that at the moment the *Infanta María Teresa* emerged from the channel, only the two guns in her bow turret were usable against more than one hundred guns in the American fleet.

Naval strategists have always feared being the target fleet in the classic operation called "crossing the T," where an enemy fleet, crossing ahead of a squadron in column, is able to pour its broadsides on the leading ship while those behind the leader are unable to bring their guns to bear on any target.

In a way the sortie of the Spanish fleet resembled this maneuver, but it was much more hopeless for Cervera's ships. A column at sea, even if the victim of the T-crossing, has some freedom of movement. Cervera could not turn right or left in the channel without going aground. All he could do was steam straight into the American fire until he cleared the channel, and then turn along the coast before his cruisers could return the foe's fire. He had known all this before, as his own dispatches to Blanco had made clear, and Concas said that all other officers knew it, but there was no alternative save surrender.

Engine room gongs sounded in the American fleet, battle hatches open to give the sweltering crews below decks a breath of fresh air were dogged shut, and ammunition hoists hummed as shells went from magazines to gun turrets.

All this happened in less than ten minutes. It had been 9:31 A.M. when the lookouts on the *Iowa*, closest to the channel mouth, has spotted the *Teresa*. Captain Evans was enjoying a cigar after breakfast with his son, a naval cadet, when they heard the alarm. "Papa," said the boy, "the enemy ships are coming out." They had gone to the bridge to find that already some of the guns were raking the enemy flagship. It bespoke unusually high morale and efficiency for the American seamen.

Behind the *Teresa* appeared the *Vizcaya*, with an interval for maneuvering between them, then the *Cristóbal Colon*, and, bringing up the rear of the column, the *Oquendo*.

The two fleets had been watching one another for days; yet such are the exigencies of life at sea that neither side could move with absolute freedom. The American ships were motionless at the instant of discovery. Although fires were burning under the boilers, it took an agonizingly long time for the heavy vessels to gather way. Cervera's fleet, on the other hand, had to come nearly to a crawl as it rounded Diamond Bank, not only to make the turn, but to drop the civilian pilots. It was a ridiculous operation. Miguel Lopez, pilot on the flagship, recounted with awe the scene when he stood with Admiral Cervera, waiting for the moment when the *Teresa* could shift her helm to starboard to round Diamond Bank. By then shells from the *Texas* and *Iowa* were hitting the Spanish ship, some exploding deep inside.

"To starboard," said Cervera, as calm as though at anchor in his home port, according to Lopez. Then the admiral turned to the civilian pilot. "Good-bye, pilot," he said. "Go, and be sure you let them pay you, because you have earned it well."

Even in his hour of dire extremity, Cervera was a Spanish gentleman who could not forget his manners.

Each of the other cruisers made the turn to westward upon rounding the shoal, dropped her pilot, and followed in the

Teresa's wake, all the while coming under murderous fire from the converging American warships. Evans estimated that his first order to fire came at a range of five thousand yards or two and a half nautical miles, which must have appeared frightfully close to the emerging ships.

Shells from the *Indiana, Iowa,* and *Texas,* nearest the *Teresa,* were falling in a giant cascade about the flagship. They penetrated the stern, swept men and boats from the deck, and wrecked a forward turret, sending shell fragments against the bridge and wounding Captain Concas. Cervera took command, for the man who should have taken over when the captain was hit could not be reached in the shambles. It was an academic point, anyway, as the *Teresa* had but a few minutes to live.

The night before, Cervera had told his ship commanders of a plan to even some of the odds against his fleet. He knew that the *Brooklyn* and *New York* were the fastest ships in the enemy fleet. The former had maintained a post to the west of the harbor entrance, the direction in which the Spaniards had determined to move. The Spanish admiral expressed a hope that on quitting the port he might be able to get out before the American vessels could get under way. If this happened, he said, he intended to ram the *Brooklyn,* sacrificing the *Teresa* in the hope that other Spanish ships might escape. On paper, his four cruisers were faster than the American battleships. If the *Brooklyn* could be put out of commission, he had said, the three other Spanish cruisers could possibly escape from the heavier enemy ships before the *New York* could come up from the east. In a chase one enemy cruiser might be handled by his three survivors.

It was a sensible enough plan, but it could not be adhered to for several reasons. The *Brooklyn* had turned away as soon as she could get power to the main shaft, and the *Texas* and *Iowa* had moved more swiftly than contemplated and had managed to steam into a position where they, rather than the faster *Brooklyn,* would have been under the *Teresa*'s bow. Moreover, the Spanish ships were not as fast as they might have been because their bottoms were fouled from long weeks spent in warm seas.

If the Spanish officers considered their survival unlikely, this feeling did not keep their sailors from fighting bravely. As each cruiser rounded Diamond Bank, its guns barked defiantly at the American vessels. Shells whistled over the *Texas,* sending up great geysers a thousand yards or more behind her. Bravery, however, is not the same as gunnery. Many of the Spanish main batteries had not been fired from the time they were installed until they blasted away at Schley's fleet because of lack of ammunition for practice.

For only a few minutes the naval engagement was a magnificent thing to see. The American ships, lead-colored and rusty from their long stay away from drydock, contrasted strongly with the enemy fleet, which had been painted while in Santiago Bay. The Spanish vessels rode high in the water, partly from lack of coal in their bunkers. Great silk flags, heavy with gold thread, showed blood-red against the clear blue sky.

Then the scene changed as smoke from the many stacks, mixed with the heavy black smoke from the American guns, formed a blanket that often turned the battle into a ghastly game of hide-and-seek. In one of the periods of near blackout Captain J. W. Philip of the *Texas* heard his flag lieutenant complaining about the lack of battle flags. The younger officer, seeing the Spanish ships with flags on every staff, wanted more than one American ensign flapping on the *Texas'* stern. He asked the signal quartermaster where the flags were.

"In the locker," said another sailor, "and 'flags' has the key."

"Then smash the locker," cried the lieutenant. Out came the flags and the *Texas* charged on, resplendent as only a warship can be.

It was a pleasant interlude. A few minutes later grave danger brushed the *Texas,* frightening her skipper more than anything Cervera had been able to do.

The *Texas* and *Iowa* had pushed straight ahead toward the emerging Spanish squadron, but the *Brooklyn,* farther to the west, and totally obscured in the thick pall of smoke, had executed a turn to starboard that brought her rushing across the *Texas'* bows. Suddenly a breeze tore the clouds of smoke apart, and Captain Philip on the open bridge of the battleship saw the flagship coming up "so near that it took our breath away."

"Back both engines hard," ordered Captain Philip.

The *Texas* shuddered as the engines worked against the old ship's momentum. Those officers on the open bridge who saw the *Brooklyn* bearing down on their vessel could think of nothing but what would happen if the vessels collided. Philip wrote later that had the *Brooklyn* struck his ship, it would have been the end of the older warship and her five hundred men. Had the *Texas* rammed the armored cruiser, it would have been equally disastrous as the *Texas* was not built for ramming and, he said, "would have doubled up like a hoop." The *Brooklyn's* speed saved the great cruiser. She thundered past just ahead of the battleship.

Schley's maneuver is still the subject of debate in wardrooms and classrooms. He explained that he wanted to use first his port and then his starboard batteries in rapid succession, but somehow the Commodore's propensity for getting into trouble had done him a new disservice.

While the two vessels were thus engaged, the *María Teresa* had led her sister ships along the coast, the flagship already afire and the *Vizcaya*, next in line, taking a terrible beating from the guns on the *Indiana, Oregon,* and *Iowa.* After the early confusion, the battle became a race, the enemy doing its best to escape, and the American flotilla building up speed and taking station alongside at a distance of less than two or three thousand yards. At this range the thirteen-inch guns on the battleships and the eight-inch guns on the cruisers did incredible havoc to the enemy. There was a sort of pageantry to it for a few minutes. When the *Teresa* first emerged she was under attack from the entire blockading fleet for about ten minutes. Then as each Spanish cruiser came out, she fired as she came broadside on. There were many things wrong with the Spanish fleet: decks were of wood and much of the superstructure was fashioned from the same highly flammable material. After a few well-placed shots from the American guns, the Spanish ships' top hamper were blazing like torches. And the enemy had done little practicing because of lack of ammunition.

But this did not detract from their brave efforts. Shells whistled over the American ships, but some hit their targets. The

Texas was struck three times, once on the open bridge just after Captain Philip and his aides had gone to the conning tower.

The *Oregon,* fastest of the battleships, had kept all her main boilers on and surged ahead of the *Texas,* which had had to stop dead in the water after the near collision, standing toward the west almost abreast of the *María Teresa.* The *Iowa,* which was closest in, followed in the *Oregon*'s wake, her starboard batteries pounding both the Spanish flagship and the *Vizcaya.*

Two of the *Iowa*'s twelve-inch shells struck the *Teresa* just forward of the stern, breaking one of her main steam lines and causing an immediate loss of speed. Captain Concas, on the *Teresa,* had believed that she could outrun all the American ships on the scene except the *Brooklyn,* but this hope was dashed by the *Iowa*'s projectiles. It was at this juncture that Concas was wounded, and Admiral Cervera, taking command, turned toward the shore. The steam from the burst pipes scalded many of the men in the after sections of the ship. Some men in the after turrets were asphyxiated. Fires in the small-caliber ammunition magazines were spreading rapidly. One shell set fire to the Admiral's cabin. The after deck and chart house were blazing. Men who went below to flood the after magazine were suffocated in the live steam. Cervera decided that further fighting was senseless and he ran the *Teresa* aground on a small beach just west of Punta Cabrera, six and a quarter miles from the point where she first came under American fire.

Five minutes later the *Oquendo,* from which towering sheets of flame and smoke were pouring, was beached at Cabrera Point, a half mile beyond the Spanish flagship. Although last in line, she had taken more punishment than the *Vizcaya* or the *Colon.* The reason was obvious, once the smoke cleared away. When the *Teresa* came out of the harbor, most of the American ships trained their guns on her. Then as the *Vizcaya* rounded the shoals, she too came under heavy fire. The smoke of battle hid all the ships for a time, and the black curtain of haze from the furiously burning flagship blanketed the second in line. Untouched for a short period, the *Vizcaya* raced westward ahead of most of the American battleships. When the latter could see again, it was the *Oquendo* which was closest, and she came under a devastating fire from the *Brooklyn, Oregon, Texas* and *Iowa*.

The Caribbean forms a small bight between Diamond Bank and Punta Cabrera, pushing in toward shore several thousand feet. Taking advantage of this, the *Cristóbal Colon* had steamed inshore from the *Oquendo* and had escaped what Captain Philip called the "thrashing" the latter ship was getting from the *Texas'* guns.

Just a few minutes before the *Teresa* hauled down her colors, the remaining two ships of Cervera's squadron—the torpedo boats *Pluton* and *Furor*—were spotted coming out of the harbor.

A signalman on the *Indiana* hoisted flags warning, "Enemy torpedo boats coming out." The doughty little armed yacht *Gloucester,* which had been hanging back for this very purpose, opened her throttle all the way and charged straight for the enemy's rear guard. Someone on the *Gloucester* misread the *Indiana*'s signal, thinking the flags spelled "Gunboats close in," and Lieutenant Commander Richard Wainwright steered between the last of the American battleships, now turning westward, and the torpedo boats.

Captain Evans of the *Iowa* and Captain Taylor of the *Indiana* were both fighting "fools." Although their main batteries were firing at the Spanish cruisers, they ordered their rapid-fire guns to pepper the *Pluton* and *Furor*. Only luck saved the *Gloucester* from being hit by her own sister ships. Shells from enemy and friend fell around the little yacht, kicking up huge geysers that nearly swamped her.

Lieutenant Commander Rodgers, Captain Evans' executive officer, saw her plight. Hurrying to the bridge, he cried, "Look out, Captain, you will sink the *Gloucester.*" Evans ordered, "Cease firing," and the crisis passed.

Wainwright had "bottled" his steam and had no trouble reaching top speed. When within twelve hundred yards of the enemy gunboats he ordered his two small Colt rifles to open fire. They spit out a steady stream of small bullets that raked the enemy decks. The foe was using Maxim automatic one-pounders. Wainwright could see the splashes from their projectiles "walking" closer and closer to his frail little ship. Just before the range was

perfected, the firing ceased. One of the big shells from the battleships had disabled the *Pluton*'s machinery. As the American
gunners on the *Gloucester* looked on, the *Pluton* piled up on a
rocky ledge just west of the landing beach at Cabanas and then
blew up in a shattering explosion.

Bereft of her sister's support, the *Furor* turned bows on to the
Gloucester, as though to ram her or perhaps, Wainwright
thought, to fire her torpedoes. Instead the Spanish gunboat continued to turn, executing a tight circle. Her rudder was out of
commission.

Wainwright turned aft to see Sampson's flagship, the *New
York,* racing into battle from the east, under fire from the batteries at Morro Castle. Ignoring the land guns, the *New York*
let drive several shots at the circling *Furor* as the *Gloucester*
signaled the big cruiser, "Enemy's vessels destroyed." Sailors on
the flagship gave three cheers as the *New York* plunged on.

Within minutes the *Furor*'s aimless circling ceased. The little
torpedo boat trembled and went down bow first. There was
nothing for the *Gloucester* to do now but rescue the crews of the
two small vessels and aid in the same work alongside the burning *María Teresa.*

Sampson and Captain French Chadwick of the *New York*
were galled by the fear that they might not see action before the
fighting was over. They had asked the chief engineer to give
them his top speed, and as the big cruiser raced past the *Gloucester* the flagship was doing a little better than seventeen knots.

As she came abreast of the burning *María Teresa,* a Spanish
sailor was seen struggling in the water. An American sailor,
hearing his cries for help, picked up the chaplain's reading desk,
stowed on the main deck, and tossed it over. The desk had a
cross emblazoned on it.

"Cling to the cross," yelled the American seaman, "and you'll
be saved." Minutes afterwards men on the *Gloucester* rescued
the Spaniard, still clinging to the chaplain's desk.

Meanwhile the battle in the van was going badly for the two
surviving enemy cruisers. Captain Clark had taken the *Oregon*
close inshore and was cutting down the distance between his
battleship and the fleeing *Colon* and *Vizcaya.* The *Brooklyn,*

farther offshore, could not take advantage of her superior speed at once, but her forward turrets were pounding the *Vizcaya* mercilessly. From farther astern and to seaward, the *Texas, Iowa,* and *Indiana* were sending their heavy shells at her too. She was on fire, forward and astern, but her guns were still defiant. Far ahead the *Colon* seemed to be drawing away from all the ships but the *Oregon*.

By about eleven o'clock the seventeen knots she was making took the *New York* past the slower battleships, and her forward guns began to fire at the *Vizcaya*. The crippled Spanish cruiser swung to starboard toward the shore, and she crossed the *New York*'s bows less than a mile ahead of Sampson's flagship. Fires were raging below decks in the *Vizcaya* as the *New York* came close alongside, and the Spanish sailors were coming up to the open deck and crowding into the bows. Captain Chadwick described the scene:

The crews were face to face, and we looked at each other—victors and vanquished—the former without a cheer, the latter huddled forward, clear of the flames, without sound or movement, but with emotions of the sort for which no dictionary has a transliteration. We were abreast of her almost at the moment of her striking on the reef, inside of which is the little harbor of Aserraderos, and above which, on the hill, was the Cuban camp where, on the 20th of June, Garcia had met our Admiral and General Shafter.

As the *New York* steamed on after the *Colon,* her men saw a great cloud of smoke mount a thousand feet into the sky as the *Vizcaya's* forward magazine blew up.

Sampson ordered the *Iowa* to drop out of column to aid in rescuing men from the *Vizcaya*. Captain Philip on the *Texas,* playing the odds, ordered his engine room crew to keep the boilers under forced draft. He pondered the chance that something might happen to the *Oregon* and also the statistics indicating that the *Colon* was stronger than the *Brooklyn*. Why leave it all to the *New York,* he wondered? Later, he wrote of it: "That ship [the *Colon*], wiliest of all the Spanish vessels, was making a great race for liberty. . . . It was very clearly the duty of the *Texas* to keep along in the chase, with all her energies. It gives me pleasure to be able to write that, old ship as she is, and not built for speed, the *Texas* held her own and even gained on the *Colon* in that chase."

It was now not so much a battle as a chase. The fleeing Spanish cruiser was straining to put every ounce of power on her main shaft. For about two hours it was a grim, relentless, and strangely silent race over a smooth sea just offshore from the southern coast of Cuba. But the end was certain even at the beginning. The *Colon* was boxed in. The fleet-footed *Brooklyn* had swung out and around toward a point of land projecting several thousand feet into the Caribbean, thus making an escape farther down the coastline impossible. The *Oregon,* her engines still not overhauled from her race around Cape Horn from the Pacific, was nearly abeam the *Colon* and the *Texas.* Her engines pounding valiantly as sweating, nearly exhausted firemen stoked the boilers almost to the danger point, she brought up the rear.

To the correspondents scattered on the various warships it was the *Oregon* that seemed the key to victory. She had shelled every one of the three enemy cruisers now ashore and had built up her speed until she virtually tore through the water. She moved up ahead of her sisters at a better than fifteen-knot gait, smoke pouring from her funnels and a great white "bone in her teeth" as the water built up under her bows and cascaded out in foaming waves.

Sampson's navigators and aids established after the battle that the *Colon* was making 14.25 knots during the long reach down the shore. The logs of the American ships showed that the *Oregon* was doing 15.42 knots, the *Brooklyn* 14.6 knots, and the old *Texas* 13.8 knots.

At ten minutes before one o'clock Captain Clark gave orders to try a thirteen-inch shell against the enemy. It fell short. Every few minutes his gunners tried again, increasing the range as crewmen on the *New York,* several miles astern, cheered each near miss. At 1:15 P.M., the fifth shot, fired at a range of 9,500 feet or nearly five and a half land miles, sailed over the *Colon,* as did a sixth. Those two shots ended all chance for the *Colon.* They meant Clark could pound her into submission while safely staying out of range himself. Commodore Don José de Paredes, second in command to Admiral Cervera, who was on the *Colon,* decided it was best to run aground and save the lives of his men. He turned in toward the mouth of the Turquino River, hauled down his colors, and ran onto the beach at a speed of thirteen knots, a figure he testified to but which was doubted by the American commanders on the scene.

It had been a gallant chase, nonetheless. The mouth of the Turquino is seventy-five miles west of the entrance to Santiago harbor. It was nothing less than a miracle that one of Cervera's doomed ships could have made it so far in the face of such overwhelming odds.

Schley sent Captain Francis Cook of the *Brooklyn* off in the gig to accept the *Colon*'s surrender, and his signalman put up flags spelling out, "The enemy has surrendered." Men on the *Oregon* and *Texas* could read it, but they were already aware that the battle had been won. When the *New York* steamed within sight Schley ordered a new signal put up. It said, "A glorious victory has been achieved. Details later." When there was no reply from Sampson's ship, the signalman sent flags up the mast with still another message: "This is a great day for our country." Then came a reply from the admiral, but it contained no congratulatory words, just: "Report your casualties." Commodore Schley spun on his heel and turned away, a reporter wrote to his paper, "a pained expression on his face."

Rescue work had started long before the chase of the *Colon* had been won. The *Gloucester* took on board men from the torpedo boats and the *Teresa;* and the *Indiana,* too slow to follow after the fleeing cruiser, had been ordered to the side of the *Vizcaya.* Two small craft, the *Hist* and the *Ericsson,* which had been patrolling toward Siboney, joined in, and later the *Iowa* and the armed merchantman *Harvard* were assigned to the same duty.

Wainwright's boats pulled survivors from the *Furor,* which was a shattered wreck, and then hauled men from the *Pluton* out of the water. Moving on to the *Teresa* and *Oquendo,* the yacht's skipper found them flying white flags from all parts of the burning vessels. Lines were strung from the Spanish warships to the beach, and the American sailors helped their enemy to the shore. It was a ferry service with ships' cutters serving as the ferryboats. By this means 480 men were saved from the *Teresa,* on which small explosions were occurring below deck almost constantly.

Many of the Spanish sailors who had jumped over the side to escape the flames swam to a narrow spit of sand about three hundred yards off shore, where they stood in water up to their armpits. Captain Evans saw them and sent boats to rescue them from under the rifles of Cuban insurgents who were firing at the miserable seamen.

A boatswain's mate from the *Iowa,* at the tiller of a small lifeboat, looked up at the deck of the burning *Vizcaya* and saw three men hanging over the rail of the almost red-hot ship.

"Without orders he [the boatswain] jumped overboard," Captain Evans reported, "then swam to the side of the *Vizcaya,* clambered up to the deck at imminent risk of his life, kicked the three men overboard, took a header himself, and succeeded in rescuing all three of them. The water was full of sharks snapping at the Spanish dead and wounded."

Far to the westward, men from the *Oregon* were performing the same merciful chores for the victims of the *Colon.* To their surprise, they found most of the Spanish firemen and coal-passers roaring drunk. Later they learned that these men had been ashore in the trenches outside Santiago for thirty-six hours, and by mistake no food was prepared for them when they re-embarked before the fleet sortied from the harbor. To compensate for this, they were "liberally dosed" with brandy to brace them for the ardor of battle in the depths of the ship where the temperature was never under 110 degrees. The brandy kept them at their stations until the *Colon* went ashore, when most of the poor devils collapsed in a stupor.

One of the men taken from the burning flagship was Admiral Cervera, who was rowed to the *Gloucester* clad only in soaking wet underclothes. Remembering how kind the Spanish admiral had been in rescuing Hobson and providing for his safekeeping, Wainwright said he felt "like a culprit" when the gallant old admiral came up the ladder. Shedding no tears, Cervera asked to visit his wounded and walked among them, consoling each one.

The press boats, which had been steaming in and out of the battle's fringe, often in great danger themselves, helped with the rescue work. The *Wanda,* a chartered boat flying the British flag which was hired by the Associated Press, picked twelve men from the torpedo boats out of the water and then went to deliver them to the *Gloucester.* Wainwright did not think this was quite correct. He did not want a vessel flying the Union Jack to be rescuing prisoners for the American Navy. There was a discussion over protocol which got nowhere until Captain Diego Carlier, commander of the *Furor,* solved the sticky international problem. He signed a paper ordering his men to "report" to the *Gloucester,* and they did so. It was a singularly wise and comfortable solution.

With few supplies and no fancy stores on board, Commander Wainwright still managed to put forth a pleasant lunch for his high-ranking prisoners. Admiral Cervera sat at the bottom of the wardroom table, his son and flag lieutenant, Don Angel Cervera, beside him. Captain Carlier was on one side and Captain Pedro Vasquez of the *Pluton* on the other. Wainwright stayed on the bridge, but the paymaster acted in his stead. He asked his guests why they had insisted on coming out into the face of such tremendous odds. The Admiral's son answered: "Your army surrounds the city, and can enter when it chooses; we were driven out."

Lieutenant Harry Huse, executive officer on the *Gloucester,* was in an expansive mood. The victory was ours, the guests had fought valiantly, and he saw an opportunity to use his knowledge of French on an occasion not likely to be repeated. Turning to Don Angel, he said:

"Nous avons remporté la victoire, mais la gloire est à vous."

Young Cervera translated it into Spanish for his father, and the old Admiral replied: *"C'est très bien."* One of the officers, showing the strain of battle, broke down, and tears rolled down his cheeks.

Luncheon was barely over when the men on the *Gloucester*

saw the *Vixen* steaming past under forced draught, carrying
Sampson's victory message to Siboney. The little craft was hardly
hull down on the horizon when word came from the lightly
armed auxiliaries *Harvard* and *Resolute* that an enemy cruiser
had been spotted to the east, obviously headed toward the beachhead at Siboney, bent on sinking the Army transports. The
Indiana was the nearest man-of-war capable of handling such a
situation, and Captain Taylor was ordered to intercept the
stranger. His men had been under strain for days and at battle
stations since breakfast, yet they cheered when told a new battle
might be imminent. Standing in to within a few miles of the
approaching cruiser, the *Indiana* trained her guns on the suspect,
but at the last minute, when within six thousand yards, flags went
up in international code identifying the newcomer as the Austrian cruiser *Kaiserin Maria Theresa*. A lieutenant all decked
out in dress uniform with a fore-and-aft hat came aboard the
Indiana. After the amenities were over he asked:

"Then there has been a battle?"

"Yes," replied Captain Taylor.

"And the result?"

"We have defeated them."

"But where is Cervera's fleet now?"

Taylor pointed out where black smoke was still pouring up
from the three nearest Spanish cruisers and told the Austrian
officer that the *Colon* was ashore much farther to the west. The
American commander also revealed that only a few men had
been killed or wounded in the victorious fleet.

"*Mein Gott!*" exclaimed the Austrian officer. "Admiral Sampson's fleet has destroyed these great Spanish ships, and without
injury to his own squadron! Sir, it is unheard of. I must go to
inform my captain."

The *Vixen* had been detached to help run down the strange
cruiser, so the message Sampson wanted wired to Washington
finally was sent to Siboney aboard the torpedo boat *DuPont*. By
the time it was carried ashore by Sampson's assistant chief of
staff, S. A. Staunton, it was 2 A.M. of the day after the battle
and the courier found Commodore Schley's flag lieutenant waiting at the cable office.

An unpleasant exchange of words ensued, but Staunton pointed out that all communications to the Secretary of the Navy had to go through the senior officer present, so that Schley's message would have to be approved by Sampson. So the first word of the complete annihilation of the Spanish fleet arrived in Washington over Sampson's signature. It was more than twelve hours old, but the news it carried was balm to the jangled nerves of Mr. McKinley, Secretary Long, and millions of Americans who read it later in the morning editions of their papers on July 4. It read:

The fleet under my command offers the nation as a Fourth of July present the whole of Cervera's fleet. It attempted to escape at 9:30 this morning. At 2 the last ship, the *Cristobal Colon,* had run ashore seventy-five miles west of Santiago and hauled down her colors. The *Infanta Maria Teresa, Oquendo* and *Vizcaya* were forced ashore, burned, and blown up within twenty miles of Santiago.

Stephen Crane had missed the great sea battle. Returning from a trip to Port Antonio, he found the American fleet, without visible signs of injury, still lying in the usual semicircle off Santiago harbor.

"The squadron hadn't changed a button," he wrote. "There it sat without even a smile on the face of the tiger. And it had eaten four armored cruisers and two torpedo-boat destroyers while my back was turned for an instant."

It seemed as if everyone had to play a role in the victory. Mr. Hearst, who, like Crane, missed the battle, returned in the *Silvia* in time to pick up twenty-nine Spanish seamen discovered huddled together on the shore near the still burning *María Teresa.* Taking them on board his yacht, the publisher sought out the admiral himself to report on his find. Sampson thanked him courteously and asked him to transfer the prisoners to the *St. Louis.* Sampson's good manners had little effect on Hearst. A few days later his New York paper, the *Journal,* waded knee-deep into the dispute over whether Schley or Sampson deserved the kudos for Cervera's defeat. An editorial contained these words: "It was Schley who originally bottled up Cervera in Santiago harbor. He ran the Spaniards to earth, kept guard over them until Sampson joined him, and now has exterminated them as a fighting force. Schley is as much the hero of Santiago as Dewey is of Manila."

Of the approximately 2,225 men who went to battle stations on the Spanish ships on the morning of July 3, there were more than five hundred officers and men killed and wounded. On the American side the casualty list was incredibly low, with one man dead and ten wounded.

Naval historians were to marvel at the one-sided victory for years to come. Fighting admirals wondered what meat it was upon which the American naval colossus fed to make it so powerful. It was no wonder every sailor in Sampson's fleet felt a little cocky. Something of this feeling was communicated to the flag lieutenant of the *Kaiserin Maria Theresa* when he paid a courtesy call on Commodore Schley. After an exchange of pleasantries the Austrian officer asked where his ship should go the night after the battle.

"Twenty miles off the coast, at least," replied Schley. "This is a bad coast tonight for strangers."

The Austrian understood.

"We will go forty miles off," he said, and clambered down into the gig.

16

★   ★   ★   ★   ★   ★

The Flags Change
over Santiago

IN ONE WAY, it was about as cheap a victory as any nation ever won at sea. Admiral Sampson calculated that the cost of ammunition had amounted to a mere $85,000. The total number of shots fired by the various ships in the engagement was divided as follows: *Brooklyn,* 1,973; *Oregon,* 1,903; *Indiana,* 1,876; *Iowa,* 1,473; *Texas,* 835; and *Gloucester,* 1,369.

The ammunition fired was broken down thus: thirteen-inch, 47; twelve-inch, 39; eight-inch, 319; six-inch, 171; five-inch, 473; four-inch, 251; six-pounder, 6,553; three-pounder, 780; one-pounder, 466; and one-pounder and 3-mm, 330—totaling 9,429 projectiles fired at the six Spanish men-of-war.

Such statistics are dear to the hearts of naval strategists, but they had little meaning to the men in Shafter's Fifth Corps, lying in the trenches facing the Spanish lines outside Santiago.

The commanding general sent messages into his lines, telling the soldiers of the sortie by the Spanish fleet, and followed it with others telling of the progress of the great naval engagement and the final victory. Weary fighters, many weakened by illness, shouted and cheered at the bulletins, which were announced against the distant sound of cannonading. The men realized when the firing died down completely that a new frontal assault on the city would probably not be required and, remembering the bloody hours before El Caney and San Juan Hill, were gratified beyond measure at their sister service's achievement.

But General Toral did not like the idea of surrender. A very proud man, he knew his signature would go on any document signed with the Americans. It would be a hollow honor to have taken over command from the wounded Linares only to be known as the man who surrendered a few hours later.

White flags went back and forth between the lines as Shafter pressed for an end to the war without having to launch a new attack. Toral agreed to many things; he would allow noncombatants to leave the city; he would exchange Hobson and his gallant crew for Spanish officers captured at El Caney; he would do virtually anything except surrender. Toral may have sensed that Shafter's demand was nothing more than sheer effrontery, for he must have received information as to the weakened condition of his enemy.

The Fourth of July, celebrated with exultant happiness in the United States, was anything but a cheerful holiday in the American trenches. Men were going on sick report in ever-growing numbers, and the lines now stretching from the very edge of Morro Castle clear around the harbor to the El Cobre road west of Santiago were so weakened that a sortie by Spanish troops concentrated at one or two spots could hardly have been beaten back.

There were never enough rations in the front lines to meet even limited needs. What there was turned the noses and tortured the stomachs of hungry men. George Clark Musgrave, the British correspondent, described the rations for his readers in words that few Americans saw, obviously, or the loved ones at home would have stormed the halls of Congress demanding heads on pikestaffs.

The hardtack was excellent when shipped, the British newspaperman said, but the Quartermaster Corps had used wooden cases to pack it. "It was soaked first in seawater," he wrote, "then by rain; the boxes lay around in thick mud which oozed into the badly made joints, and much of the hard bread was soon unfit for consumption."

Other rations were little better. Pork and bacon were wrapped in cheesecloth—nothing else.

"It was thus very difficult for the men to carry forward the slimy sides of bacon," said Musgrave. "It speedily became rotten, also, from sun and rain."

His worst adjectives were saved for the canned beef, which he said was "execrable—simply the offal of a beef extract factory." Canned beans were so heavily soaked in pork fat, he reported, that they were "nauseating even to the Massachusetts troops."

If all had gone well at sea, and it seemed that it had, the same could not be said about the forces ashore. Besides the shortage of food, even bad food, there was a continuing lack of blankets, tentage, and tarpaulins. Men slept drenched to the skin, and every few hours a man would collapse from fever. A few complained of nausea, said their bones ached, and showed the yellow-tinted eyeballs that meant they had yellow fever. Within five hours such men had to be carried on stretchers to the hospital, so swift was the onslaught.

The night of the naval battle General Escario led more than four thousand troops from Manzanillo through the Cuban lines west of town without the insurgents firing a single shot. Shafter was furious. He knew that Toral now had enough healthy reinforcements to make an American assault unwise, in view of the weakened condition of his own men.

Much of what Colonel Roosevelt had to say about the conduct of the campaign reflected his own conceit and the conviction that he could do anything better than most other officers in Cuba. But he was aware of the dangers that would come from a renewed attack against Santiago and of the more insidious dangers of exposure and disease. On the day of the sea engagement he wrote Lodge:

Tell the President for Heaven's sake to send us every regiment and above all every battery possible. We have won so far at a heavy price but the Spaniards fight very hard and charging these entrenchments against modern rifles is terrible. We are within a measurable distance of a terrible military disaster; we *must* have help,—thousands of men, batteries and guns and ammunition.

While the Americans suffered from the maladies of hunger, disease, and indecision, the Spaniards in the city gave way to strange expressions of simultaneous bravery and stupidity. Toral warned the civilian inhabitants that they might be bombarded at any moment by the victorious American fleet. Then he conferred with the commander of the one man-of-war still left in the harbor—the *Reina Mercedes*. Toral thought the warship might aid in defending the city if she were moved out into the channel.

It was a foolhardy undertaking. The *Mercedes* was an iron cruiser of only 3,090 tons, built in 1887. Her machinery was "hopelessly out of condition" according to Captain Chadwick, and most of her guns had been dismounted and carried ashore to support the men in the trenches.

Nonetheless, on the night of July 4, the old relic was moved out toward Morro Castle. Lookouts on the *Texas,* acting as supporting ship to the *Massachusetts,* which had the searchlight duty, spotted the ancient Spanish vessel. The *Texas* opened fire and the *Massachusetts* joined in. Within minutes the *Mercedes* was struck by a twelve-inch projectile from the former and a thirteen-inch shell from the latter. She rolled over, canted to port, and then sank, her one side still above water. She had been worthless as a fighting ship and was now of no use in blocking the channel as she was too far from deep water.

The sound of heavy gunfire at midnight terrified the people of Santiago, who assumed the enemy fleet was on the way into the harbor. Old men and women, children, the weak and the ill, all who thought the countryside was a safer place, started walking out of the city. Stephen Crane watched them, "tottering upon the verge of death," and another reporter said the refugees stretched twenty miles along one road.

The scene was too much for the American soldiers. Quitting the trenches, many of them helped the involuntary pilgrims on their way and shared their meager rations with the refugees. One

Rough Rider from Arizona carried several old women and little children as far as El Caney. The regimental surgeon heard about it and ordered the men to desist, fearing they would pick up yellow fever germs from the emaciated refugees. The Arizonan persisted, but stopped long enough to tell Colonel Roosevelt, "God wouldn't let a fellow catch yellow fever while he was doing a good turn for them kids."

General Shafter made several requests of Admiral Sampson, asking that the Navy break into the harbor and bombard Santiago. In one note he said it would save one thousand lives. Sampson brushed the demands aside, pointing out that the Army had not reduced the fortresses of Morro Castle or Socapa Point and that plunging fire from those locations high above the channel would do terrible damage to the fleet. Eventually the impasse reached Washington. The Army and Navy marshaled their leading exponents. Mr. McKinley was lectured on the relative points of view by Secretary Alger and Captain Mahan. The President, averse to having the final word left in his care, sent off a message to Cuba that was a masterpiece of political dodging. It said in part: "General Shafter and Admiral Sampson should confer at once for cooperation in taking Santiago. After the fullest exchange of views they should determine the time and manner of attack."

It did not please Shafter but it did lead him to devote his attention to the enemy rather than the Navy. He began a veritable fusillade of notes demanding that Toral surrender. It was not diplomacy alone that led Shafter to do this. He was, in retrospect, using a weapon that would cost no American lives while waiting for the reinforcements that Washington was promising in nearly every message. He knew he had hunger on his side and that every day the inhabitants of Santiago were growing less disposed to continue the fight.

Sampson bridled under attacks from the Secretary of War, the worst being a suggestion to Shafter that he take a few transports, armor them with bales of hay, and force the entrance to the harbor in that manner. But the admiral felt he knew best how to use the fleet and refrained from ordering it to attempt the entry.

Both Sampson and Shafter were ill while the exchange of dispatches with Washington was going on, Sampson with a temporary malaise and Shafter with his continuing illness born of great corpulence and extreme heat. Because of the admiral's indisposition, he sent Captain Chadwick to confer with the general. During the conference the captain of the *New York* drafted a message to Toral that was nothing less than brilliant. It suggested that Toral might wish to communicate with his home government about a surrender and that a truce could be extended until the Spanish commander had had time for a reply from Madrid.

Toral agreed to the truce and during it exchanged Hobson and his seven men for a number of Spanish officers and men seized at El Caney. The actual ceremony was an emotional highlight of the war. The whole Army, it seemed, was drawn up along the road from Santiago to El Pozo, and when the American heroes appeared, cheers went up that could be heard on the warships offshore. Richard Harding Davis described it as not unlike an important ball game with the sun-drenched bleachers crowded to the topmost row. There was at first a solemn moment when soldiers removed their hats in honor of Hobson. But then a trooper called for three cheers, and the freed sailors, rollicking in a wagon drawn by six stubborn mules, their faces wreathed in smiles, and rolling over one another with glee, were huzzahed to the echo.

Reinforcements started arriving off the beaches at Siboney before the week was out. General Miles, with 1,800 men of Garretson's brigade, came on the *Yale,* followed closely by the First Illinois Infantry, and Brigadier General W. F. Randolph with the Fourth and Fifth Artillery. The District of Columbia Infantry came the next day.

Now that Shafter had his big guns, all that troubled him was getting them to the front. The road had grown even worse under the pounding of equipment and the heavy rains. The fords had not been bridged. Moving supplies from shipboard to beach was such a constant hazard that small boats and barges overturned and broke on the rocks. If the war with Spain did nothing else for American arms, it proved the need for joint command in amphibious operations. Sampson answered a grouchy note from Shafter about the whereabouts of two lighters in a message that struck straight to the heart of the trouble: "Lighters brought by *Fern* and *Niagara* were received and turned over to the quartermaster at Siboney and anchored. One the following day was ashore and destroyed. Until the embarkation, transport and disembarkation of troops and supplies come under the control of the navy as in England this muddle will continue."

With new troops fed into the lines, Shafter felt easier and called for a fleet bombardment of Santiago. On July 10 and 11 the big guns on several of the warships began firing over the hills at Santiago. Arrangements for spotting the hits were unsatisfactory, and not all the shells fell in the city. General Wheeler commented on this, apparently unaware that firing at an invisible target is not the easiest of operations. In the midst of the bombardment Shafter notified Sampson of another temporary truce, and all firing, from sea and from the American lines, stopped completely.

On the twelfth, Shafter asked Toral for another parley between the lines, saying that he would have General Miles with him. Unknown to the Americans, on the same day, General Linares, from his hospital bed, sent his government in Madrid a message outlining the dire straits of the defenders. He mentioned hunger, heavy casualties, a lack of ammunition, and his inability to put more than a third of his men into the lines at any one time. Surrender, said the badly wounded officer, was inevitable. The message was almost lyric in its description of the situation:

Santiago is no Gerona, a walled city, part of the mother country, defended inch by inch by its own children without distinction—old men, women and children, who encouraged and assisted the combatants and exposed their lives, moved by the holy idea of independence, while awaiting aid which they received. Here is solitude; a total emigration of the population, insular as well as peninsular, including the public officials with rare exceptions. Only the clergy remain, and they wish to leave the city today headed by their archbishop. . . . The honor of arms has its limit, and I appeal to the judgment of the government and of the entire nation, whether these long-suffering troops have not saved that honor many times since the eighteenth of May, when they sustained the first bombardment.

If Shafter had known half of what was in the minds of his enemy, he would not have complained again about the refusal of the Navy to try to force its way into Santiago harbor. Miles, however, did seem to side with Sampson by keeping so many troops on the transports, ready for a landing at Cabañas. Washington may have been growing a bit tired of Shafter's whining, as Alger's office sent a message on July 13 addressed to Miles, granting him the privilege of accepting a surrender if on unconditional terms. This was a complete reversal of earlier orders saying that Shafter was to exercise supreme command despite Miles's arrival.

During one of the many truce conferences under a big ceiba tree between the lines, Miles informed Toral that he had left Washington but a few days before and knew the temper of the government. He called for unconditional surrender but softened the demand by telling Toral that the United States would undertake to move all Spanish troops back to Spain.

Two things broke Toral's resistance: the realization that the fleet could bombard Santiago at will, and the arrival of more ships with reinforcements. The clincher was the movement of three of Sampson's ironclads to a position just off Cabañas and the sending of the transports to the same location.

On the fourteenth Toral sent a message of surrender to the American generals, which was approved by Mr. McKinley and Secretary Alger. Two days later Toral signed the necessary documents completing the unconditional capitulation.

The next morning—July 17—was a Sunday, just two weeks after the victory of the American fleet over Cervera's squadron. Toral, a stickler for military decorum, paraded the best of his units in the central plaza of the city, saluted the Spanish colors on the palace flagstaff, and ordered them hauled down. Then he rode out of town with his aides and surrendered personally to Shafter, who had managed with considerable pain and difficulty to rise from his sickbed and mount a horse for the ceremonies. The American general presented Toral with the sword and spurs of General Vara del Rey, the hero of El Caney, and then rode into the heart of Santiago. Along the way Shafter and his staff took notice of the many lines of entrenchments and barbed wire entanglements. There was no American in the group who was not thankful it would now be unnecessary to launch an assault against such barricades.

General Shafter was happy at the way things had turned out and just as happy at his opportunity to even scores with the Navy. Although Sampson had requested that a naval representative be present at the surrender ceremonies, Shafter delayed sending word until it was too late. Sampson's man reached the scene of the ceremony when it was all over.

Food by the wagonload was sent into Santiago to help feed the inhabitants. Other supplies went to El Caney, where the refugees, according to one reporter, were crowded together like ants in the remaining houses. Miss Barton ordered virtually every bit of special food, medicine, and clothing on the *State of Texas* put ashore, and the Red Cross workers probably saved the lives of hundreds of starving Cuban children.

On the day of the formal takeover of Santiago, Shafter was in a particularly bad mood. He still lumped all newspaper correspondents together—the good with the bad, the lazy with the energetic, those who liked him and those who thought him a gross caricature of a general. When reporters asked him if they could go into the city to watch the American flag hoisted above the palace, he thundered that not one newsman could enter the city.

The more enterprising men walked away from the conference, joined various bodies of troops heading for the city, and watched from side streets and windows. Sylvester Scovel, of the *World,* who had done what he pleased from the days before the war started, went up on the roof of the palace and was there when the soldiers assigned to raise the flag reached it. Shafter ordered him down. The correspondent and the commanding general confronted each other in the central square while hundreds looked on. Accounts differ as to what happened, but some saw Scovel strike, or try to strike, Shafter, and Shafter strike back, or make the attempt.

In a towering rage Shafter ordered Scovel arrested and held in the Spanish *calabozo* overnight. Some Army officers thought he should be shot, but Shafter was astute enough not to risk the displeasure of the people back in the States. He ordered him sent home instead.

Shafter did not see fit to honor the volunteers in Wood's brigade. The Rough Riders remained on the ridge of San Juan Hill as regulars marched into town to take part in the flag raising. But the general could not control the feelings of the men in the ranks. As the First Illinois Volunteers, one of the newly landed units, saw the Rough Riders standing on the crest of the hill up which they had charged so gallantly long days before, they began cheering Roosevelt and his troopers. Then one of the Rough Riders called for three cheers for the colonel and "the whole army replied with one great voice," according to the regiment's historian, Edward Marshall.

One enemy was defeated but another had risen in his place. Perhaps it was the relaxation of military discipline or perhaps the sudden mingling of troops with civilians, but whatever the reason, malaria and yellow fever now struck with terrifying virulence. Soldiers succumbed by the dozen. Hospital orderlies were so overworked that the Army sent the Twenty-Fourth Infantry to Siboney to nurse the fever victims. There still existed the unfounded belief that Negro soldiers had a certain immunity to the diseases.

Roosevelt wrote on July 19 that he had only half of the six hundred men who had landed with him still on duty. The rest were on sick call. He and other officers moved many of the regiments up into the foothills to get away from the malarial mists that shrouded the lowlands. Fifty of the men fell from heat prostration on the way but were replaced by others who quit the crowded hospitals to recuperate in the open. Most of these said they would rather die in the hills than stay longer in the dirty, sweltering field hospitals.

On July 23 the future President wrote Secretary Alger urging that the Rough Riders be sent to help in capturing Puerto Rico —next stop on the government's road to expansion.

Between that day and early August the rapid increase in the number of malarial fever cases, and the growing signs that yellow fever was in fact spreading among the troops, changed Roosevelt's mind, or his point of view. He wrote a long letter to General Shafter suggesting that conditions were bad enough to warrant sending the troops that had been in Cuba longest to some healthy place like the northern coast of Maine. He said that if the men remained longer in the Tropics, half the Army would die, citing estimates given him by regimental surgeons. He forecast "an appalling disaster" if the troops were not put aboard transports for home immediately.

On August 3 the field commanders drew up another statement and sent it to Shafter. It was a singularly strong document, demanding that the Army be removed from Cuba and sent north to a spot where the civilian population would not be infected.

"The army must be moved at once, or perish," the round-robin letter stated bluntly.

It was signed by virtually every important commanding officer in the field, including Kent, Bates, Chaffee, Sumner, Ludlow, Wood and, of course, Theodore Roosevelt.

The leader of the Rough Riders gave a copy of his letter to the Associated Press correspondent, and the round robin, which had been left with Colonel Wood, also came into the hands of the same newspaperman. The next morning it was in every paper in the United States. Mr. McKinley was shocked beyond words and called on Shafter for an explanation. The general said he knew nothing of how it had come to be made public.

It was, of course, one of those coincidences that make the annals of warfare so strange, but three days later transports were quitting Siboney and Santiago, loaded to the rails with happy soldiers, bound north to Montauk Point, Long Island. Among them were "Teddy" and his Rough Riders.

Years later Roosevelt stated publicly that the letters had been "suggested" by Shafter, but there was now no danger in thus throwing the charge of hypocrisy straight in the commanding general's teeth. General Shafter had died some time before.

To the men who had fought in Cuba, there was no other war, for this is ever the way with fighting men. Yet during most of the period between the blockading of Cervera's fleet and the final act of surrender at Santiago there had been a strange business going on involving another squadron of Spanish warships. This one was commanded by Rear Admiral Camara, or so the orders at the ministry of marine in Madrid showed it, but both the admiral and the squadron were, in fact, puppets on strings held tightly by the minister himself.

In the very earliest days of the war this official, Admiral Aunon, had sponsored a grandiose scheme involving Cervera's force in the West Indies and Camara's as a nuisance factor raiding cities on the North Atlantic coast of the United States. Before it could be put into effect, Cervera was bottled tightly in Santiago harbor, and Dewey had annihilated the Spanish Asiatic Squadron.

For a time Camara was sent hither and yon, down the African coast, out toward the Canaries, and then along the home coast on the Iberian Peninsula as a sort of psychological support to the folks in Spain.

Then Aunon dreamed up what some called a zany scheme and others a master stroke of naval diplomacy. No matter which it was, it came to naught, but for a time the American War and Navy departments, the President, various consuls and ambassadors, and the fleet commanders were all making plans to counter the danger implicit in Camara's force.

Aunon ordered Camara to head for the Philippines by way of the Suez Canal, after feinting toward the West Indies by daylight. When it was dark, Camara was to retrace his steps and head into the Mediterranean. His force was made up of the battleships *Carlos V* and *Pelayo;* two converted cruisers of no great fighting quality, the *Patriota* and *Rapido;* and three destroyers, the *Audaz, Osado,* and *Proserpina.* The destroyers were to turn back at Suez.

Poor Admiral Camara! His instructions were so long and detailed they resembled a hybrid document half diplomatic and half naval. He was told his main purpose was to appear in the Philippine archipelago to reinforce Spain's claims that the islands belonged to her even if Dewey was sitting in Manila Bay like a cat that had just devoured a tasty canary and even if Aguinaldo was rampaging through the island of Luzon, stirring up a movement for independence. But he was warned to stay out of Dewey's way.

Eventually Camara quit Cádiz with four thousand troops on board and twenty thousand tons of coal. The cloak-and-dagger precautions did him no good, since American diplomats in Portugal and Gibraltar alerted Washington, from which orders sped to many out-of-the-way consular offices. So when Camara reached Port Said on June 25, he found that the American deputy consul-general, Ethelbert Watts, had taken a lien on every ton of coal in that part of Egypt. The Egyptian government would not even let the poor admiral take on coal from his own colliers in their waters; they maintained that international law forbade it as he had enough in his bunkers to get him to a home port.

On July 29 the Egyptian officials ordered him to leave port, for he had already overstayed the twenty-four hours to which belligerents are entitled. Camara tried refueling in the Mediterranean, but the seas were too high and rough. While he was failing in this attempt, Cervera's squadron was being destroyed by the Americans.

The victory won by Sampson and Schley freed enough ships for the Navy Department to feel safe in sending a squadron after Camara. Commodore John Crittenden Watson was named to head it. Sampson received a telegram instructing him to assign certain ships and, if need arose, to accompany Watson as far as the Suez Canal. Sampson knew little of Camara's movements and replied to the department that his ships were in dire need of refitting and overhauling. On the day Sampson was told to prepare for a transatlantic crossing, President McKinley had signed a resolution annexing the Hawaiian Islands. There was obviously a feeling of great power, and perhaps even cockiness, in the nation's capital. This may have been why Sampson was asked by return telegram if he meant the vessels he commanded could not cross the Atlantic and back "in view of the importance of re-enforcing Commodore Dewey."

There had to be a non sequitur in the message somewhere. How could such a voyage reinforce Dewey in Manila? But Sampson, a good public servant, sent back word that the *Oregon, Massachusetts, Newark,* and *Dixie* would be ready to sail east in two days.

Fortunately for the sanity of the admiral, General Miles began pleading for ships to cover his landings in Puerto Rico, and the big warships never did start for the east. Merritt and his men in the convoy headed for Manila were left unguarded, true, but there was no Spanish man-of-war worthy of the name within five thousand miles.

If the statesmen in Washington were showing signs of strain, those in Madrid were no better off. Camara reached Cartagena on July 23 to find new orders from Admiral Aunon: "When the torpedo-boat destroyers have rejoined your squadron, start for Cadiz with the *Pelayo, Carlos V, Rapido, Patriota, Buenos Aires* and the destroyers, keeping close to the shore, so as to be seen from Spanish cities, exhibiting, when near them, the national flag, illuminated by search-lights, which are also to be thrown upon the cities."

17

Picnic on Puerto Rico

THE WAR WITH SPAIN was only one war, but the authorities appeared totally incapable of keeping track of the various segments of the conflict. At the very moment that Washington was demanding of Sampson that he send almost his entire battle force to chase that ineffectual will-of-the-wisp, Camara, General Miles was beseeching the same admiral to supply a squadron to cover Army landings in Puerto Rico.

Sampson responded quickly and assigned the *Yale, Columbia, New Orleans,* and *Cincinnati.* It must be remembered that, as of that day in July, there was no Spanish warship nearer than Gibraltar except a few gunboats blockaded in San Juan harbor and one in a southern Cuban port, also bottled up. Yet for about a week messages went back and forth among Washington, Santiago, and the fleet, discussing whether the assigned vessels were sufficiently powerful for the task at hand. Miles, knowing nothing of the orders to send the heavy ships to Gibraltar, thought Sampson was stingy with his battleships and cruisers.

Some of his fear about protection for his convoys was transmitted to Washington and, naturally enough, various Secretaries, together with the President, fired off angry telegrams to the fleet commander. One would have thought Sampson was abandoning Miles to the combined fleets of Britain and Germany with a few

others thrown in for good measure. The admiral sent off a message to Miles listing the gunpower of the four ships and making
it clear that they could handle any eventuality except the reduction of stone forts and the silencing of heavy guns in position.
He did more. He rounded up the *Annapolis, Wasp,* and *Leyden*
and then added three monitors from Key West. Finally he ordered the *Gloucester,* that fearless vessel that had tackled the two
Spanish gunboats at Santiago, to go along too.

With this assemblage of fighting craft Miles was content, and
went on planning to attack Puerto Rico. It was high time. Spain
was negotiating with France to arrange a peace conference.
McKinley, Lodge, and other expansionists wanted the island
under the Stars and Stripes before a treaty was agreed upon.

Miles intended to use the three thousand troops he had kept
on transports off Siboney to avoid exposing them to yellow fever
germs, plus contingents embarking at Charleston, South Carolina; Newport News, Virginia; and Tampa. He informed the
War Department that he planned to make a landing at Cape
Fajardo on the easternmost tip of Puerto Rico and then march
on San Juan from the rear. Alger and the President gave him
carte blanche to go anywhere he pleased, which could have been
a mistake, and the transports began moving from the United
States.

Major General James H. Wilson sailed from Charleston with
3,500 troops and Brigadier General Theodore Schwan led 2,900
out of Tampa. Major General J. R. Brooke, with 4,000 soldiers,
waited impatiently at Hampton Roads, Virginia.

All of the transports set courses straight and true for Cape
Fajardo. In the meantime Miles himself had quit Santiago and
Siboney, well convoyed by a battle squadron which had had its
components shaken up again at the last minute. It included the
Massachusetts, Dixie, Gloucester, Columbia, and *Yale.*

As the convoy from Cuba passed along the north coast of
Haiti, General Miles changed his mind. He thought about all
the publicity that had been given to a landing at Fajardo and
thought it would be pleasant to win Puerto Rico with a minimum
of assistance from the Navy. The result of his deep conjecturing
was an unexpected change of destination. He would make a feint

at the original landing point and then continue halfway around the island to Puerto de Guánica, on the southwestern tip.

Once ashore he could sweep across Puerto Rico at will, winning his battles before Spanish troops could move from San Juan and Fajardo.

Remembering that the rest of his troops were at sea or about to leave American ports with every reason to believe Fajardo was the rallying point for the invasion, the general belatedly notified the War Department that he was heading for Ponce, up the coast from Guánica. Before the message got to shore and to the States, the press knew of it. Understandably, this created pandemonium in Washington. No wonder, then, that General Brooke received this wire from the Adjutant General: "Press dispatches say that General Miles is disembarking at Ponce. The secretary of war does not credit it, and yet feels that it may be so. He says that you should sail for Fajardo; not finding him there, to then proceed to Ponce. Some notice will doubtless be waiting at Fajardo."

Down in the West Indies the general with the restless mind ordered a new course and sailed through the Mona Passage straight for Guánica.

At dawn on July 25 the main convoy stood in toward the town, a village with one main street and a few side lanes crowded with huts made of palm leaves. The *Gloucester* was instructed to probe the harbor to see if there were mines, and Wainwright steamed boldly in. There were no mines, no enemy vessels, no shore batteries. So the troops began landing from the transports, only to find that the American flag was flying over the main building, a squalid old structure housing the post office, the court, and the police barracks.

Commander Wainwright had landed a party of sailors under Lieutenant Huse—the young officer who had spoken French with Admiral Cervera after the battle of Santiago—and the Navy men had shot four Spanish soldiers and taken possession of the village.

A regiment or two of troops went ashore at Guánica, but others were held for a landing the next day at Ponce, second largest city in Puerto Rico. When the Army contingents stepped ashore in Ponce, the Stars and Stripes were flying over the city hall there also, having been run up by naval Cadet G. C. Lodge, a midshipman whose temporary appointment had been easy to arrange. All it had required was a note from his father, Senator Lodge.

The *alcalde,* a mayor of sorts, and the city dignitaries paid General Miles homage, not as a conqueror, but as a benefactor, when he went ashore from the *Yale* after a restless night caused by the sound of firing behind town. The *alcalde* assured him the shots were not fired in anger but in delirious joy. If a commanding general had to invade foreign territory, surely this was the pleasantest of all possible ways to do it. The *Puertoriqueños,* with minor exceptions, were so happy that their affectionate greetings were almost embarrassing. When the local fire company paraded in the Americans' honor, they ran over three of their own men. The local Red Cross workers picked them up and rushed them away on stretchers, the men all the while protesting that they would rather walk.

The citizens of Ponce were not satisfied with an official surrender on the balcony of the local palace, nor with the firemen's parade. Several thousand waited until the soldiers started coming ashore in large numbers and then rushed down to the harbor, wading into the water, nearly upsetting the boats, and screaming *"Viva!"* until the troops were deafened.

Miles issued a proclamation containing certain words that left no doubt that the United States was not going to fool around while desirable islands were waiting, ripe and valuable, for a conqueror to collect. Those words were: "The first effect of this occupation will be the immediate release from your former political relations, and it is hoped a cheerful acceptance of the government of the United States."

The natives thought it a capital idea. They liked surrendering to the United States so much, Richard Harding Davis said, that they surrendered four times to different officers in the one city of Ponce. When the troops went to the third port, Arroyo, about thirty miles east of Ponce, the *Gloucester* led the way again. The mayor, priests, and virtually every inhabitant gathered on the beach to welcome the Americans. An officer from the ship read the surrender terms, the local officials nodded pleasantly, and the young naval officer ran the Stars and Stripes up over the custom house.

During the days that followed these friendly acceptances of American suzerainty, some of the troops marched inland. In the hills they ran into a little scattered opposition, but skirmishing lasted only a short time in each case. Several units of Spanish snipers tried to guard bridges or narrow roads, but the Americans found that the simple technique of wheeling the dynamite gun into position and lobbing a few shells at the enemy always routed them.

All along the routes on which the four-pronged advance was staged, natives fell over one another surrendering their small villages. Davis, who had managed to have his correspondent's uniform laundered, went with General Wilson's vanguard and, with three other newspapermen, managed to reach the town of Coamo ahead of the Army's scouts. All four were mounted on ponies, and that was enough—together with the campaign ribbons Davis wore on his breast—to convince the citizens that they were dealing with very important American officials. Davis accepted the surrender with theatrical finesse and was conferring on terms with the mayor when the soldiers arrived.

Stephen Crane, who never cut the martial figure his friend Davis did, had his brief hour of glory too—at a crossroads village called Juana Díaz. Several of the townsmen surrendered the hamlet to Crane, and the correspondent was sipping black coffee with them at a sidewalk café on the central plaza when the troops came marching in.

There was so much hilarity, so much flag-waving and happiness, on the part of the *Puertoriqueños* that the serious aspects of the invasion could have been overlooked. Although there was not enough resistance to dignify the name, Miles's plans were well made and deserve some attention.

The strategic purpose was to drive any enemy forces ahead of him to the vicinity of San Juan. There they would be compressed in the city, which would have to surrender because it would be caught in the jaws of a trap formed by the Army onshore and the American fleet offshore.

Miles had sent Schwan on an end run from Guánica toward Mayagüez, an important city on the west coast of the island. Wilson had marched from the same port to the east and then northward into the mountains in the center of the island. Brigadier General Guy V. Henry's column disembarked at Ponce and struck inland to find itself unopposed. Brooke landed with his men at Arroyo and nearby Guayama and headed straight across the island toward San Juan.

The movement of these four columns would have cut the island up and made resistance most difficult, had there been any eagerness on the part of the Spanish troops to resist. While the Army was advancing, the Navy seized Cape Fajardo, which was undefended, but finding it of no real value, withdrew.

On August 12 the fleet commanders in Cuba and Puerto Rico and the Army commanders on both islands received terse orders from Washington: "Suspend all hostilities." It was all over. An armistice had been agreed upon between the United States and Spain.

It had been a picnic. Miles led fifteen thousand young and healthy men eager to see action. Spanish forces totaled about seven thousand troops worn out by the thankless chores of occupying an unfriendly colony. There was never a confrontation worth mention. What had happened at Santiago—both on land and at sea—had destroyed any will to fight in the hearts of the defenders.

After the victories in Cuba, the seizure of Puerto Rico was an anticlimax. It pleased the American public but ordinary folk become more excited about gory battles than they do over the acquisition of foreign real estate in bloodless campaigns. On the other hand, there was no lack of excitement within the inner circle at Washington.

Events had been happening with great rapidity, each one portentous and intriguing. General Merritt had landed in the Philippines on July 25, hard on the heels of diplomatic messages from the consul in Manila telling of the formation of an independent government headed by Aguinaldo. The next day Miles occupied Guánica, signifying that that invasion was starting well. The day after that the French ambassador to the United States handed the State Department a message authorized by the Spanish throne. It called for a peace conference.

Like so many of the events of this strange war, the offer to seek peace became embroiled in something else close to slap-stick comedy. France was acting in behalf of the Spanish, but the Spanish note reached the French embassy in diplomatic cipher which the French could not break because the code was in the safe of the Austrian minister. That gentleman had fled Washington to seek relief from the almost unbearable heat and humidity along the Potomac, and the French officials had no way to decode the note from Madrid. By the time this was done Miles was on Puerto Rican soil and harvesting surrenders right and left.

Sampson must have been one of the happiest men in uniform when he received his orders to suspend hostilities. For days he had nursed the feeling that the idea of sending a fleet into Euro-pean waters after Camara's puny squadron was not only foolish, but not even in keeping with the true wishes of the President and the State Department. Delay followed delay, substantiating his hunch. So when the message arrived on August 12, he must have been greatly relieved. His orders read:

Suspend all hostilities; blockade of Cuba and Porto Rico is raised. Howell ordered to assemble vessels at Key West. Proceed with the *New York, Brooklyn, Indiana, Oregon, Iowa* and *Massachusetts* to Tompkinsville [Staten Island, N.Y.]. Schley to come north in *Brooklyn*. Place the monitors in a safe harbor in Porto Rico. Watson to transfer his flag to *Newark* and remain at Guantánamo. Assemble all cruisers in safe harbor. Order marines north in *Resolute*.

Hurricanes were brewing far out in the eastern wastes of the Atlantic, and it was time to move. The *Texas* was already on the way north, her main deck so warped by the blasts of her twelve-inch guns that further firing might have cracked it. No naval commander likes his fleet in tropic waters when the big winds blow, so Sampson steamed north behind her, well contented.

18

★ ★ ★ ★ ★ ★

Manila Falls into
the American Basket

WITH THESE LOOSE ENDS neatly tied, Washington authorities could ponder the next steps. The expansionist clique, ecstatic over Spain's peace feeler, was convinced that speed was essential to grasp whatever territory it could before negotiations got under way. Brigadier General T. M. Anderson, with the advance contingent of troops sent to Manila, had established a camp on land, well south of the city line. Using a potpourri of captured Spanish tugs and lighters, smallboats from Dewey's squadron, native craft, and sleds dragged by water buffalo, he had put the first men ashore on July 19 and had the full two thousand on dry land by July 24, which was the day before Miles reached Guánica in Puerto Rico.

It was no surprise to anyone when he designated as Camp Dewey the patch of ground once used for growing peanuts.

All this was known to Mr. McKinley and his cabinet as they discussed the Spanish peace note. Several of the secretaries wanted to settle for Puerto Rico and a naval base near Manila, but they were outvoted. We had won what Ambassador John Hay in London, in a private letter to Colonel Roosevelt, had called "a splendid little war," and they saw no reason to neglect the spoils of that conflict. The President went along with the land-grabbers.

On July 30 the French ambassador was given our terms to transmit to Spain. We wanted the Spaniards to relinquish all sovereignty over Cuba, to cede us Puerto Rico, and to give us one of the Ladrones in the South Pacific, which we would select at a time convenient to us. Moreover, the message said, with an amazing lack of clarity considering how many lawyers were available, "the United States is entitled to occupy, and will hold, the city, bay, and harbor of Manila pending the conclusion of a treaty of peace which shall determine the control, disposition, and government of the Philippines." Or perhaps it was meant to be ambiguous.

Poor Spain. Defeat would cost her a heavy price in indemnity. The Teller Amendment would ultimately prevent American control of Cuba, but all her islands in the Caribbean, one in the Pacific, and possibly the Philippines would be lost, after approximately four centuries of overlordship.

There was a certain *ex post facto* character to the demand for one of the Ladrones. It was already in our hands, having fallen there in as ludicrous a bit of comic opera warfare as history records.

When Anderson took the first troops to Manila, he was ordered to stop en route at Guam to capture any Spanish craft there and to subdue the fort. The cruiser *Charleston,* which had joined the three transports at Honolulu, found nothing in the capital of Agana, so it proceeded to San Luis d'Apra, hoisting a Japanese flag as a ruse to fool the inhabitants. There was not a single Spanish vessel in the port, but to the great embarrassment of the Americans, there was a brigantine—a Japanese brigantine with a Japanese flag at the main truck. Captain Henry Glass fired a few rounds from his three-pounders at Fort Santa Cruz. Nothing happened. No one seemed the least bit interested in an American cruiser flying a Japanese flag, followed by three transports, that was bombarding the walls of the ancient fort.

After an annoying delay a small boat did come out, and three uniformed officials clambered up the Jacob's ladder to the *Charleston*'s deck.

"You will pardon our not immediately replying to your salute, Captain," said one, "but we are not accustomed to receiving salutes here and are not supplied with proper guns for returning. However, we shall be glad to do our best to return your salute as soon as possible."

"What salute?" asked Glass.

"The salute you fired," said the Spanish officer, a naval surgeon. "We should like to return it and shall do so as soon as we can get a battery."

Later it was revealed that Guam had had no word from Manila since mid-April, had not been visited by a Spanish warship in eighteen months, had no coal in port, and did not know a war had been begun and was well on the way to being finished. The next day, June 21, the American flag was run up over the fort. The convoy moved on to Manila, not bothering to leave a single man to represent the new ruler. All the Spanish officers and soldiers cheerfully went along as prisoners of war.

Conditions in Manila were just below the boiling point. Emilio Aguinaldo was laying claim to widespread support on most of the islands of the Philippine archipelago. This did not sit well with our diplomats there, or in Washington. Consul General Williams sent letter after letter to the State Department extolling the virtues of the islands and urging their commercial development under American control. He had a low opinion of the native population, except as laborers, and painted a picture of vast American agricultural projects using Filipino labor. As he saw it, our entrepreneurs would not even have to learn Spanish to deal with the inhabitants. "Let natives learn English," he wrote in one message.

Dewey's blockade fell into a routine made more pleasurable by the arrival of sheet music from home. The songs were full of praise for the admiral, even if the music was generally bad, and it was pleasant to know that relatives back in the states were singing songs with names like "What Did Dewey Do to Them?" and "Dewey's Duty Done."

Within a few weeks the pleasure was diluted by the appearance in Manila Bay of warships from other nations. The men in the fleet expected such arrivals, as it is an old naval custom to "show the flag," particularly at a time like this one. But the German fleet—and it was a fleet that might have outfought Dewey's in battle—seemed to be intent on fishing in troubled waters. The French and British ships behaved with punctilious correctness, but the German vessels steamed in and out of the anchorage, almost colliding with our ships on patrol, and signaling with searchlights at night.

American officials knew that other nations were on the prowl for new territory. Not many months before the invasion of the Philippines, Russia, Germany, and Great Britain had all bitten off pieces of China, or had extorted special concessions and spheres of control. They did not know, however, that the German Emperor had enunciated a policy under which his diplomatic corps, his army, and his fleet were instructed to acquire any maritime footholds in eastern Asia that were not tightly nailed down.

The same general policy motivated other European powers, but the French and British captains in Manila Bay appeared only to wish to see how things were progressing with the American operations there.

German Vice-Admiral von Diedrichs arrived about the time that Aguinaldo's insurgents extended their control to the bulk of the Bataan Peninsula and the shores of Subic Bay, an excellent anchorage to the northwest of Manila. The Filipino leader notified Dewey of his success but said he had no way of driving the Spanish out of a small naval base on Isla Grande, an islet in the bay.

Von Diedrichs was no tyro in diplomacy. He knew that the American forces had control of a very small section of the island of Luzon. He also knew that no other big power would object too strenuously if he saw fit to establish a protectorate over another part of the Philippines "in the name of humanity" or "to avoid useless bloodshed," reasons often used by nations as they seized backward areas.

Dewey learned of the German plan just in time. He sent the *Raleigh* and *Concord* off to scout the Spanish naval station, not knowing that von Diedrichs had just ordered the German man-of-war *Irene* to take over the installation. The American captains saw the other vessel, cleared for action, and started in her direction; but the *Irene* had no stomach for a fight and fled around the other end of Isla Grande. The Spanish force in the base surrendered to the two American cruisers.

The Americans found the German truculence most unsavory. Nothing overt was attempted, but the harassing behavior continued until Dewey bluntly asked the German admiral if Germany and the United States were at war. If the opposite were true, and the nations were at peace with one another, he said, he expected the Germans to respect international rules governing the American blockade. Commodore Chichester, commanding the British warships at Manila, backed Dewey to the hilt, and von Diedrichs decided to behave from then on. A short time later, his squadron quit Philippine waters to gather up the Caroline Islands, which the poor Spaniards were in no shape to hold.

Secretary of State Long cabled Dewey not to enter into any formal agreement with Aguinaldo "that would incur any liability to maintain their cause in the future." The way things were going in Washington, no official wished to see barriers erected to their own take-over of the Philippines, if such a course seemed wise.

Until Dewey had a sufficiently large force of troops on shore, he could do little but maintain the blockade. He took note of a shipment of three thousand Mausers sent to the insurgent leader from China and urged his superiors to expedite the sending of more troops and several monitors to beef up his squadron.

On July 17 an additional 2,900 troops arrived at Cavite under Brigadier General Francis V. Greene. They were volunteers from Colorado, Nebraska, and Pennsylvania, two battalions each from the Eighteenth and Twenty-Third Regular Infantry, some engineers, and two batteries of the Utah Light Artillery.

On paper this massing of men looked eminently pleasing to most commanders, but not to Admiral Dewey. He was on the uneasy seat because it still appeared that Camara would come all the way from Suez. Dewey, who knew the forces he was fighting, realized he had no ship capable of standing up to the *Pelayo*. The Admiral and General Anderson put their heads together and tried to figure out a timetable for possible eventualities.

They knew that two monitors, the *Monadnock* and the *Monterey,* were en route from the west coast of the United States, making between six and seven knots. General Merritt, with the third contingent of men from San Francisco, was at sea somewhere between Honolulu and Manila. Both the American monitors and the Spanish squadron had about seven thousand miles to steam but there was little doubt that the enemy fighting force could make faster time than the heavy, awkward monitors.

Dewey was in a precarious position. On his fleet rested the entire responsibility for the protection of the Army and its transports as well as the maintenance of the American presence in the Philippines. To fight Camara before the monitors arrived would be to go into battle outgunned by the enemy. If the monitors did not arrive in time and Merritt's convoy reached Manila before them, the chance for disaster was greatly increased.

Dewey finally told Anderson that he would wait another week. If by then he had heard nothing to indicate that Camara was not coming, he would take his squadron and all the American transports, sail north of Luzon, and then head east to rendezvous with the monitors. With them he would then return to Manila and destroy the Spanish fleet. He could have taken the troops back aboard the transports, but he asked General Anderson what he would do if he had to leave Manila with his ships.

Anderson's reply was both courageous and typically American. He said he would take thirty days' rations, march into the hills about twenty miles east of Cavite, entrench, and there await the return of the fleet.

None of this came to pass, as Dewey received word that the Spanish government had recalled Camara because of fear that Watson's flotilla—which never existed anywhere but on paper—would ravage the Spanish coast. Merritt arrived on July 25, three days before the time Dewey had estimated. The *Monterey,* with her twelve-inch guns, steamed past Corregidor on the very day the Admiral had figured Camara would show up.

General Merritt, who was to exercise overall command on

land, brought with him an expeditionary force of 197 officers and 4,650 men under the immediate command of Brigadier General Arthur MacArthur. It was composed of an amazing assortment of regulars and volunteers, gathered up from virtually every regular Army post and National Guard armory in the western states.

Infantry regiments predominated, but there were engineers and artillery, regular and volunteer (the latter included the famed Astor Battery from New York City and vicinity), medical units, Signal Corps men, even several bands.

With these new arrivals Merritt could put about 8,500 in the field. Most of them were put ashore at Pasay, three miles south of the Spanish lines at the edge of Manila. Outposts were set up, trenches dug, and sentries set to marching along the perimeter of Camp Dewey, but there was no real danger of a surprise attack. This was due not only to what General Greene had mentioned when he reported to a superior that "the Spaniard, like the Turk, is not given to offensive operations," but also to the existence of hundreds of Philippine insurgents who dug their own entrenchments between the Americans and the city.

From reports of deserters, spies, and Filipino informers, the Americans estimated that General Don Fermin Jaudenes y Alvarez commanded thirteen thousand Spanish troops in Manila, a total found numerically correct when the enemy surrendered. Merritt and his generals were not disturbed by the disparity in forces because of their faith in their troops' fighting spirit and the knowledge that Dewey's warships could support them from the bay with destructive firepower.

While all this movement of men and ships had been going on, Emilio Aguinaldo had declared himself leader of the Independent Republic of the Philippines, stating that he would rule by decree until an elected government could be set up. He was displeased by the build-up of American forces ashore, since he had wished to capture Manila—with the aid of Dewey's squadron, of course.

First the Admiral, and then General Anderson, engaged in sporadic communications with the insurgent chief, but they had each received so many warnings from Washington not to enter into any alliance or entanglements with him that they barely managed to preserve the appearance of cooperation. Dewey said he thought Aguinaldo was suffering from a "big head." On one occasion the Filipino leader sent a message "forbidding" the landing of American troops for fear his people would think it an infringement of their national rights, but men, guns, stores, and ammunition continued to be transported from ship to shore.

The arrival of the monitor *Monterey* on August 4 provided the American forces with the fuse that set off the real explosion. She had two twelve-inch and two ten-inch guns, powerful additions to the eight-inch guns which were Dewey's largest. With these Dewey had no doubt he could silence the guns of the city's old forts and the blockhouses that had been built at the edge of the old city. He informed Merritt that the Navy could now support the Army in any operation that seemed desirable.

American officers knew they held still another ace in the game they were playing for such high stakes. Word had come out of Manila that conditions growing out of the siege, which the insurgents had maintained for many weeks, were worsening with each passing day. There was, despite the open hostilities, a modicum of communications between the enemy forces, made possible by the presence of noncombatants in the city and in the foreign ships in the bay. The Belgian consul, M. Edouard André, served as an unofficial go-between, and several British and French businessmen made it a practice to board their country's ships for conferences, and even to visit American vessels. One way or another the dire straits of the inhabitants became common knowledge among the besieging troops. The Spanish citizens had been reduced to eating horseflesh for some weeks and, the story went, the inhabitants of Manila's small Chinatown were eating cats and dogs.

These conditions within the beleaguered city led Admiral Dewey to counsel delay. A calm and humane man, the naval hero believed that a few more days or even weeks of sporadic firing between the trenches would sap the Spanish will to fight. He also saw the value of the insurgents in applying pressure that would react against them and not the Americans.

"It is better," he told General Greene, "to have small losses,

night by night, in the trenches than to run the risk of greater
losses by premature attack," but he left the decision to Merritt
and his staff. They had agreed upon a signal that would bring
down on the enemy the full firepower of the squadron. It was
to be the igniting of a blue fire on the shore at Camp Dewey,
and this was what the Admiral referred to as he continued, "If
you burn the blue light on the beach, the *Raleigh* will immediately open fire, and the *Charleston* will go to her assistance,
and the *Boston* and *Monterey* will follow if the engagement continues . . . but I hope you will not burn the blue light unless you
are on the point of being driven out."

Each night the Spanish opened fire on the American positions
at about 7:30 o'clock, and each night the Americans, sure the
musketry was a sign of an attack, returned the fire. "As usual,"
wrote Greene later, "the mistake was made of thinking the
Spaniards were advancing and our men fired away nearly 20,000
rounds."

Aguinaldo's men joined in the nightly exchange, but there was
almost no attempt to maintain liaison between him and our
forces. Frank D. Millet, correspondent for the London *Times*
and *Harper's Weekly,* expressed amazement over the situation:
"Until the campaign before Manila I always believed it to be an
elementary military axiom that if two armed bodies jointly
occupy a territory they must be either enemies or allies. In the
investment of Manila the insurgents were not recognized by us
in either of these capacities."

Millet would have been less amazed if he had known the
contents of some of the secret dispatches that had been going
back and forth between the American commanders and Washington.

The first American soldiers had been killed on the night of
July 31, and as each succeeding darkness had brought on more
firefights, our men were growing impatient. They had extended
their trenches from the water's edge inland for a mile and a half
either by digging them themselves or by cajoling the insurgents
into giving up some of theirs.

The nearest Spanish positions consisted of Fort San Antonio
Abad, on the beach, a stone structure called Blockhouse No. 14

almost a mile inland, and trenches and breastworks connecting the two strong points. The area to the east of the city was less well fortified because the swampy terrain, drainage ditches, and meandering waterways made attacks from that side impracticable. There were a few Americans scattered around the outer districts of the city, but they were more valuable as spotters than as assault troops. Manila's main section lay about three miles north of the most advanced American trenches, with the Pasig River looping around it to the north and east. Geography and terrain together made it almost inevitable that any attack on what was known as Manila Intramural would have to be mounted along the high ground just behind the shoreline through suburbs known then and now as Malate and Ermita.

Greene held the left of the American line from the beach to the edge of a small rice paddy seven hundred yards inland, with Fort San Antonio a mile in his front. MacArthur's men held the right flank, extending from his link-up with Greene to where the land fell off in another swamp drained by a small stream called the Estero Tripo de Gallina. In front of him was Blockhouse 14. Anderson's reserve regiments were just to the rear.

Naturally, as Manila had been in Spanish hands for many years, there was a main road called Calle Real, or Royal Road. It paralleled the shore a short distance in from the water, and the American troops would be astride the highway when they moved north to attack.

The First Colorado Volunteers and the Eighteenth Regular Infantry shared the van of Greene's brigade, supported by two batteries from Utah. MacArthur's forward lines were supported by the Astor Battery, an elite volunteer unit raised and equipped by John Jacob Astor. It was commanded by Captain Peyton C. March, who would one day be Chief of Staff of the American Army.

What Colonel Roosevelt's Rough Riders were to the Army under Shafter in Cuba, the Astor Battery was to Merritt's in the Philippines, with the one difference that there was no swashbuckling politician at its head. Astor was content to finance the unit, and the artillerymen were content to serve their country.

The battery had many a famous athlete on its roster, as well as socialites and prominent men in other walks of life. There were J. W. Beacham, the Cornell football great; Harry Esselstyn, champion bicycle racer; Frank Jay Hutchinson, captain of the football squad at New York's City College; Charles C. Webster, son of the president of the Dry Dock Savings Bank in New York and a noted equestrian; and Robert A. Burbank, a noted athlete at Swarthmore and Harvard.

As these men and their companions in arms fretted for action, their commanding general and Admiral Dewey opened a diplomatic attack upon General Jaudenes, who had taken over command in Manila with the resounding title of Governor General and Captain General of the Philippines. A joint letter was sent to Jaudenes on August 7 warning that an attack might be launched at any time and that noncombatants would be given a limited time to leave the city. Within hours an answer came back pointing out that as the insurgents surrounded the city there was no place for noncombatants to go to seek safety. It was a touching message, revealing the very heart of the problem faced by the Spanish, and it was signed: "Very respectfully, and kissing the hands of your excellencies, Fermin Jaudenes."

Monsieur André told Millet that the Spanish military could not envision surrendering to Aguinaldo's insurrectionists, both as a matter of honor and because of fear of reprisals. Admiral Chadwick put it this way: "*Pundonor* was the real stumbling block; there must be at least a semblance of attack and defense to fulfill the demands of the Spanish military code."

Merritt and Dewey exchanged other letters with Jaudenes, arguing in their own messages that with the loss of the Spanish fleet there could be no hope of succor and that surrender to vastly superior forces would in no way sully the honor of the defenders. The governor general asked for time to consult with his government and the use of a boat to carry his cables to Hong Kong, but the request was turned down. Days went by, with evidence growing that the Spanish would not give in without an attack but that if an attack were made it would not be too strenuously opposed.

At a council of war on board the *Olympia,* Dewey's flagship, a most strange decision was reached to attack on Saturday,

August 13, but to do it in such a way that loss of life might be avoided where possible. In compliance with this consensus, General Merritt issued General Order No. 4, providing for a combined land and naval attack but one limited to artillery fire in the beginning: "Our lines will make no advance, but hold the trenches, the infantry covering the artillery."

A more explicit memorandum to general officers explained that the troops were to move forward only after a bombardment and were to refrain from advancing unless it could be done "without disadvantage." Dewey, Merritt said, would steam to a point just off the walled city after the initial artillery barrage and would hoist the international signal, "Surrender." Merritt established headquarters on the *Zafiro,* a British steamer that Dewey had purchased to use as a supply ship when leaving Hong Kong. The memorandum was explicit about what was to be done if a white flag showed on the inner walls of the fort and even more explicit when it said: "It is intended that these results shall be accomplished without the loss of life; and while the firing continues from the enemy with their heavy guns, or if there is an important fire from their entrenched lines, the troops will not attempt an advance unless ordered from these headquarters."

It was a most peculiar set of orders for an assault upon one of the most important cities in all Asia, defended by more than thirteen thousand troops. More significant by far was a second memorandum to both brigade commanders, Greene and Mac-Arthur, advising them not to permit any armed men to advance close to the city unless they were Americans. "Pillage, rapine, or violence by the native inhabitants or disorderly insurgents must be prevented at all costs," the instructions added.

It was going to look like a battle between Americans and Spaniards. The villains had been the Spanish, but now they were the good guys and without altering the cast of characters one iota, the insurgents had become the ones to hiss.

"The question was one of gaining an end," said Admiral Chadwick, "not of slaughtering men."

During the night of August 12–13 Greene and MacArthur moved their men as far forward as they could, without actually forcing the insurrectionists out of their trenches. When the Utah

Battery, to which two three-inch boat guns had been added, tried to drag their pieces into position, there was some resistance from the Filipinos but it was quelled without bloodshed. The athletes and socialites in the Astor Battery also wheeled their guns into place behind some native huts near Blockhouse No. 14. That done, the artillerymen and their supporting infantry regiments tried to get some sleep, resting by the guns.

At 9 o'clock on the morning of August 13 the flagship *Olympia* made the signal, "Ships take their stations," and the warships executed the order immediately. This resulted in the *Concord* standing a thousand or so yards off the mouth of the Pasig River, the *Boston, Baltimore, Charleston,* and *Monterey* off the walls of the inner city, and the *Olympia, Raleigh,* and *Petrel* off Fort San Antonio. With the latter force were the captured gunboat *Callao* and the tug *Barcelo.* General Merritt waited in the *Zafiro,* behind the cruisers.

It was a most warlike scene. If there had not been a soldier on Luzon, Dewey's powerful squadron could still have blasted Manila to rubble in a matter of hours. With the Americans ready to advance from the south, the defenders did not have a chance. Yet ordinary men are usually brave under such conditions, and as Governor General Jaudenes and his officers had not let the men in the ranks know of the overall plan to make the defense look real, most of the Spanish soldiers took up their arms determined to give a good account of themselves. Had they understood the hidden nuances of the situation and known the behind-the-scenes maneuvering, they might have been depressed at their superiors' duplicity and surely a little less valiant.

But as it was, when the American warships steamed into formation and took their prearranged positions off the city walls, they sensed nothing of the hidden humor behind the choice of the music played by the band on the British flagship *Immortalité.* It was "See, the Conquering Hero Comes."

A few minutes later the *Olympia* opened fire on Fort San Antonio. Other vessels joined in, followed by the barking of the field artillery onshore. It had been raining most of the night, but at the outset of the bombardment dark gray clouds coming in from the Pacific dumped torrential showers on the bay and

city, leaving them enveloped in shifting white mists. Onshore
winds scattered these clouds of vapor just as the guns stopped
firing. To watchers in the trenches the fort seemed deserted.
Men from the Colorado Regiment streamed out of their ditches
and rifle pits, overran the fortifications, and discovered it had
been abandoned. There were two dead men and one wounded
soldier left behind. Utah cannoneers were surprised to find that
all the breech blocks had been removed from the Spanish guns.

Greene's men scurried up the Camino Real, peppering the
retreating enemy soldiers who thought it their sworn duty to
defend the city. At the suburb of Malate, which they reached
about 10 o'clock, the Americans saw a white flag flying over
the citadel. Their officers ordered them to form a protective ring
around captured enemy soldiers, more as a defense against the
insurgents than because they represented any menace in themselves.

Out from town dashed a carriage drawn by two horses. There
were two men in livery up on the seat but no one else. One of
them had a message for General Greene. It contained instructions for him to enter the fort and to order his men to cease
firing as an armistice was being signed. Greene found Governor
General Jaudenes, his predecessor in that office; Admiral Montojo, the commander with no fleet to command; and other
Spanish officials together with Lieutenant Colonel C. A. Whittier of Merritt's staff, who had come ashore under cover of the
rain squalls. Papers were already being signed for a surrender.
The white flag on the wall, Greene noted, was a white bedsheet
from an officer's bunk on the *Olympia,* tied to a bamboo pole.

It was relatively easy for Greene to stop his men from further
firing, and he moved the brigade into the heart of Manila and
beyond the bridges over the Pasig River, where they could prevent further advances by Aguinaldo's men.

On the right of the American advance, however, no word
came to General MacArthur indicating a change in the instructions given the night before. He could not see the fleet or the
white flag flying over the captured citadel. Naturally, he proceeded to execute his orders.

The Thirteenth Minnesota led the attack with the Astor Battery, two regular infantry regiments, and the North Dakota Volunteers in close support. They found Blockhouse No. 14 abandoned and ran up the Stars and Stripes, but as they moved along toward the suburb of Singalong they fell under a loose, scattered fire that built up steadily until the van was engaged in a brisk firefight. Rifle bullets spurted from another blockhouse, No. 20, in which a small number of Spanish soldiers, serving as a rear guard, seemed determined to hold on at all costs.

It was a sticky situation. A few men from the Minnesota unit, a few from the Astor Battery, Captain March of the artillery, and Captain Sawtelle, a member of the brigade staff who joined the van as an individual volunteer, undertook the task of moving up under cover of their comrades' fire, edging their way through bamboo groves, rice paddies, and clutches of small palm-thatched huts to within eighty yards of the blockhouse.

There they ran into a hailstorm of bullets and were driven back into the center of the village of Singalong where they improvised hastily erected defense works. A shell from an enemy field piece struck the barrel of one of the Astor Battery's guns and failed to explode, fortunately, but killed a cannoneer and wounded three others.

The fifteen men in the center of town held the temporary firing line while MacArthur had the battery placed behind the village church. The supporting infantrymen dug in behind stone walls built to enclose adjacent gardens. March and Sawtelle kept their men intact while the guns behind them roared in support, the shells striking the blockhouse and nearby trenches with deadly accuracy.

It was a bitter battle, even though it involved a relatively small number of men on both sides. One thing was certain. The high command may have been staging an attack aimed at making the Spanish surrender appear legitimate, but the Spanish and American soldiers near Blockhouse No. 20 had no reason to believe that they were not engaged in a titanic struggle for the city of Manila.

Those who died were as dead as any who expired on the battlefields at Brandywine, Antietam, or Gettysburg, and the wounded suffered in the same way.

Contact with the enemy on the right had been made at noon. It was now about 1:30 P.M., and the American spearhead at Singalong had ground to a complete halt. The men in the Astor Battery served their guns with dogged determination, and the defenders opposing them must have thought there were three or four times as many field pieces as the three that were actually in action.

Corporal Burbank explained this in a letter home, saying that he and other cannoneers fired their guns so fast that the barrels grew too hot to touch. Between rounds, however, they began to wonder when relief would come to extricate them from their dangerous position. They did not have long to wait.

Up from the bamboo groves to the left and rear of the heroic little band holding on in Singalong came a battalion of the Twenty-Third Regular Infantry, whose commander, without orders from above, had decided to advance, remembering the classic adage that no soldier errs who marches toward the sound of guns. He moved four companies to an intersecting road to the west of where the fifteen men were holding fast, and the danger passed. Fearing they would be outflanked, the enemy withdrew and a few minutes later all firing ceased, except where small bands of insurgents were shooting at Spanish troops from hidden points at the edge of town. MacArthur led his brigade into the city through the Paco district and the action was completed.

MacArthur did not fail to note the valor of the few men from Minnesota and the Astor Battery who had held on so valiantly in the narrow streets in Singalong. Writing of them in his report, he said: "Aside from conspicuous individual actions in the first rush, the well-regulated conduct of this firing-line was the marked feature of the contest, and it is proposed, if possible, to ascertain the names of the men engaged, with a view to recommend them for special distinction."

All through the afternoon of August 13 and most of the next day the friction between American and insurgent troops stayed just below the point where it might have ignited a full-scale conflict. Shots were exchanged sporadically, but always at long distance, and no one was killed. On August 14 a commission including high-ranking Spanish and American military and civil officials drew up a document of honorable capitulation. It contained the kindest of terms for the vanquished, allowing officers to retain their sidearms, horses, and private property, permitting all soldiers to move about freely after turning in their equipment, and it guaranteed freedom of religion, acknowledgment of private property, and the protection of all Manila "under the special safeguard of the faith and honor of the American Army."

This was not going to be easy, because of the truculence of the Filipino insurrectionists. Merritt and Dewey, even before the battle was actually over on August 13, cabled Washington about the difficult situation and asked how far they should go in "forcing obedience" on the insurgents who were pressing for joint occupation of the city.

The reply set the stage for the future, making a war with the Filipinos almost certain and underlining our intention to hold the master's hand in the islands. As it is such an important document, it is given in full:

The President directs that there must be no joint occupation with the insurgents. The United States in the possession of Manila City, Manila Bay, and harbor must preserve the peace and protect persons and property within the territory occupied by their military and naval forces. The insurgents and all others must recognize the military occupation and authority of the United States and the cessation of hostilities proclaimed by the President. Use whatever means in your judgment are necessary to this end. All law-abiding people must be treated alike.

It was not until the exchange of this and other messages that American and Spanish commanders learned that the battle for Manila had been fought after the war was over. On August 12 Secretary Day and the French ambassador, Jules Cambon, acting in Spain's behalf, had signed a protocol of an agreement preliminary to the establishment of lasting peace.

None of these agreements, decisions, or events interested Emilio Aguinaldo. Boiling mad at the American success in winning the engagement without his help, and bitter over his failure to play a role in the capitulation agreement, he moved his headquarters to Malalos and sulked there while his men launched a hit-and-run campaign against the Spanish soldiery, residents of the city with valuable property, and Filipinos who leaned toward American control. Merritt used his troops to push the insurgents into the bush, but pillage, and the murder of natives who collaborated with the occupying force continued. Aguinaldo convened what he termed the Filipino congress for a session in the hills, and the way was opened for the bitter war that followed.

19

★ ★ ★ ★ ★ ★

Silent Now, the Guns

THE PEACE AGREED UPON in Washington, to be implemented in full at a later date, caused great elation in the United States, but it fell far short of the Biblical peace that surpasses all understanding.

All the rival hatreds, ambitions, and opinions exploded, not in one mighty blast, but more in the manner old-fashioned Chinese firecrackers, tied together in bundles, go off. There was enmity between field commanders, and it came swiftly to the surface. The typhoid, malarial, and yellow fevers that were killing American soldiers were mild compared to the mass fever that drove many at home to criticize the way the war had been managed.

Democrats and Republicans argued bitterly in Congress. The newspapers championed or reviled Mr. McKinley, and Secretary Alger, who had labored mightily to support the troops in the field, became a scapegoat for all the things that had gone wrong. The President did his best to soft-pedal criticism, but once the cohesive force of the war was dispersed by victory, divergent elements in the population took up a hue and cry against almost everything they did not like, and they disliked a lot of things.

Then a new cause for deep concern arose—fear that yellow fever would sweep the country as infected men came home from

Cuba. Some newspapers belabored this fear by referring to the returning transports as "horror ships," and many correspondents never wrote of the port of Siboney without calling it "that charnel house."

Shafter's corps was being evacuated from Cuba as fast as troops from Southern states could replace them. The surgeon general believed that these replacements would be immune, but it proved he knew little of how the infection was spread or controlled. Negro and white soldiers alike contracted the disease, as did the Red Cross workers and newspapermen.

Terror rode the waves as the ships loaded and moved from port to port. When men became ill, some captains forced them to go ashore. Others were compelled to sleep on the aftermost section of the open decks and would have died had their comrades not cared for them and shared their rations with them. John M. Maxwell, correspondent for the Chicago *Tribune,* reported two hundred ill with yellow fever at Siboney. Malcolm McDowell of the Chicago *Record* told of two companies of the Negro regiment, the Ninth Regular Infantry, who were guarding warehouses at Santiago although of the 110 men involved only 29 were able to man their sentry posts, and they were so weak they were allowed to sit down while doing it.

For those left behind in Cuba the fruits of victory turned sour. Americans who understood Spanish were disturbed to overhear the natives indicate they had no more use for the victors than the vanquished. Men sent as replacements when wars are over lead lives of limited horizons. There is no patriotic excitement to buoy them up, only the dull business of being good soldiers.

Such a one must have been Lieutenant Herbert Sargent, whose wife journeyed to Santiago with the Fifth U.S. Volunteer Infantry and lived with him eight months in a tent pitched on a hill outside the city. From there, in the weeks after Toral's surrender, she could see the smoke rising from where the authorities were burning the bodies of yellow fever victims. She wrote in her diary that it made her think of Coleridge's line in "The Ancient Mariner," "Christ, that such things should be."

After a snake was found in the bedding of an officer not far away, she became accustomed to shaking hers out at night. Even so, she said, "a scorpion on my skirt . . . warned us to keep our eyes open for crawling things."

Illness among the troops continued to worry the officials. Mrs. Sargent wrote that "the sick report ran up at one time to 275 out of a regiment of 1,000, but conditions are better now [October 9, 1898], there being no new cases of yellow fever."

Some of these soldiers were the ones being sent home on the transports called "horror ships." The first, the *Seneca,* reached New York on July 20, but more followed, reeking of crude disinfectants, all through the fall. Most of the ships, however, carried the returning troops directly to Montauk Point, Long Island, where a camp was hastily erected on the sand dunes more than a hundred miles from the nearest large city.

Politics got in its licks, now that the enemy was no longer a menace. It is an American phenomenon that parties work together rather well in time of grave danger but fall out immediately the peril is past. It was so after this short war. Having no external foe to chastise in their columns, papers supporting the Democratic Party crucified Republicans for their mistakes.

As the war-weary, fever-ridden heroes of Santiago disembarked at Montauk, all the stops were pulled out in the antiadministration organs. Within a week or so the rest camp at the end of Long Island was dubbed a pest house, a public shame, and a hell hole by the Democrats.

As a matter of fact it was nothing of the sort. It was surprisingly well laid out, and although there was some confusion in the first few days, it was efficiently operated. Relatives and friends and those who were curious enough to endure the long, hot, sooty ride on the steam cars flocked to the encampment bearing with them food, delicacies, civilian clothing, and other gifts.

Here, as elsewhere, the Rough Riders fared better than other regiments. Their brothers-in-arms who had not served in Cuba, but had stayed on in the crowded camps of the south, came home by train to Jersey City. They had little or nothing to eat en route and were depressed at having failed to see action. Factory girls from nearby plants welcomed them and shared their lunches with them.

But the heroes from San Juan Hill—six troops of them— landed at Montauk directly from the steamer *Miami*. Their transport was met in the harbor by sleek white-sailed yachts, steam yachts, and tugboats hired for the purpose. Skippers of these craft tied down their whistles, and a few even fired welcoming salvos from saluting cannon.

With the Rough Riders were four troops of the Third Regular Cavalry accompanied by Fighting Joe Wheeler and his son, a lieutenant. Bands played "When Johnny Comes Marching Home Again," and the volunteers answered with their cowboy yell as the ship tied up at the dock. Suddenly the people on land spied Colonel Roosevelt on the bridge. As the regiment's historian said, "the crowd on shore went mad."

As the troopers walked down the gangplank, the crowd's demeanor changed. Men and women looked at the bronzed, emaciated veterans, many in ragged uniforms, most of them unshaven, and the shouting died out. Civilian men took off their hats and for a while there was only the sound of shuffling feet on the sun-dried boards of the dock.

Such scenes were not duplicated at the Southern camps. Those in Florida, filled with soldiers who had been denied the glory— and the danger—of war, had suffered from heat and ennui. Soldiers at Chickamauga were in far worse shape. Typhoid had struck there soon after the first troops moved out, and succeeding regiments were decimated by disease. There were five hundred cases of typhoid at the Georgia camp at one time. It was not much better at Camp Alger near Washington. By the end of September, Americans were horrified as statistics became known.

At Chickamauga 425 men died of disease; at Jacksonville, Florida, 246 died; at Camp Alger, 107; and in the various California camps where men headed for the Philippines had stayed or were still waiting, another 139 died. It did no good to say that the disease rate in the Civil War had been much higher. The public was incensed and wanted to find villains to blame. Roosevelt, fresh from his scene of triumph, took up his pen again and dashed off scathing criticisms in which condemnation of Secretary Alger, the chiefs of the Quartermaster Corps, and General Shafter was a constant theme.

Buffeted by these attacks, Mr. McKinley acceded to Alger's request that he appoint a commission to investigate the war. It served his purpose well, as it dug so deeply into every nook and cranny that its report came out long after the November elections. As always, such reports have a basic ambivalence. The best they do is to highlight what all sensible men know: democracies are never ready for the wars in which they become involved, no matter how well they do when the battles are fought.

Of the many complaints looked into by the commission appointed by the President the most explosive dealt with the rations served the Army in Cuba. Men had complained bitterly in letters home and to their Congressmen. The strange thing about the hearings was that they had been under way for three months, at seventeen different cities and camps, before anyone broached the subject. When it did come out into the open, it was in the testimony of General Miles, the major general commanding the Army of the United States.

Miles charged that the canned beef sent to the soldiers in the field was prepared experimentally, that such beef was not on the list of approved rations, and that a chemical had been injected into the meat to preserve it. He referred to the meat as having been "embalmed."

For a reason known only to himself, General Miles refused to be sworn before testifying, although the other 495 witnesses who appeared before the commission did so under oath. His accusations stirred up a dozen hornet nests, and he was interviewed everywhere he went after the hearings. The meat packers marshaled their arguments to prove his statements were false, but when the commission finally published its findings no one was really satisfied. The tribunal said it had heard nothing to lend foundation to the charge that canned beef was not a part of the regular, authorized ration, that it had been furnished as the pretense for experiment, or that it was the pulp of beef from which the extract had been removed.

It is too long after the event to add other testimony, but it is apparent that while the meat was not actually spoiled or illegally tampered with by adding chemicals, it must have been horrible food in camp and on the battlefield. The commission properly decided that it was a most unpalatable ration, that it was not too bad in permanent installations where there were stoves and plenty of other supplies to add to it, especially vegetables, but that when it was eaten from the can, without being cooked and without condiments being added, it was just barely acceptable.

While tempers flared over these hearings, other Americans became embroiled in the personality conflict over whether Sampson or Schley had the better claim to fame for the victory over Cervera's fleet. McKinley was on the former's side. Just as the fleet was coming home, the President promoted Sampson by eight numbers on the Navy seniority list and Schley by only six. Each became permanent rear admirals, but their relative seniority was shifted. Schley had been senior to Sampson when the war started, but now was junior.

Hearst was in Schley's corner and used his chain of papers to lash out at McKinley for honoring the man who had not been in the battle until it was almost over. It did not matter to him that nearly every turn of the propellers, nearly every decision on the bridge of the warships, had been provided for in orders written by Sampson. The public supported Schley, always championing the underdog, but even its demands for an inquiry served its hero little. The inquiry dragged on and never came up with a firm determination. Sampson died first, his life shortened by the vitriolic criticism. Schley grew older, and more bitter, angry that the board of inquiry had not supported his claims.

The fragments of the conflict by now were scattered in many ways and places. Mr. McKinley named a commission to go to Paris to arrange a permanent peace treaty at about the time some of the returning regiments and units were being acclaimed by cities on both coasts.

The Rough Riders, finally done with their mustering-out procedures, descended on New York City in droves. Everywhere they appeared they were lionized, some at the Stock Exchange, some at City Hall, and most of them in the best hotels in town. Their uniforms distinguished them from all other units, and women found them irresistible, kissing them with wild abandon on the streets and in the theaters.

Roosevelt's famous regiment had barely left town when the Astor Battery returned from its duties in the Philippines. The volunteers had left New York seven months before, looking like civilians in uniform. They returned lean, tanned, and sure of themselves.

A committee gave them a breakfast at the Grand Union Hotel, at which speeches were made and fulsome words spoken of their courage and fortitude. Some of the speakers were long-winded, and some tried to weave into the proceedings such foreign ideas as that the cannoneers had been motivated not alone by love of country, but affection for such institutions as Cornell, Harvard, and other colleges. It was a far, far simpler day than those that were to follow. When all the speeches were done, soldier and civilian alike joined in singing the Doxology.

As autumn advanced and the corn went into the cribs and reapers cut great swaths through the prairie wheat fields, Mr. McKinley took the campaign trail to insure control of Congress. He reiterated in one village after another, and at every whistle stop, that he was not a Republican President but the chief executive of all the people. He talked, but he also listened to what the men and women of America had to say. Representative "Uncle Joe" Cannon of Missouri claimed McKinley kept his ear so close to the ground that it was full of grasshoppers. It couldn't have been so, because the message McKinley heard was one of support for the expansionists. We had won the war with Spain, was the central theme of the arguments heard all across the land. Why shouldn't we get the spoils?

The American peace commission, motivated by those same arguments, held fast against the Spanish envoys' efforts to put the Philippines in a separate category. Long after the parties at the conference had agreed that Cuba must be left independent and that Puerto Rico and Guam should belong to the United States, the emissaries from Madrid contended that as Americans held only a small segment of one island in the Philippines, the balance should stay under the Spanish crown.

It was no use. The delegates from the United States, constantly in touch with the President, could not let go their bulldog grip. The Spanish commissioners might have saved themselves time and breath if they had realized how definitely the American people had come to look upon expansion as their God-given prerogative. So, on December 10, the peace treaty was signed in the opulent Old-World surroundings of the French ministry's Quai d'Orsay.

Ratification took a long time too. It might have taken longer, or there might have been no approval in the Senate at all if, far around the globe, Emilo Aguinaldo had not made a serious mistake. In January he proclaimed himself head of the Philippine Republic. It was the second time, or the third, perhaps, but he changed the phrases to explain the repetition. On February 4 there was the crackle of rifle fire near the palace in Manila as American soldiers and Filipino militiamen, probably through failure to understand one another, shot several rounds at one another. That was all it took to clinch matters in Washington. On February 6, two days later, the Senate voted to ratify the peace treaty.

Henry Cabot Lodge thumped his Republican colleagues on the back, happy at the result, but wishing no public congratulations for his success in steering the treaty to a successful ratification.

"We were down in the engine room and do not get flowers," he said, "but we did make the ship move."

That "ship," which carried the United States well along the road to expansion, to a role of great importance in global politics, and to a secure place among the great powers, functioned well. The same could hardly be said of another, true ship—the Spanish man-of-war *Infanta María Teresa*.

Salvaged from the Caribbean and patched together by commercial wrecking crews, the cruiser was ordered north to Norfolk. While the statesmen were wrangling at the peace table in Paris, she wallowed along under her own power until overtaken by a fierce Atlantic gale. She was abandoned by the wrecking crew near San Salvador Island in the Bahamas, and sank in waters near where Columbus had made his first landfall and claimed the island in the name of their Spanish Majesties, Ferdinand and Isabella.

It was altogether fitting that this was where Spain's glory had begun and her ignominy ended in the New World.

Select Bibliography

ORIGINAL SOURCES

Notes on the Spanish-American War, A series of translations of Spanish documents, articles, and reports, made by the Office of Naval Intelligence, U.S. Navy.

Record of Proceedings of a Court of Inquiry in the Case of Rear-Admiral Winfield S. Schley, U.S. Navy, Convened at the Navy Yard, Washington, D.C., September 12, 1901.

Report of the Commission Appointed by the President to Investigate the Conduct of the War Department in the War with Spain. Sen. Doc. 221; 56th Congress, 1st Session.

Report of the Secretary of the Navy of the United States for 1898.

Report of the Secretary of War of the United States for 1898.

PERIODICALS: MAGAZINES

American History Illustrated
Century
Forum
Harper's
McClure's
North American Review
Review of Reviews
Scribner's
Yankee

PERIODICALS: NEWSPAPERS

London *Times*
New York *Journal*
New York *Post*
New York *Times*
New York *Tribune*
New York *World*
Philadelphia *Inquirer*
Pittsfield (Mass.) *Eagle*
Pittsfield (Mass.) *Journal*

BOOKS

Abbot, Willis John. *Blue Jackets of '98.* New York: Dodd, Mead & Co., 1899.
Alger, R. A. *The Spanish American War.* New York: Harper & Bros., 1901.
Atkins, John Black. *The War in Cuba.* London: Smith, Elder & Co., 1899.
Barrett, John. *Admiral George Dewey.* New York: Harper & Bros., 1899.
Berryman, John. *Stephen Crane.* New York: Sloane, 1950.

Bonsal, Stephen. *The American Mediterranean.* New York: Moffat, Yard & Co., 1912.
———. *The Fight for Santiago.* New York: Doubleday & McClure Co., 1899.
———. *The Real Condition of Cuba Today.* New York: Harper & Bros., 1897.
Brown, Charles H. *The Correspondents' War.* New York: Charles Scribner's Sons, 1967.
Carlson, Oliver, and Ernest Sutherland Bates. *Hearst, Lord of San Simeon.* New York: Viking Press, 1936.
Chadwick, French Ensor. *The Relations of the United States and Spain* (3 vols.). New York: Charles Scribner's Sons, 1911.
Churchill, Allen. *Park Row.* New York: Rinehart & Co., 1958.
Churchill, Winston. *My Early Life.* London: T. Butterworth Ltd., 1930.
Cisneros, Evangelina, and Karl Decker. *The Story of Evangelina Cisneros.* New York: Continental Publishing Co., 1898.
Davis, Richard Harding. *Cuba in War Time,* New York: R. H. Russell Co., 1898.
———. *The Cuban and Porto Rican Campaigns.* New York: Charles Scribner's Sons, 1898.
———. *The Notes of a War Correspondent.* New York: Charles Scribner's Sons, 1910.
———. *A Year from a Reporter's Note-Book.* New York: Harper & Bros., 1898.
Dewey, Adelbert M. *The Life and Letters of Admiral Dewey.* New York: Woolfall Co., 1899.
Downey, Fairfax. *Richard Harding Davis; His Day.* New York: Charles Scribner's Sons, 1933.
Dyer, John Percy. *"Fighting Joe" Wheeler.* University, La.: Louisiana State Univ. Press, 1941.
Esposito, Vincent J., ed. *West Point Atlas of American Wars.* New York: Frederick A. Praeger, 1959.
Evans, Robley D. *An Admiral's Log.* New York: D. Appleton & Co., 1910.
———. *A Sailor's Log.* New York: D. Appleton & Co., 1901.
Freidel, Frank. *The Splendid Little War.* Boston: Little, Brown & Co., 1958.
Goode, W.A.M. *With Sampson Through the War.* New York: Doubleday & McClure Co., 1899.
Hobson, Richmond Pearson. *The Sinking of the Merrimac.* New York: The Century Co., 1899.
Hohenberg, John. *Foreign Correspondence: The Great Reporters and Their Times.* New York: Columbia Univ. Press., 1964.
Lee, Fitzhugh, and Joseph Wheeler. *Cuba's Struggle Against Spain.* New York: American Historical Press, 1899.
Leech, Margaret. *In the Days of McKinley.* New York: Harper & Bros., 1959.
LeFur, L. *Etude sur la Guerre Hispano-Americaine de 1898.* Paris: Libraire de la Cour D'Appel et de L'Ordre Des Avocats 1899.
Lodge, Henry Cabot. *The War with Spain.* New York: Harper & Bros., 1899.
Mahan, Alfred Thayer. *Lessons of the War with Spain.* Boston: Little, Brown & Co., 1899.
Marshall, Edward. *The Story of the Rough Riders.* New York: G. W. Dillingham Co., 1899.
Mason, Gregory. *Remember the Maine.* New York: Henry Holt, 1939.
Miles, Nelson A. *Serving the Republic.* New York: Harper & Bros., 1911.
Miley, John D. *In Cuba with Shafter.* New York: Charles Scribner's Sons, 1899.
Millis, Walter. *The Martial Spirit.* New York: Literary Guild of America, 1931.

Morgan, H. Wayne. *America's Road to Empire.* New York: John Wiley & Sons, 1965.

Morison, Elting E., ed. *The Letters of Theodore Roosevelt.* Cambridge, Mass.: Harvard Univ. Press, 1951.

Musgrave, George Clarke. *Under Three Flags in Cuba.* Boston: Little, Brown & Co., 1899.

Musick, John R. *History of the War with Spain.* New York: J. S. Ogilvie Publishing Co., 1898.

Parker, James. *Rear Admirals Schley, Sampson and Cervera.* New York and Washington: Neal Publishing Co., 1910.

Post, Charles Johnson. *The Little War of Private Post.* Boston: Little, Brown & Co., 1960.

Quinlan, Michael. *The Spanish American War.* Written and printed by himself while serving as printer on the cruiser *New York,* 1898.

Robinson, Albert Gardner. *Cuba and the Intervention.* New York: Longmans, Green, 1905.

————. *Cuba, Old and New.* New York: Longmans, Green, 1915.

————. *The Philippines: The War and the People.* New York: McClure, Phillips & Co., 1901.

Roosevelt, Theodore. *The Rough Riders.* New York: Charles Scribner's Sons, 1900.

Russell, Henry B. *Our War with Spain.* Hartford, Conn.: A. D. Worthington & Co., 1898.

Sargent, Alice Applegate. *Following the Flag; Diary of a Soldier's Wife.* Kansas City, Mo.: E. B. Barnett, n.d.

Sargent, Herbert H. *The Campaign of Santiago de Cuba.* Chicago: A. C. McClurg & Co., 1907.

Sargent, Nathan. *Admiral Dewey and the Manila Campaign.* Washington: Naval Historical Foundation, 1947.

Schley, Winfield Scott, *Forty-five Years Under the Flag.* New York: D. Appleton & Co., 1904.

Sigsbee, Charles D., *The "Maine."* New York: Century Co., 1899.

Society of the Army of Santiago de Cuba. *The Santiago Campaign.* (Written by participants and published by the Society.) Richmond, Va.: Williams Printing Co., 1927.

Spears, John R. *The American Navy in the War with Spain.* London: Bickers & Son, 1899.

Stallman, R. W., and E. R. Hagemann, eds. *The War Dispatches of Stephen Crane.* New York: New York University Press, 1964.

Watterson, Henry. *History of the Spanish-American War.* Louisville, Ky.: Courier-Journal Pub. Co., 1898.

West, Richard Sedgewick. *Admirals of American Empire.* Indianapolis: The Bobbs-Merrill Co., 1948.

Wheeler, Joseph. *The Santiago Campaign.* Boston: Lamson, Wolffe & Co., 1899.

White, Lillian C. *Pioneer and Patriot: George Cook Sweet, Commander, USN.* Delray Beach, Fla.: Southern Publishing Co., 1963.

Wilson, Herbert W. *The Downfall of Spain.* London: Sampson Low, Marston & Co., 1900.

Wisan, Joseph E. *The Cuban Crisis as Reflected in the New York Press.* New York: Octagon Books, 1934.

Wormser, Richard. *The Yellowlegs; the Story of the United States Cavalry.* Garden City, N.Y.: Doubleday & Co., 1966.

Young, Louis Stanley. *Life and Heroic Deeds of Admiral Dewey.* Philadelphia: World Bible House, 1899.

Index

Aguadores, Cuba, 120
Aguadores River, Cuba, 137
Aguinaldo, Emilio, 62, 218, 222, 224, 226, 227, 236, 237, 245
Akiyama, Saneyuki, 116
Alfonso XII (cruiser), 37
Alger, Russell, 27, 50, 51, 87, 92, 113, 173, 176, 178, 203, 206, 208–209, 214, 238, 242
Alliança (steamer), 1, 2, 6, 10–11
Almirante Oquendo (cruiser), 46, 184, 188–189, 193, 197
Altares, Ensenada de los, 120
American Transatlantic Line, 66
Amphitrite (monitor), 47, 76
Anderson, General T. M., 220, 221, 225, 226
André, M. Edouard, 227
Anna Karenina (Tolstoi), xi
Annapolis (ship), 214
Arango, Clemencia, 19–20
Archibald, James F. J., 89
Arroyo, Puerto Rico, 216, 218
Associated Press, 110
Astor, John Jacob, 229
Atkins, John Black, 149
Atlantic Monthly, 73
Audaz (destroyer), 210
Austria, 116, 196

Bahama Banks, 80
Bahama Channel, 84, 98

Bahama Islands, 246
Balloons, 151, 152–153, 155
Baltimore (cruiser), 56, 57, 60, 232
Baltimore *American,* 65
Bancroft (ship), 120
Barbados Island, 79
Barcelo (tug), 232
Barton, Clara, 171, 207
Bataan Peninsula, 223
Bates, John C., 121, 140, 156, 164, 169, 209
Bay of Pigs incident, 4
Beacham, J. W., 230
Belmont, Mrs. August, 89
Bennett, James Gordon, Sr., 9
Berriz, José, 24–25
Blanco, General Ramón, 29, 37, 42, 49, 92–93, 179, 180, 181, 184
Blockhouses, 145–146
Blue, Victor, 113
Bly, Nellie, 10
Bolívar, Simón, 4
Bonsal, Stephen, 118–119
Boston (cruiser), 56, 57, 228, 232
Brazil, 78, 79
Breakwater (transport), 174
Bridges, Robert, 73
Brooke, Major General J. R., 214, 215, 218
Brooklyn (cruiser), 80, 82, 83, 100, 104, 120, 183, 185, 219
Brooks Brothers, 63

Bryan, William Jennings, 17
Buena Ventura (steamer), 47
Buenos Aires (destroyer), 212
Bull, Henry, 90
Burbank, Corporal Robert A., 230, 235

Cabanas Bay, Cuba, 88, 120, 126, 206
Callao (gunboat), 232
Camara, Rear Admiral, 210–211, 212, 213, 219
Cambon, Jules, 236
Camino Real, Cuba, 137, 139, 144, 159
Camino Real, Philippines, 229, 233
Camp Alger, 241
Camp Chickamauga, 241
Camp Dewey, 220, 226, 228
Camp Thomas, 86
Cannon, Representative Joseph, 244
Canones Point, Cuba, 105
Canovas del Castillo, Antonio, 7
Cape Fajardo, Puerto Rico, 214, 215, 218
Cape Haitien, Haiti, 81
Cape Verde Islands, 66, 82
Capron, Allyn K., 130, 142, 145, 146, 147, 148, 163, 164, 166, 169
Carbonelle, Carlos, 25–26
Carlier, Captain Diego, 195
Carlos V (battleship), 210, 212
Castilla (man-of-war), 55, 59
Castine (gunboat), 114, 120
Casualties, 71, 72, 168–169, 172, 173–174
Censorship, 93
Century, 73
Cervera, Don Angel, 195
Cervera, Pascual, 46, 47, 65, 66, 67, 73, 141, 151
Chadwick, French Ensor, viii, 70, 118, 155, 190, 191, 202, 204, 230, 231
Chaffee, Adna R., 143, 145, 146, 148, 209
Chamberlain, Joseph, 163–164
Chandler, Senator William E., 41, 43
Charette, George, 101–102, 103, 104, 105, 106

Charleston (cruiser), 221, 222, 228, 232
Cherokee (transport), 174
Chicago (ship), 101–102
Chicago *Record,* 239
Chicago *Tribune,* 239
Chickamauga National Park, 86
Chile, 98–111
China, 3, 54, 56, 62, 223, 224
China Sea, 55
Churchill, Sir Winston, 12
Cincinnati (cruiser), 47, 213
Cisneros, Evangelina, 23–25
City of Washington (steamer), 37, 115
Civil War, 3, 48, 49, 52, 53, 151, 168, 241
Clagett, J. C., 90
Clark, Captain Charles E., 78–79, 81, 190, 192
Clausen, Rudolph, 104
Cleveland, President Grover, 3, 14, 15, 16, 30, 147
  as a humanitarian, 17
Coamo, Puerto Rico, 217
Cody, William "Buffalo Bill," 48
Columbia (cruiser), 80
Competitor (schooner), 16
Concas, Captain Victor, 183–184, 185, 188
Concord (cruiser), 56, 57, 223–224, 232
Cook, Captain Francis, 193
Corbett, Jim, 48
Corregidor Island, 56, 57
Cowboy Regiment, 75
Crane, Stephen, 117, 131, 151, 153, 155, 197, 202, 217
Creelman, James, 164
Christóbal Colon (cruiser), 46, 84, 85, 184, 189, 190–191, 192, 193, 194, 196, 197
Cuba, vii, 1–8, 27–33, 62, 218, 221, 239, 244
  annexation of, 2
  business interests in, 15
  Daiquirí, 112–127, 128, 129, 148, 178
  famine in, 22, 28, 29
  Las Guásimas, 128–144, 148, 156
  the *Maine* incident, 35–44
  money for relief donated by Mc-Kinley, 29–30

newspaper coverage, 4–5, 9–26
reconcentration decrees, 28
Santiago, 98–111, 118, 120–121,
    126, 129, 134, 135, 137, 139,
    141, 143, 144, 147, 151, 163,
    166, 167, 176, 177, 199–212,
    239
Cuban fever, 138
Cullom, Shelby M., 2, 3
Curaçao, 77
Cusco Hill, Cuba, 117

Daiquirí, Cuba, 112–127, 128, 129,
    148, 178
Dana, Charles, 48, 49
Davis, Mrs. Jefferson, 24
Davis, Richard Harding, 19–20, 22,
    94, 118, 124, 126, 129, 131,
    132, 137, 144, 159–160, 162,
    174, 204, 216, 217
Dean, Dudley, 89–90
Decker, Karl, 25, 26
Deep Sea Sounding and Dredging
    (Sigsbee), 33
Deignan, Oscar, 101, 102, 103, 104,
    105
De Lôme, Dupuy, 15
Del Rey, General Vara, 138, 148,
    163, 166, 207
Derby, George M., 151, 152, 153
Detroit (cruiser), 47, 114, 120
Devereaux, Horace, 90
Dewey (tug), 88
Dewey, Commodore George, 30, 40–
    41, 45, 46, 54–71, 97, 111,
    210, 211–212, 222–225, 227–
    228, 230, 231, 232, 236
Diamond Bank, Cuba, 183, 184,
    186, 189
Diego Perez Island, 68
Dixie (battleship), 212, 214
Don Antonio de Ulloa (gunboat),
    55, 59
Donderio, Enrique, 15–16
Don Juan de Austria (gunboat), 55,
    59
Dorst, J. H., 177
Dos Caminos, Cuba, 141
Dry Tortugas Islands, 114
Ducoureau House, 140, 167
Dupont (torpedo boat), 80, 82, 196
Dutch Antilles, 77

Dygert, Walter Grant, 14
Dysentery, 138, 173

Eagle (gunboat), 68, 113, 114, 120
Egypt, 211
El Caney, Cuba, 138, 139, 140, 141,
    143, 145, 146, 147, 148, 149,
    154, 155, 156, 157, 163, 164,
    166, 168, 180
Elliott, G. F., 117
El Pozo Hill, 138, 139, 140, 142,
    143, 144, 148, 149, 151, 154,
    159, 167, 168
El Viso (fort), 141, 146, 147, 164
Ericson (torpedo boat), 114
Ericsson, 193
Esselstyn, Harry, 230
Estero Tripe de Gallina (stream),
    229
Estrella Point, Cuba, 98, 108
Evans, Captain Robley, 80–81, 100,
    182–183, 184, 189, 194
Ewers, E. P., 157

Fajardo, Puerto Rico, 214, 215
Famine, 22, 28, 29
Farragut, David Glasgow, 56
Fern (ship), 205
First Volunteer Cavalry, 112
Fish, Hamilton, 130
Fitzsimmons, Bob, 48
Florida (steamer), 93–94
Flying Squadron, 77, 80, 81, 82, 83,
    84, 85
Fort Canosa, 141, 163, 177
Fort San Antonio Abad, 228–229,
    232
Fort Santa Cruz, 221
Forum, 2
Fraile, El (islet), 56, 57
France, 116, 214, 219, 223
Frye, Senator William Pierce, 65
Furor (torpedo boat), 189, 190, 193,
    195

García, Calixto, 11
García, José, 11
Germany, 94, 116, 123, 213, 223–
    224
Glass, Henry, 221, 222

Gloucester (yacht), 120, 136, 189, 190, 193, 194–196, 199, 214, 215, 216
Gómez, Máximo, 7, 11, 12, 15, 22, 92
Grandpré, Clément de, 116
Great Britain, 54, 97, 116, 213, 223
Greely, A. W., 93
Greene, General Francis V., 224, 226, 227, 228, 229, 231, 233
Grimes, George S., 149, 158, 159
Grito, 6
Guadeloupe Island, 66
Guam Island, 221, 222, 224
Guantánamo Bay, Cuba, 84, 116, 117, 137, 139, 219
Guayama, Puerto Rico, 218
Guerrilla warfare, 49, 118–119
Gussie (side-wheeler), 88–89, 93–94, 115

Haiti, 75, 83, 214
Hamilton, John M., 160
Hanna, Mark, 27
Harden, Edwin W., 55, 61
Harper's Weekly, 94, 228
Harvard (steamer), 66, 67, 83–84, 193, 196
Havana, Cuba, 139, 180
Hawaiian Islands, 2, 3, 17, 211
Hawk (ship), 82
Hawkins, H. S., 154, 157, 159, 160, 162
Hay, John, 220–221
Hearst, William Randolph, 136, 164, 197
Helena (ship), 120
Hemingway, Ernest, 144
Henry, Guy V., 218
Hobson, Richmond Pearson, 98–111, 200, 204
Hong Kong, China, 40, 45, 54, 55, 62, 64, 230, 231
Hornet (ship), 120
Howe, Julia Ward, 24
Hudson (revenue cutter), 68
Hugh McCullough (revenue cutter), 55, 56, 57, 60, 64
Hurricanes, 97, 219
Huse, Lieutenant Harry, 195, 215
Hutchinson, Frank Jay, 230

Immortalité (flagship), 232
Inagua Island, 115
Indian fighters, 48, 49
Indiana (battleship), 47, 75, 76, 114, 120, 185, 187, 219
Infanta María Teresa (cruiser), 46, 84, 183, 184, 187, 188, 193, 194, 197, 245–246
Iowa (battleship), 47, 75, 80, 81, 100, 120, 182, 183, 184, 185, 219
Irene (man-of-war), 224
Isla de Cuba (cruiser), 55, 59
Isla de Luzon (cruiser), 55
Isla Grande (islet), 223, 224

Japan, 56, 116, 123, 221
Jaudenes y Alvarez, Don Fermin, 226, 230, 232, 233
Juana Díaz, Puerto Rico, 217
Juragua Ore Mining Company, 124

K Troop volunteers, 89–90
Kaiserin Maria Theresa (cruiser), 196
Kane, Woodbury, 90
Katahdin (ram), 80
Kelly, Francis, 101, 103, 105, 107, 109
Kendrick, Marion, 24
Kent, Jacob F., 120, 121, 126, 139, 140, 142, 143, 148, 149, 151, 152, 153, 154, 155, 157, 163, 205
Kettle Hill, 139, 141, 142, 144, 148, 149, 158, 159, 160, 162, 163
Key West, Florida, 114, 116, 214, 215

Ladrones Islands, 221
La Redonda, Cuba, 156
La Reforma, Battle of, 12
Las Guásimas, Cuba, 128–144, 148, 156
Lawton, Henry L., 120, 121, 124, 126, 128, 132, 134, 136, 139, 140, 142, 143, 145, 146–148, 149, 153–154, 155–156, 163, 166, 167
Lee, Captain Arthur H., 116, 166–167

Lee, General Fitzhugh, 16, 24, 28, 31, 32, 33, 37
Lee, Robert E., 16, 53
Leona (ship), 115
Leyden (ship), 214
Linares, General Arsenio, 119, 122, 133, 135, 141, 142
Lincoln, Abraham, 52
Lodge, G. C., 216
Lodge, Henry Cabot, 2, 3, 17, 30, 40, 43, 91, 112, 113, 175, 177, 178, 201, 214, 216, 245
London *Times,* 94–95, 228
Long, John D., 27–28, 38, 39, 40, 41, 77, 197
Lopez, Miguel, 184
Lopez, Narciso, 4
Ludlow, William, 145, 146, 147, 164, 209
Luzon Island, 56, 223, 225, 232

MacArthur, Arthur, 226, 229, 231, 233, 234, 235
McCalla, B. H., 68, 71
McClernand, E. J., 114, 151, 172, 177
McDonald, William, 25
McDowell, Malcolm, 239
Maceo, José, 11, 12
McKinley, William, vii, 17, 22, 24, 26, 27–32, 38–44, 147, 168, 197, 203, 206, 209, 211, 214, 220, 221, 238, 242, 243, 244
  chooses Shafter as field commander, 52–53
  donates money for Cuban relief, 29–30
  Roosevelt on, 41
Mahan, Captain Alfred T., 49, 55–56, 66, 78, 79, 88, 203
Maine (battleship), 31–33, 35–44
  sinking of, 35–44
Malaria, 138, 173, 208, 238
Mangrove (tender), 136
Manila, 218, 220–236
  battle of, 60–61
Manning (ship), 114
Manzanillo, Cuba, 139, 201
Marblehead (cruiser), 47, 68, 69, 71, 82, 83, 84, 116, 117
March, Peyton C., 229, 234

Maria Christina, Queen Regent, 40
Marianage, Cuba, 140, 156, 167
Marietta (torpedo boat), 79
Marques del Duero, 55, 59
Marshall, Edward, 90, 131
Martí, José, 5–6
Martinique, 66, 77, 78, 79, 80, 84
Massachusetts (battleship), 80, 101, 120, 202, 212, 214, 219
Matteawan (ship), 114
Maxfield, Joseph E., 151, 152
Maxwell, John M., 239
Mayagüez, Puerto Rico, 218
Merrimac (collier), 81, 83, 97–111
Merritt, General Wesley, 62, 92, 212, 218, 225–226, 227, 229, 230, 231, 236, 237
Miami (steamer), 115, 241
  conditions aboard, 115
Migration, 4
Miles, Colonel Evan, 145, 146
Miles, General Nelson A., 50, 51, 52, 73–74, 87, 119, 156, 164, 204, 205–206, 212, 213–219, 242
Miley, John D., 158
Miller, J. M., 100
Millet, Frank D., 228
Millis, Walter, 175
Minneapolis (cruiser), 80, 83
Mirs Bay, China, 54, 55
Mona Passage, 75, 80
Monadnock (monitor), 225
Monocacy (ship), 40
Monroe Doctrine, 8
Montague, Daniel, 102
Montauk Point, Long Island, 209, 240, 241
Monterey (monitor), 225, 227, 228, 232
Montgomery (cruiser), 47
Montgomery, L. M., 90
Montojo, Rear Admiral Patricio, 55, 57, 58, 233
Morgan, John T., 2, 3
Morro Castle, 76, 98, 136, 140, 183, 190, 202, 203
Mosquitoes, 51–52
Mullen, James, 101, 102–103
Murchie, Guy, 63, 90
Murphy, J. E., 103
Musgrave, George Clarke, 23, 24, 25, 200–201

Nanshan (collier), 56
Napoleon Bonaparte, 75, 121
Nashville (gunboat), 47, 68, 69, 71
Negroes, 126, 160, 208, 239
New Orleans, 120, 213
New York (cruiser), 46, 47, 75, 76, 80, 120, 182, 185, 219
New York and Cuba Mail Steamship Company, 37
New York *Herald,* 144, 174
New York *Journal,* 110, 131, 136, 155, 164, 197
New York *Post,* 163
New York *Sun,* 48
New York Times, The, 7
New York *Tribune,* 7
New York *World,* 94, 155, 207
Newark (battleship), 212, 219
Newfoundland, 67
Newspapers, 4–5, 9–26
Niagara (ship), 205
Nicaragua Canal, 2
Norris, Frank, 174
Norway, 116

Old Bahama Passage, 80
Olivette (steamer), 18, 19–20, 114, 174
Olympia (cruiser), 41, 56, 57–58, 230, 232
Oregon (battleship), 41, 75, 77, 78, 79, 80, 81, 86, 120, 219
Osado (destroyer), 210
Osceola (ship), 114, 120

Pact of Zanjon, 5, 16
Palo Seco, Puerto Rico, 76
Panther (cruiser), 116
Paredes, Don José de, 192–193
Parker, John H., 142, 159, 160, 162, 170
Pasig River, 229, 232, 233
Patriota (cruiser), 210, 212
Pelayo (battleship), 210, 212, 225
Pershing, General John J., 152–153, 154, 155
Petrel (gunboat), 56, 57, 59, 60, 232
Philip, Captain J. W., 100, 186–187, 191
Philippine Islands, 30, 41, 46, 62, 218, 220–236, 245
    annexation of, 86

Phillips, John P., 101, 103, 105, 107
Pluton (torpedo boat), 108, 189, 190, 193
Ponce, Puerto Rico, 215–216
Powell, J. W., 110
Proserpina (destroyer), 210
Puerto de Guánica, Puerto Rico, 215, 218
Puerto Rico, 64–65, 75–76, 212, 213–219, 220, 221, 244
Puget Sound, 81
Pulitzer, Joseph, 155
Punta Cabrera, Cuba, 188–189
Punta Estrella, Cuba, 105
Puritan (monitor), 47

Rafferty, William A., 121
Raleigh (cruiser), 56, 57, 223–224, 228, 232
Randolph, W. F., 204
Rapido (cruiser), 210, 212
Reconcentration decrees, 28
"Red Badge of Courage Was His Wig-wag Flag, The" (Crane), 117
Red Cross, 171, 207, 216, 239
Reina Cristina (ship), 55, 57, 59
Reina Mercedes (cruiser), 108, 109, 111, 202
Remington, Frederic, 18–19, 20, 22, 118
Resolute (auxiliary), 196
Rodgers (torpedo boat), 114
Ronalds, Pierre Lorillard, 89
Ronalds, Reggie, 89
Roosevelt, Theodore, vii, 17, 22, 40–41, 43, 48–49, 89–91, 92, 130, 132–133, 140, 149, 152, 155, 159, 160, 163, 209
    appointed Assistant Secretary of the Navy, 30
    becomes Lieutenant Colonel, 89
    on McKinley, 41
    on Shafter, 175
Root, Elihu, 43
Rough Riders, 87, 89–91, 112, 121, 124, 129, 131, 132, 137, 140, 149, 159, 160, 176, 177, 178, 203, 208, 209, 229, 240–241, 243–244
Royal Road, 137, 138, 139, 229
    See also Camino Real

Rustler Regiment, 75

St. Louis (steamer), 66, 67, 197
St. Paul (merchantman), 81, 83
Samoa, 2, 3
Sampson, William T., 65, 66, 67, 135–136, 142–143, 190, 243
Sandoval (gunboat), 116
Sandwich Islands, 64
San Francisco *Post,* 89
San Juan, Puerto Rico, 215, 217–218
San Juan Hill, 139, 141, 142, 144, 148, 149, 157–167, 168, 169, 171, 177, 180, 208, 241
San Juan River, 137, 139, 143, 152–153, 158, 182
San Luis del Caney (church), 145, 170
San Martin, José de, 4
San Nicolas Channel, 81, 113
San Salvador Island, 246
Santiago, Cuba, 98–111, 118, 120–121, 126, 129, 134, 135, 137, 139, 141, 143, 144, 147, 151, 163, 166, 167, 176, 177, 199–212, 239
Santo Domingo, 75, 121
Sargent, Herbert, 239
Sargent, Mrs. Herbert, 239–240
Saturn (collier), 69
Schley, Winfield S., 46, 77, 80, 81, 82, 83–85, 219, 243
Schley's Flying Squadron, 66
Schwan, Theodore, 214, 218
Scorpion (ship), 120
Scovel, Sylvester, 155, 207–208
Scribner's Magazine, 73
Segurança (ship), 114, 118, 119, 121, 134, 140, 174
Seneca (steamer), 26, 240
Seventh Regiment of New York City, 51
Shafter, General William R., 52–53, 74, 75, 88, 92, 112–113, 114, 116, 117, 118, 134, 136, 137–138, 139, 140, 142–143, 144, 148, 149–150, 151, 155, 156, 229, 239, 242
  chosen as Field Commander by McKinley, 52–53
  Roosevelt on, 175

Sherman, John, 15, 16, 27
Sherman, William Tecumseh, 53
Siboney, Cuba, 119–120, 122, 126, 128, 129, 131, 132, 135, 136, 137, 138, 144, 148, 169, 172, 173, 178, 196, 208, 214, 239
Sigsbee, Charles, 31–33, 35–38
Silvia (yacht), 136, 197
Socapa Point, Cuba, 203
Spain, 1–8, 28–29
  armada, 66
  the *Maine* incident, 31–33, 35–44
Spanish American War
  background of, 1–8
  Daiquirí, 112–127
  Las Guásimas, 128–144, 148, 156
  Maine incident, 31–33, 35–44
  the *Merrimac,* 81, 83, 97–111
  newspapers in, 4–5, 9–26
  Santiago, 98–111, 118, 120–121, 126, 129, 134, 135, 137, 139, 141, 143, 144, 147, 151, 163, 166, 167, 176, 177, 199–212, 239
Squier, George O., 93
Star Point, Cuba, 105
State of Texas (passenger ship), 171, 207
Staunton, S. A., 196–197
Subic Bay, 223
Suez Canal, 211
Sumner, Samuel S., 120, 140, 142, 143, 148, 149, 151, 153, 154, 158, 163, 209
Suwanee (gunboat), 117, 120
Sweden, 116

Tampa, Florida, 93, 94, 95, 117, 138, 151, 171, 214
Tampa Bay Hotel, 74, 91, 95
Teddy's Terriors, 75
Teller Amendment, 62, 221
Ten Years' War, 4, 5, 16
Terror (monitor), 47, 76
Texas (battleship), 80, 82, 84, 104, 117, 120, 186, 219
Tiffany, William, 89
Tolstoi, Count Leo, xi
Toral, General José, 170, 180, 200, 203, 204, 205, 206
Torpedoes, 99–100, 106, 107, 108–109, 179, 189

Trinidad, 67
Triton (tug), 88
Trocha, 11
Turquino River, 193
Typhoid, 238, 241

Union of Soviet Socialist Republics,
116, 223
United States
annexes Cuba, 2
annexes Philippines, 86
Maine incident, 31–33, 35–44
Merrimac, 81, 83, 97–111
newspaper coverage, 4–5, 9–26
U.S. National Guard, 50, 51, 86, 226
U.S. Navy, 30
U.S. Senate Foreign Relations Com-
mittee, 6, 14–15
U.S. Volunteer Cavalry, 87

Valdez, General Saurez, 12
Vanderlip, Frank, 55
Vaquero, José, 142
Vasquez, Captain Pedro, 195
Virginius (steamship), 4, 5
Vixen (ship), 120, 196
Vizcaya (cruiser), 32, 46, 181, 184,
187, 188, 190–191, 193, 194,
197
Volz, Robert, 70, 71

Wainwright, Richard, 35, 189, 193,
195, 215
Wanda (boat), 195
Ward Line, *see* New York and Cuba
Mail Steamship Company

Wasp (ship), 114, 120, 214
Watson, John Crittenden, 211, 225
Watts, Ethelbert, 211
Wellington, Duke of, 75
West Indies, 66, 80, 127, 210, 215
Western Regiment, 75
Weyler y Nicolau, General Valeri-
ano, 12–13, 14, 16, 18, 19,
22, 24, 25, 29, 92–93
Wheeler, Joseph "Fighting Joe," 53,
120, 121, 124, 126, 128–129,
130, 131, 132, 134, 136, 138,
139, 140, 143, 158, 177, 178,
205, 241
Whitney, Caspar, 118, 174
Whittier, C. A., 233
Williams, Oscar F., 55, 57, 222
Wilson, James H., 214, 217
Windom (revenue steamer), 69, 71
Windward Passage, 75, 84
Winslow (torpedo boat), 67–68
Winslow, Cameron, 68, 69–70
Wompatuck (tug), 84, 114, 120
Wood, Colonel, 74–75, 90, 128, 129,
130, 134, 140, 208, 209
Woodford, Stewart Lyndon, 28–29,
40, 41, 43

Yale (ship), 83, 204, 214, 216
Yankee (gunboat), 116
Yellow fever, 51–52, 73–74, 138,
203, 238, 240
Young, S. B. M., 128, 129, 131, 140
Yucatan (ship), 112, 113, 114, 115,
118, 123
Yucatán Channel, 81

Zafiro (supply ship), 56, 231, 232